Nurturing Happiness

Nurturing Happiness

How Religion Shapes Emotional Practice

ROBERT WUTHNOW

OXFORD
UNIVERSITY PRESS

Oxford University Press is a department of the University of Oxford.
It furthers the University's objective of excellence in research, scholarship,
and education by publishing worldwide. Oxford is a registered trade mark of
Oxford University Press in the UK and in certain other countries.

Published in the United States of America by Oxford University Press
198 Madison Avenue, New York, NY 10016, United States of America.

Library of Congress Cataloging-in-Publication Data
Names: Wuthnow, Robert author
Title: Nurturing happiness : how religion shapes emotional practice / Robert Wuthnow.
Description: 1. | New York, NY : Oxford University Press, [2025] |
Includes bibliographical references and index.
Identifiers: LCCN 2025013429 (print) | LCCN 2025013430 (ebook) |
ISBN 9780197807040 paperback | ISBN 9780197807033 hardback | ISBN 9780197807064 |
ISBN 9780197807057 epub | ISBN 9780197807071
Subjects: LCSH: Happiness—Religious aspects | Religion and sociology—United States
Classification: LCC BL65.H36 W88 2025 (print) | LCC BL65.H36 (ebook) |
DDC 306.60973—dc23/eng/20250409
LC record available at https://lccn.loc.gov/2025013429
LC ebook record available at https://lccn.loc.gov/2025013430

DOI: 10.1093/9780197807071.001.0001

Paperback printed by Marquis Book Printing, Canada
Hardback printed by Bridgeport National Bindery, Inc., United States of America

The manufacturer's authorized representative in the EU for product safety is
Oxford University Press España S.A., Parque Empresarial San Fernando de Henares,
Avenida de Castilla, 2 – 28830 Madrid (www.oup.es/en or product.safety@oup.com).
OUP España S.A. also acts as importer into Spain of products made by the manufacturer.

Contents

Preface

Much of what we read about religion and happiness describes a straightforward relationship. Religious belief encourages us to feel that things will work out because God is in charge. Religious belonging gives us supportive contact with like-minded people. Belief and belonging, therefore, promote happiness. But if we dig deeper, the relationship is less clear. A growing body of literature stresses that happiness is something people do—a practice made up of dispositions, expectations, decisions, and interpretations, as well as feelings. Happiness takes place in social situations that provide cues about what to feel and how to express those feelings. It is guided by the habits we bring to those situations, influenced by the power dynamics present, and guided by social norms and institutions.

For many people, religion is one of the institutions that shapes their views about happiness and their experiences of it. Many faith communities encourage people to think about the joy to be experienced with God in heaven and to relate that joy to the happiness (or sorrow) they experience in this life. Many faith communities provide occasions for experiencing exuberant emotion. They promote happiness when they encourage participants to enjoy socializing with one another. They sometimes organize dual-purpose events that promote happiness while raising money. They often try to persuade participants that happiness can be achieved by doing good deeds. They draw moral distinctions between the kinds of happiness that believers should experience within the faith community and the kinds that may tempt them in other venues. Some faith communities encourage participants to be playful, finding happiness by combining worship with music and dance. Sometimes their participants pursue happiness in illicit ways, necessitating efforts to curb the fallout. This list covers many of the ways in which faith communities nurture the pursuit of happiness. Each has a history.

Examining the history of these practices is a way to better understand how faith communities have come to guide the pursuit of happiness in the ways they do. When did faith communities start encouraging people to believe that they could find heavenly happiness in this life rather than having to wait until they were in heaven? How did faith communities come to believe that extravagant emotion at revival meetings was appropriate? What was the thinking that led churches to start having church suppers, parties, and fairs? When did service to one's neighbors become an emphasis in faith communities' ideas about happiness? When did faith communities start imagining that play was a way of relating to the sacred? Has spiritual practice become so serious that it is hard work rather than a source of happiness? What happens when the pursuit of happiness leads to sexual abuse? These are the questions this book addresses.

My approach draws on social practice theory. In the contributions of Pierre Bourdieu, Alasdair MacIntyre, Jeffrey Stout, and others, practice theory brings together ideas about how our activity, thoughts, and feelings are shaped by habits, dispositions, intentions, and social interaction. In this approach, power figures importantly. Authorities influence how emotions are experienced and expressed. The shaping occurs through the rules, scripts, and definitions that are built into the situation. My writing about religion as a social practice in *What Happens When We Practice Religion: Textures of Devotion in Everyday Life* (2020) and *Religion's Power: What Makes It Work* (2023) provides background for what I offer here.

I conceptualize happiness (building on the important work of historian Monique Scheer and sociologist Arlie Hochschild) as an emotional practice composed of situated dispositions, improvisations, and social interaction guided by formal and informal feeling rules. I show how religious authorities create the social spaces in which emotional practices take place and regulate what happens in those spaces. The success of these efforts, I argue, has hinged on working out compromises between conventional norms of religious practice and opportunities for happiness to be experienced in new ways and put to new uses.

As I familiarized myself with the popular literature on happiness, I realized that one of its central claims is that happiness is a choice. To be happy, a person should think happy thoughts, adopt a positive outlook, and do something to have a good time. From that perspective, "nurturing happiness" would mean taking responsibility for one's happiness. I am not suggesting that people shouldn't do that. But choosing to be happy involves more than simply making up one's mind about it. The choices are shaped by the opportunities available.

The popular literature includes another view of happiness that may be misleading. In that view, happiness is a stable attitude toward life that can be measured with a simple question or two. The polling industry has been measuring happiness this way for decades. I understand the value of such information. But happiness fluctuates. Its meanings are shaped by our upbringing and our situations. Happiness cannot be understood apart from those influences.

The idea that faith communities do things to facilitate, shape, and otherwise nurture happiness differs from the current perception of religion that regards it mostly through the lens of contentious political issues. Those issues grab headlines because they are in fact contentious and do have political implications. But anyone who spends much time in faith communities realizes that a lot more happens there. Much of what they do and say is about happiness. All that takes planning and organizing. The planning and organizing have evolved in tune with religious traditions and in response to changing social conditions.

At this moment in our nation's history, there is a widely shared sense that American religion is going through a transition that may not bode well for its future. Behind the headlines about declining attendance and rising rates of nonaffiliation are stories of small congregations shutting their doors, startup congregations failing, layoffs happening, and budgets shrinking. Religious leaders are rolling up their sleeves, working harder in their various venues to reorganize, engage in relational evangelism, preach better sermons, and win over the public with media campaigns and social advocacy. These efforts notwithstanding, there is also the long tradition in American religious history that emphasizes the value of being inspired by joy, rejoicing in God, having a cheerful countenance and a merry heart—in short, the relevance of faith to the pursuit of happiness.

This tradition acknowledges the pain and suffering of human life but takes to heart the scriptures' emphasis on finding happiness in worship, through service, and in obedience to God. Religious leaders in the past incorporated this emphasis in the various ways that made sense in their given times and places—in testimonials about heavenly joy, at camp meetings, through fairs and festivals, in teachings about serving the needy, and in thoughts about finding joy in useful work. They tried not only to guide the faithful in deepening their faith but also in finding happiness in ways they deemed to be morally appropriate.

These traditions are currently being rediscovered and adapted to new conditions. There are experiments in the arts and liturgical practice, ideas about God as a playful deity, movements toward having fun with Jesus, and sober assessments of the hard spiritual work that may be necessary to find true happiness. Nobody, as far as I can tell, argues that religious leaders doing a better job of promoting happiness in these ways is the key to religion's future. But the possibilities are stirring new interest in looking again at how religious leaders have managed happiness in the past, what has been happening recently, and how the meanings of happiness are being shaped. This book is a modest attempt to examine these traditions and stirrings.

Introduction

Perspectives on Happiness

Surveying the religious scene in America today, a thoughtful observer could hardly be blamed for concluding that religion mostly spreads displeasure and conflict. Preachers in well-heeled pulpits rail against the sins they believe are leading the nation to perdition. Pastors of a different stripe lament the decline of their denominations. In the political sphere, faith communities divide along partisan lines. Christian nationalism arguably threatens the principles of American democracy. The nation's most influential preachers seem obsessed with protecting their constituents' rights to do whatever they want whether it violates the rights of others or, for that matter, compromises public health and safety. The wealthiest churches have been scandalized by sexual harassment and toxic work environments. The image that faith communities have cultivated for themselves is less often about peace and love than it is about contention, division, and anger. Little wonder that the number of Americans who claim to be without religion has risen dramatically.

Set aside the angriest, most divisive segments of American religion. Leave those contentious churches for other discussions. Focus on the mainstream, the people of faith who quietly practice what they believe to be true. Certainly, there are many people who take their faith seriously. *Seriously* is the watchword. They work hard at their faith, study scripture, confess their sins, do good deeds, meditate, help their neighbors, and feel they have not been doing enough. Their religious practice is hard work. They struggle to get right with God, to rid themselves of their afflictions, avoid temptation, deepen their faith, and discipline themselves. They find it important to have a spiritual director, diligently spend time in prayer, faithfully attend worship services, go on weekend retreats, and serve on church committees. The journey is slow and the road is long.

Where is the joy in all this? Isn't religion supposed to proclaim a message of good news? Doesn't good news imply hopefulness? Hasn't religious faith encouraged believers in the past to live in ways that promote

Nurturing Happiness. Robert Wuthnow, Oxford University Press. © Oxford University Press 2025.
DOI: 10.1093/9780197807071.003.0001

their and others' happiness? Aren't the scriptures rich with teachings about wonder and rejoicing? Through most of our nation's history, haven't faith communities achieved success as much or more by nurturing happiness than by proclaiming doom?

Popular religious practices have certainly encouraged seekers of spirituality to find hope and to pursue happiness. Yet it often seems difficult to find studies that examine the details of this strand in our religious history. It is an aspect of religion that comes up as if by chance in treatments of other topics, leaving many important questions to be asked. Are there uniquely religious ways of thinking about joy? Is happiness so subjective that it can be experienced only in deeply personal ways? Are there social customs that tell why certain kinds of emotion are morally acceptable and others are not? Does religion influence these customs? How has religion shaped our understandings of happiness? How have these understandings changed?

Scholars of religion have been exploring these questions with increasing interest in recent years. Studies have long dealt with religious authorities' role in guiding what people were expected to believe, the creeds they were expected to affirm, where they worshipped, and how they behaved morally. Recent scholarship has addressed similar questions about religious authorities' efforts to manage feelings. For example, studies have examined the emotional aspects of religious experience, the layering of emotional norms in racial and gender distinctions, the relative salience of emotion and rationality in moral arguments, and a host of related topics.[1]

Feelings are of interest in the study of religion, Wayne Proudfoot has argued, because they are so profoundly personal that they are hard for institutions to manipulate, and yet all religious traditions have sought to give them moral meaning.[2] Feelings are of growing interest because they serve as moral guides, providing justifications for courses of action that do or do not "feel right."[3] The "triumph of the therapeutic," as Philip Rieff termed it some years ago, is evident in devotional literature dealing with happiness, in the growth of congregation-based counseling programs, and in sermons emphasizing subjective well-being.[4] Pastoral leadership is concerned with parishioners' mental health; congregations sponsor care ministries; music is geared toward emotional uplift; and greater interest is evident in the emotional aspects of mindfulness, meditation, and prayer.[5] For the study of religion, these developments pose important questions about how religious authority influences adherents' emotional lives. These are questions that have required looking again at historical sources.

When Thomas Jefferson enshrined life, liberty, and the pursuit of happiness in the Declaration of Independence, the claim that these were self-evident truths was beyond dispute. The question, then as now, was how best to facilitate the pursuit of happiness. A large part of the answer was of course democratic government, enacted in laws that protected property and public safety. As the nation advanced economically, a large share of the pursuit was associated with westward expansion and industrial development. Insofar as inalienable rights were endowed by the Creator, it was understood, too, that religious faith in its various manifestations was important.

Over the years, faith communities have played their part in offering guidance about the pursuit of happiness. They provided moral frameworks that connected the pursuit of happiness with loving God and neighbor, with arguments about justice and mercy, and with expectations of eternal joy in heaven. They created the lived practices through which the faithful experienced and expressed happiness in worship, fellowship, and service. The frameworks and practices adapted to changes in the social environment. At critical times, faith communities responded to these changes by experimenting with new ways of promoting—and controlling—the pursuit of happiness.

This book describes how American faith leaders at pivotal moments in their history grappled with changing ideas about happiness, how they took advantage of new opportunities for nurturing it, and how they dealt with the attendant challenges of maintaining order within their communities. The ideas, opportunities, and challenges required religious authorities to engage in theological reflection about the afterlife, keep emotional enthusiasm under control while also encouraging it, tackle such practical matters as organizing church fairs and festivals, figure out how to attract newcomers, promote charitable service, and embrace new ideas about entertainment. As they adapted their programs to changing conditions, religious authorities showed a remarkable capacity to use happiness to their advantage, arguing that faith should not only be taken seriously but also be practiced joyfully. Happiness was in these important respects an emotional practice that religious authorities worked at—both to facilitate and to manage. In this introductory chapter, I set the stage for examining happiness as a religiously shaped emotional practice by, first, summarizing the primary approaches through which happiness is currently studied; second, introducing the concept of emotional practice as the approach to be taken here; third, summarizing the aspects of religious institutions that may influence emotional practice; and fourth, providing a brief overview of the following chapters.

Scholars who have examined the history of happiness, starting with Aristotle and Plato and reaching into the modern era, largely agreed on the following: first, that happiness originates in sources outside the individual, either from fate or the gods, but is nevertheless subject to improvement through human activity; second, that happiness has undergone a kind of secularizing development through which it has ceased to be as much about heaven and more about the sensations and experiences of everyday life; and third, that the relationship of happiness to morality has been an enduring concern that has nevertheless gravitated between ideas about goodness as the source of happiness and ideas about happiness being only modestly constrained by moral considerations. Each of these trajectories remains evident in contemporary scholarly treatments of happiness.

The idea that happiness is beyond but also within the individual's control is present in contemporary discussions of social and neuropsychological determinants of happiness and of agentic possibilities for enhancing the pursuit of happiness within these determinants. The secularization of happiness is the background against which the relationship between religious and secular pursuits of happiness is considered. And the relationship between morality and happiness is a crucial consideration in present discussions of the norms under which expressions of happiness are deemed appropriate or inappropriate. The impetus for much of the scholarly work on happiness in recent years is not only that happiness is of popular interest but also that happiness is a feature of these concerns about constraint, agency, religion, everyday life, morality, and social norms.[6]

Scientific studies of happiness have grown on such a scale over the past half-century that several thousand peer-reviewed scholarly articles, books, and reports are currently being produced each year. Much of this research is concerned with the neuroscience, physiology, psychology, and sociology of happiness and the therapeutic, occupational, and economic implications of happiness. For our purposes, several of the main conclusions are worth summarizing. The conclusions reflect the various approaches that have been taken, starting with observations about happiness at the personal level and moving to ideas about happiness at the cultural and institutional levels.

Happiness is neurochemical. Scientists have identified four primary brain chemicals that play a role when happiness is experienced: serotonin, dopamine, endorphins, and oxytocin. Acting together, these neurotransmitters promote feelings of well-being and overcome feelings of stress or discomfort. They are associated with feelings of joy, pleasure, satisfaction, and contentment. Happiness in this respect is truly internal. However, neurochemistry does not act independently of other endogenous and exogenous factors, including diet, exercise, general health, social interaction, and social conditions.[7]

Happiness is subjective. Psychologists argue that happiness is truly known only to the person who feels that he or she is happy. Happiness in this respect is self-referential and self-reflective, meaning that a person whose body was experiencing well-being could nevertheless be unaware of being happy or could say that he or she was happy without necessarily having the neurochemical evidence for saying so. In other words, subjective happiness amounts to assessing one's self and determining that one's self is happy. Thus, self-reports are commonly used in research as the preferred measure of happiness. Some scholars equate self-reported happiness with subjective well-being, which they find is empirically associated with the frequency of feeling happy, infrequency of negative feelings, and believing oneself to be highly satisfied with life. A notable feature of the happiness-as-subjective-well-being approach is its emphasis on a broad range of positive thoughts and feelings. Rather than happiness being understood as a highly specific neurochemical or affective condition, happiness is often studied through questions and activities having to do with gratitude, kindness, optimism, empathy, peace of mind, purpose in life, and clarity about life goals. Self-report assessments often show high correlations among these words, yet their distinct meanings and usages remain important as topics of investigation. The simplest one-question quantitative self-report studies do not investigate other important aspects of the subjectivity of emotions, such as what a person is angry about, why a person feels happy, what does happiness mean to the person, and what personal narratives and memories are associated with feeling happy. Qualitative studies more often take their cues from the theoretical literature in which happiness is understood as a feeling to which the person deliberatively or not deliberatively attaches meaning, rather than only a pleasurable feeling. The more sophisticated quantitative studies are also based on the premise that happiness is referential, thus prompting subjects to locate it with reference to such words, places, and experiences as "life," "the way I am," "rewarding," "laughing," "control," and "elation." Responding to these references facilitates subjects' mental association with times when their thoughts were likely to have included a positive outlook on life.[8]

Happiness is somatically communicated. Although scholars argue that happiness is subjectively experienced, happiness in many instances is also public. We perceive when others are or are not happy and we are able to express our own feelings willingly and unwillingly in ways that others understand. How is this possible? In 1872, Charles Darwin tackled this question in his book, *The Expression of Emotion in Man and Animals.* Drawing widely on the studies and anecdotal information he could find, Darwin argued that happiness was communicated by laughter, smiling, tears of joy, color in the cheeks, and, when intense, by "dancing about, clapping the hands, [and] stamping." Happiness, he said, was similar in these ways to high spirits, tender feelings, and some manifestations of insanity but different from religious devotion, which was often combined with fear. The most distinguishing features of happy faces, he thought, were a "bright and sparkling eye" and "the drawing backwards and upwards of the corners of the mouth." Today, there is consensus among scientists that fine-grained wrinkles near the eyes and a smiling mouth are the features through which the face communicates happiness. These signals appear to be more readily and more universally recognized than anger, disgust, sadness, and distrust, which vary from culture to culture. Social psychophysics emotion recognition research using digital imagery has probed the details of which facial muscles are involved and how faintly or distinctly the distinguishing features can be recognized—all of which has proven useful in applied disciplines such as robotics, animated cinematography, forensic national security, and artificial intelligence.[9]

Happiness is dispositional. To say that it is "dispositional" means that levels of overall happiness are relatively stable over time within individuals and are stabilized by personality traits, lifestyle choices, and perhaps also by genetic characteristics. A person who is disposed toward happiness, psychologist Daniel Haybron writes, "is prone to take greater pleasure in things, to see things in a more positive light, to take greater notice of good things, to be more optimistic [and] less likely to become anxious, fearful, angry, or despondent." Dispositions are habits born of previous experiences and familiar ways of responding to the point that they are largely nondeliberative. In popular parlance, an individual may be known as a fretful or angry person, having a dyspeptic or abrasive personality, or being cheerful and well dispositioned. One approach has associated these differences with extroversion and introversion—the former being happier on average because of a more engaging personality that easily makes friends while the latter is withdrawn or fearful and thus less happy. This approach, however, has been criticized on the grounds that personality differences themselves are insufficiently understood or exaggerated and fail to account for the more enduring traits that distinguish some people as happier than others. Whatever the source of these characteristics may be, they are reinforced both by the fact that significant others *perceive* the person to be this way and by the fact that the person *adopts* a self-referential identity that conforms to the perception. Facial morphology is one of the ways in which evidence—accurate and inaccurate—of such presumed personality traits as "cheerful" and "dour" is communicated. "Positive psychology" and "well-being research" are among the specialties in which long-term dispositions are emphasized. That happiness is stable is also the basis on which survey research studies operationalize happiness with questions asking respondents to rate their happiness on a simple scale and with which broad comparisons are made across regions, countries, and income groups.[10]

Happiness is episodic. Although it may be stable on average, happiness is subject to changes in mood and to fluctuations that occur at irregular intervals in response to such conditions as changes in the weather or one's health and to such events as having received good or bad news. It is commonplace that a person can be in high spirits one day, depressed the next, and overjoyed the following day. Whereas stable happiness is characterized as overall contentment or well-being, unstable happiness is described in the research literature as "momentary" happiness, "moods," or "hedonia," and as variations in duration and intensity. One approach to the relationship between unstable and stable happiness is the concept of hedonic adaptation, which suggests that humans adjust to moments of intense pleasure by returning to a more stable level of happiness. Joy is often described as momentary happiness that is particularly intense. The episodic character of happiness, though, is interwoven with the fact that these fluctuations are interpreted through the lens of the memories and habits of response that a person brings to each new situation.[11]

Happiness is conditioned by life chances. Much of the literature on the social conditioning of happiness can be summarized under the heading of life chances. The social conditions having the greatest impact on happiness are the ones that shape persons' chances of achieving what they want from life—relative to their expectations, which are also a function of social conditions. Research has found considerable support for this argument. Thus, happiness is shown to be affected by or at least correlated with higher levels of income and education, having a rewarding occupation, enjoying good health, being married, and having friends.[12] The life chances literature demonstrates the extent to which overall happiness is composed of multiple and often complex considerations. For example, a study drawing on surveys conducted in more than twenty countries found that respondents in all the countries overwhelmingly regarded raising children as one of the greatest joys in life, but those responses were tempered by perceptions about the burdens of raising children, which varied considerably from country to country because of differences in educational policies, family leave programs, and ideas about the value of traditional families.[13]

Happiness is agentic. A person can choose within limits to avoid unpleasant situations, engage in pleasurable activities, and look on the bright side when stressful occasions cannot be avoided. Making such choices is of course the point of such groups as the "Just Be Happy Club"—a personal growth through community service organization for teens—and of books such as Andreas Braun's *Practicing Happiness: Four Essential Techniques to Overcome Emotional Pain, Find Peace of Mind and Open Your Heart* and Anna Quindlen's *Short Guide to a Happy Life.* The scholarly literature in the field of positive psychology supports the claim that individuals can do things to increase their happiness, for example, by practicing kindness, engaging in physical exercise, and watching fewer hours of television. Much of the popular self-help literature is concerned with steps individuals can take to attain marginal increases in happiness. In larger terms, therefore, happiness is associated with ideas about personal influence, autonomy, and control; the ability to achieve happiness is a kind of personal empowerment.[14] However, the idea that happiness is agentic is also the focus of work that views this argument critically. The gist of this work is that agency reflects a desire to be happy, which can then be manipulated and exploited. For example, advertising plays on consumers' desire for happiness, offers a way for consumers to exercise their agency in making choices about their expenditures, but at the same time guides those choices toward specific goods and services.[15]

Happiness is cultural. Certain aspects of happiness are nearly culturally invariant; for example, one line of research called "embodied cognition" shows that metaphors such as "up" for happy and "down" for sad are not only common to diverse cultures but are also associated with bodily movement and spatial organization. These associations are such that subjects have been found to describe intense happiness as "moving up" through their torso, exhibit more pleasurable feelings or recall happier events when standing than sitting or when lifting their hands or heads, and locate words like "joy" higher on computer screens or place them higher on spatial grids than words like "sad" or "surprised."[16] However, the terms with which happiness is described and especially the meanings these words convey vary from place to place and are conditioned by the available repertoires for communicating about them. The same smile and the same fine-grained wrinkles around the eyes can be interpreted as signals of well-being in one context, as giddiness in another, as frivolity in another, and as felicity in yet another. Although the descriptions may be influenced by the duration and intensity of the specific facial expression, the choice of words and their meanings are largely independent of these physiological determinants. Thus, the analysis of culture, as Ann Swidler summarizes, is concerned with "how the larger semiotic structure—the discursive possibilities available in a given social world—constrains meaning by constructing the categories through which people perceive themselves and others or simply by limiting what can be thought and said." As the semiotic structure in which ideas are framed, these discursive possibilities are inscribed in embodied habits that exercise power and at the same time provide opportunities for improvisation. "Emotion culture" includes nuanced vocabularies for describing emotions, norms about expressing feelings, ideologies that ascribe moral meaning to emotions, and folk psychologies that account for the origin and incidence of emotions. Customs of social interaction, tradition, and language all bear on how happiness is communicated and interpreted. The interpretations, in turn, affect such matters as whether an individual is perceived to be "in the know," a welcome colleague, an outsider, confused, or troubled, and what should be done to advance or restrain certain emotions. Much interest in the cultural construction of emotions has been directed toward studies of the changing meanings associated with anger, grief, sexual gratification, love, gendered expressivity, and the languages of ecstasy and personal fulfillment.[17]

Happiness is shaped by social institutions. Institutions—schools, businesses, neighborhoods, medical establishments, mental health practices, law enforcement agencies, political parties, voluntary associations, and churches—are collections of enforceable norms that exercise power over the individuals who participate in them. Institutions' norms include expectations not only about their participants' activities but also about their feelings. These expectations include implicit—and sometimes explicit—rules about what feelings are appropriate to experience and how they should be expressed. The rules are specific to situations within institutions as well; for example, governing when school children must suppress their feelings and when their feelings can be expressed, and may vary in how they are applied to children of different genders and ethnicities. The institutional shaping of happiness has been of particular interest in studies of the effects on the meaning and expression of emotions of major institutional changes, such as the birth of insane asylums, the diffusion of the romantic novel, the mental health movement, the growth of popular psychology, the commercialization of advertising, and the prevalence of service industry work. The institutional shaping of happiness takes account of the fact that happiness as a cultural phenomenon exists beyond how individuals may experience happiness. The fact that hundreds of thousands of books about happiness, courses about it, self-help training sessions, public lectures, and therapy sessions focus on it is testimony to the fact that happiness is institutionally produced—that happiness is a cultural product rather than only a subjective experience.[18]

The literature in which these characteristics of happiness have been identified has dealt with the topic largely from the standpoint of the individual who experiences and expresses happiness physiologically in a combination of durable and fluctuating ways and is influenced by social and cultural circumstances. In much of this literature, happiness is conceived as varying in the degree of positive or negative affect the person experiences, the intensity of these feelings, and their duration. The exceptions—which have been of greater interest to sociologists and anthropologists—are the cultural and institutional conditioning of happiness. Cultural factors and institutional settings shape not only the degree of affect an individual experiences but also the meanings assigned to those experiences. In some of this literature, the individual is center stage, but the individual experiences and interprets happiness in cognitively significant ways. This approach draws from the philosophical literature in which emotions are understood to be experienced within mentally framed categories. Happiness in this understanding is not only pleasurable but also variously experienced as deserved or undeserved, as an indication of success, as a blessing, or perhaps as a harbinger of disappointment. Another approach focuses less on the individual and more on the social circumstances themselves. In this approach, the individual is no longer the measure of all things. Instead, scholars are interested in the repertoires of language, narratives, and norms about happiness that are institutionally produced and reproduced.[19]

Practice theory brings together the embodied, dispositional, and situational elements that shape social activity. A practice—playing a musical instrument, coding a computer program, filing one's taxes, cooking a meal, or participating in a worship service—is composed of a sequence of action, cognition, and communication that unfolds in a particular place and time. The components are guided by the habits that individuals carry into the situation, by the power structure of the situation, and by the purposes the individuals hope to achieve. Practices are in this respect goal oriented, although the emphasis on lived experience allows for goals to be modified and intentions to be iteratively revised.[20] Feelings are an essential feature of practices, experienced and expressed bodily, and interacting with the cognitive frames that give them meaning. In some versions of practice theory, feelings are entirely shaped by the practice with which they are associated. As Andreas Reckwitz observes, "every practice contains a certain practice-specific emotionality," which in his view means that emotions belong to practices rather than to individuals.[21] Practice-specific emotionality of this kind—what Michel de Certeau called a "feeling tone"—broadly defines the moods that are present under certain circumstances, such as a lighthearted mood at a party but a serious mood while performing surgery.[22] In other versions of practice theory, emotions are evoked by places and memories and therefore are more specific to individuals and situations, more variable and agentic, and yet are guided by social norms that influence what is experienced, what is expressed, and how these experiences and expressions are interpreted.[23]

Emotional practices are enactments of bodily dispositions, emotional know-how, and feeling rules conditioned by a social context. In this understanding, emotions are, as Monique Scheer has emphasized, not something that people simply have but things that people do.[24] Emotional practices include the activities in which people engage to achieve a particular emotional state, such as taking a walk to enjoy the beauty of nature; the activity involved in attaching meaning to an emotion, such as reading a book about nature before taking a walk; interacting with people in situations where certain emotions are experienced and expressed, such as participating in a worship service; and doing things to regulate one's own or others' emotions, such as setting up a space in which to worship and organizing how the worship is conducted. Emotional practices are dynamic, which means that they are both spontaneous and conventional, shaped by memories of past experiences, habits, cues present in the immediate situation, and expectations about the future. They are spatially located in real and imagined situations that provide affordances for their expression and presumptive definitions of what is appropriate to do, think, and feel in that space. "Feeling rules," in Arlie Hochschild's influential formulation, consist of stated norms about such things as when to smile and how much affect to display toward strangers as well as more generalized norms about the kinds of emotional temperaments that are best to cultivate for handling the ups and downs of life. Power is most obviously present in who has the authority to establish and enforce the norms.[25] Emotional know-how is the conceptual repertoire with which the meanings of feelings are shaped. Power is also present in the management of emotional know-how.

Sociologist Marci Cottingham's work on emotional practices has valuably developed practice theory's distinctive contributions to the study of emotions. She suggests, first, that the practice approach emphasizes "what happens *before, beneath,* and *beyond* individuals and their felt or managed emotions." What makes an emotion more than a feeling or mood, she argues, is "a vocabulary of knowing and feeling that allows one to match certain sensations with certain labels [and] to recognize a given sensation as distinct and in need of a label." In short, emotional practices are rooted in stocks of cultural knowledge. Second, the practice approach emphasizes the "flow of subtle and simultaneous sensations," she says, that ebb and flow in given situations and that also reflect the embodied emotional memory of previous experiences. Third, the practice approach emphasizes the "social forces that shape what happens deep within us," including how we respond and how we make use of emotions in social interaction. Finally, the practice approach emphasizes "the broader structure of the social hierarchies that shape our lives," such as gender, race, and social class.[26]

The advantage of conceptualizing happiness as an emotional practice is that happiness ceases to be understood strictly as a feeling, attitude, or construct that exists within individuals' subjectivities but becomes the nexus between those subjectivities and the norms, power structures, situations, and cultural toolkits that shape them and their expression. As emotional practice, happiness fluctuates, is influenced by situations, and is subject to the power arrangements present in those situations. It is embodied not only as a somatic sensation but also through the physical spaces in which bodies interact and the metaphoric roles that bodies play in depictions of sexual pleasure, birth, and death. Although individuals may have a great deal of discretion in what they do to achieve it, happiness is embedded in situations over which individuals have limited control. Expectations about what it is and about what is appropriate to do to achieve it are built into the situation. Happiness is in these ways regulated by the repertoires available for naming it as happiness and contrasting it with other emotions, the spatial arrangements and affordances that facilitate and constrain expressions of happiness, the intrusions that may compromise these situations and require adaptations, and the other practices from which happiness may be derived as a side benefit.

Studies of religion and happiness have mostly been concerned with religion's effects on the degree to which individuals experience pleasurable feelings that qualify as subjective indications of happiness. One approach emphasizes the role of religious beliefs. Taking its cues from religious teachings, this approach suggests that people of faith are happy because their faith in God offers hope for life after death, thereby reducing worries about dying, easing the pain of bereavement, and giving them something positive to think about from day to day whenever life seems dreary. The believer may figure that God is in control of all that is beyond the person's own control, including everything from health, personal finances, and the well-being of one's family. Belief in God may also sensitize believers to the goodness of life—the beauty of nature, small kindnesses received and given—and to the inherent meaning and purpose of life. Although the details of these arguments have seldom been examined directly, studies generally find that people who are involved in religion (and thus are assumed to believe in God) score higher on questions about happiness and subjective well-being. The strength of these relationships varies but is found among adherents of various religious traditions and is present when other factors (such as age, gender, income, and health) are taken into account.[27]

A related body of literature emphasizes the role of social factors—such as social interaction, peers, reference groups, and social contexts—as the key influences of religion on happiness. Rather than attributing the effects of religion directly to religious beliefs, these studies suggest that beliefs' effects occur by influencing the social contexts in which people spend time, make friends, and take their cues. One way this might work is that religiously motivated people simply spend more time with other people (worshipping, praying, singing, conversing) than people who sit at home watching television or working in their gardens. The religiously inclined for this reason may be happier because being with other people is a source of happiness. Additionally, it may be that associating with religious people has more of an effect on happiness than associating with other kinds of people. For instance, religious people may exude expectations about happiness because they themselves are happier, because the feeling rules that govern the places where they interact encourage expressions of happiness, because there is a sense of being among like-minded people, because religious people are somehow "nicer," or because they can be counted on whenever emotional or material support may be needed. Whatever the sources may be, studies generally support the idea that social interaction is one of the ways that religion elevates its participants' levels of happiness.[28]

Studies that focus on religion and happiness from the standpoint of their manifestations as social practices have developed alternative concepts that de-center the individual in favor of an emphasis on the repertoires of language, power structures, and social norms that influence what happiness means. These studies are less concerned with the levels of happiness or unhappiness that individuals may experience than with how happiness is understood, how its pursuit is publicly defended, what moral meanings are assigned to it, what happy people are expected to do, and why some kinds of happiness are better than others. Without obscuring the fact that individuals exercise agency in their experiences and expressions of feelings, these alternative concepts emphasize structures of power, contested definitions of reality, and the social norms that are cued in concrete situations.[29] Religious institutions put forth ideas about who God is and how God should be worshipped, they put these ideas into practice in how worship services are conducted, and they practice worship in these ways because these ways are believed to be theologically correct. Religious institutions also establish rules about how clergy should be trained, teachings about what is proper for a society's laws to say about religious freedom, understandings about how religious truth differs from scientific truth, and expectations about when and where religious services should be held. Likewise, religious institutions advance ideas about where happiness is to be found, how it should be expressed in worship services and in daily life, what roles God and the church are understood to play, and what kinds of happiness should be avoided. In these respects, as religious studies scholar Charles Mathewes writes, "churches are those institutions that aim to give us a communal and personal, intellectual and affective, structure to help cultivate joy."[30] One finds rules about the "ecclesially disciplined cultivation of joy" and expectations about "joyful praise" and "spreading the good news." Religious leaders are of course interested in whether participants understand these rules and expectations, but the rules and expectations are based on considerations of what is right, what is good, and how things have been done in the past rather than only on whether participants find them pleasing. In this respect, institutions are social arrangements that constrain the roles that are played within them and that create the opportunities through which conformity, resistance, and innovation are performed. Institutions are scenes in which social arrangements are worked out that shape what is taught, expected, and taken for granted about beliefs, activities, and feelings.

The approach that focuses on religion as a social practice offers several concepts that can be useful in thinking about religion's role in shaping the meanings of happiness. Most important is the fact that religion competes with other institutions that play a role in shaping what happiness means. Just as religion competes with science for ideas about the universe, so it competes with secular sources of happiness. The entertainment industry of course is one but so also is commercial advertising, the workplace, and the therapy industry. Institutions stake out their turf in ways that define what they do as "authentic," "scientific," "true," and in other ways compelling or gratifying, while defining their competitors' wares as inauthentic, superstitious, false, or in other ways uncompelling or unsatisfactory. When religious leaders argue against playing sports or shopping on Sundays, for example, they are talking not only about the use of time but also about how to understand and experience happiness. They are advancing arguments about why some kinds of joy are deeply fulfilling and enduring while others are frivolous and ephemeral. Moreover, these arguments are accompanied by moral justifications that, especially in the context of religion, explain why it is important to be happy in certain ways and not in other ways. Moral justifications include arguments about what is godly or ungodly, virtuous or not virtuous, edifying for one's spiritual growth or not edifying. Scholars call the deployment of these arguments "boundary work." Boundary work consists of drawing both symbolic and social distinctions that separate one group from another group. Boundary work is an important part of what religious institutions do to protect and preserve their influence. Faith communities engage in boundary work when they preach about what is right or wrong to believe, when they make membership contingent on holding to a particular creedal formulation, when they encourage the faithful to spend their time among kindred spirits, and when they discourage the faithful from interacting with "unbelievers."[31]

Related to this kind of boundary work is the task of settling major disagreements within institutions. In-fighting, theological differences, and schisms over denominational governance are among the kinds of disagreements that characterize religious institutions. Despite wanting to be known for its love, acceptance, and unity, Christianity in the United States has often been a snakepit of contention and division. How these disagreements are resolved reflects the power structures within institutions, especially who commands the largest and most prestigious pulpits, who has the best funded congregations, and who has the most access to the shapers of public opinion. Disagreements in religion have roiled into major controversies about crucial theological interpretations and about such seemingly minor issues as kinds of music. Disagreements also develop around how happiness should be attained and expressed. A perennial question is how to think about the happiness to be attained in heaven compared with whatever happiness may be experienced on earth. Happiness in these discussions is not one of degree alone but of kind, suggesting that certain practices are conducive to finding happiness by thinking about heaven, while other practices are sinful distractions. Another perennial question is how best to express happiness and whether those expressions should be taken as evidence of good standing in the community of faith; for example, is a cheerful person a better Christian than an anxious person? What about a person who has experienced ecstatic joy during a worship service versus a person who has never felt that way? These are practical questions that bear on what believers are supposed to feel and how they should show their feelings. They are questions that participants in religious institutions may also resolve through the meanings they assign to happiness. In a study of a university-based evangelical Christian organization, for example, the members spoke about their differences from non-Christians primarily in language that disallowed Christians from experiencing negative emotions, claimed that being a Christian necessarily meant being happy, and associated happiness with moral goodness. Happiness was thus a property of the group as much as it was of the individual participants, serving as a mechanism of group identity and of exclusion against non-Christians.[32]

As this example suggests, an important aspect of religious institutions is their capacity to produce ideas about happiness and to encourage those ideas to be practiced. Like other institutions, religious organizations use the time and money at their disposal to generate ideas and activities. Churches' power, for example, consists of their capacity to set aside certain times and places for worship, to certify the authority of clergy, and to establish membership criteria. Churches would rarely *require* that participants in church activities be happy, but they would likely *expose* participants to happy words, happy music, happy greetings, happy friends, and expectations about happiness. Not only do religious organizations facilitate exposure of these kinds, the organizations also function as communities of memory in which joys of the past are preserved. "All joy *reminds*," C. S. Lewis wrote. It includes "a desire for something longer ago or further away or still 'about to be.'" Religious organizations are well suited to do this because they invite participants to reflect on where their lives have been and where they are going. Additionally, the words and experiences are couched in language that deems them worthy because of values transcending personal happiness itself, such as praise, worship, divine love, and obedience to God.[33]

Language is in fact such an important aspect of religion that *how* happiness is articulated is an important topic. The literatures on discursive power and narratives suggest that references to positive concepts—God, love, salvation, forgiveness, and joy—are often embedded in stories that contrast them with negative concepts, such as evil, sin, guilt, and anxiety. Especially when extraordinarily positive concepts are described—for example, the ecstasy of heavenly joy—the narratives rely heavily on contrasts between these concepts and descriptions of mundane experiences. The sacred is thus set apart in a way that points to exceptional possibilities for happiness and to the processes through which these possibilities may be experienced without claiming to describe the indescribable. The sacred as an experience of joy or as a place where joy can be attained is also, as Émile Durkheim famously argued, a source of empowerment, an instantiation in visibly joyful celebration that the weak can be strong and the oppressed can rise up.[34]

The other kind of work in which institutions engage is forging connections where those connections can benefit the institution without compromising its identity or resources. Religious organizations borrow ideas from the wider culture, absorb practices that help them communicate better, devise strategies for earning money, forge alliances with civic organizations, start businesses, file lawsuits, and lobby for social policies. Many of these connections pose challenges to religious institutions' views about happiness. Questions arise about entertainment, sports, music, sex, gender, laughter, families, spending, leisure, and time management. The questions raise deeper concerns about what is godly, what is tolerable, and what might be worth considering in new ways. Scholars have investigated many of these topics in the terms in which they have been cast, especially whether certain activities are defensible under the law. Whether these are legitimate sources of happiness is often an issue as well.

Power is a feature of all these ways in which faith communities shape, regulate, govern, and guide how participants are expected to experience and express happiness. Happiness itself is a kind of power, as Sara Ahmed has emphasized, because we desire it and do certain things in the hope of attaining it.[35] Faith communities in this respect have power because they offer people guidance in how to achieve a happy life. Power is more specifically present as ritual power, discursive power, institutional power, identity power, and political power. Ritual power is the exercise of influence through the special practices of worship and sacred celebration of which religion is composed. It can be the occasion in which participants expect to experience happiness or joy in special ways. Discursive power is exercised through the arguments that faith leaders put forward in sermons, tracts, essays, and books and is evident, especially in how narratives are constructed to emphasize categories of feelings, such as stories that link happiness with scriptural examples of good behavior. Institutional power is a faith community's control of space, time, and money, which can be used to specify when and where a joyful or entertaining event can take place. Identity power is religion's capacity to draw boundaries between "us" and "them" and to amplify distinctions based on age, gender, and race. It can be used, for example, to define how women should express feelings differently from men. Political power is religion's capacity to use secular authorities, such as laws, the police, and government officials, to ensure that some activities do not happen or are punished if they do, such as the pursuit of illicit pleasure through sexual liaisons, drugs, or the consumption of alcohol.[36]

The pages that follow focus on moments in American religious history from the eighteenth century to the early twenty-first century when religious leaders experimented with new possibilities for bringing faith and expressions of happiness together in innovative ways. The episodes focus on Protestant and Catholic faith communities and illustrate how these communities guided the complexities of faith as it pertained to the pursuit of happiness. In each instance, a close examination of the events and arguments reveals how happiness was conceived and how those conceptions created practical problems for the communities involved. The episodes are a handful of the many ways in which faith communities have drawn nuanced distinctions among kinds of happiness, explained why and how the faithful should experience happiness in their daily lives, created real and symbolic boundaries sheltering faith-sanctioned methods of realizing happiness from doubtful methods, and adapted to new opportunities and challenges.[37]

The relation of heavenly joy and earthly joy, which had always been of interest among church leaders, underwent significant changes in the late colonial and early national periods, cautiously embracing the idea that cheerfulness and godly living went hand in hand. This was a critical period in

American religious history when improved living conditions contributed to the likelihood of enjoying longer and happier lives on this side of heaven. Anticipating happiness after death was more easily matched by expectations about happiness in the present life. The most prominent religious authorities addressed the relationship between heavenly and earthly happiness in numerous sermons, tracts, and essays. The emotion work on which they focused demonstrated several of the most enduring ways in which emotional practices are shaped. These consisted of metaphoric comparisons that contrasted and amplified the emotional valences of heavenly and earthly happiness, the use of deathbed narratives as ways of situating emotion in memorable venues, and the incorporation of authoritative advice in guidance about daily living. The eighteenth-century development of these approaches to earthly pleasure and heavenly bliss is the focus of Chapter 1.

With relatively few organized congregations, the revival meetings that began during the 1740s emerged again in the early nineteenth century as an important means of spreading the gospel. Revivalism offered participants opportunities to experience their faith in more deeply emotional ways and to express these emotional experiences more openly. Camp meetings developed at the start of the nineteenth century as ways of bringing people together and, in the process, posed new questions about expressions of ecstatic joy. The meetings were exceptional, differing from ordinary revival meetings by gathering hundreds of people together not for an evening or an afternoon but for several days or an entire week. They were thus living together, which meant that a wider variety of emotions were likely than the ones typically experienced at an ordinary church meeting. The key to a successful camp meeting was careful management. Clergy and appointed camp managers organized every detail, from selecting and clearing a space to providing seating, and from specifying where men and women and people of different races were to sit or stand to patrolling the grounds for visits from liquor dealers and prostitutes. Careful camp meeting organization also required monitoring emotions. People came to enjoy socializing with friends and neighbors, to enjoy singing and listening to sermons, and in some cases to experience the holy spirit in emotionally extravagant ways. How the camp meeting managers dealt with these multiple emotions is an instructive example of religion's shaping of emotional practice. I show in Chapter 2 that spatial arrangements, precedents, and authoritative interpretation were the keys to sorting out the differences among convivial happiness, worshipful enjoyment, and ecstatic joy.

As churches grew, especially in larger cities, they required more money to build larger buildings, to maintain these buildings, and to better serve the public needs of their communities. Before large city-wide expositions became popular, urban congregations determined that a good way to raise money was to organize church fairs. These were festive occasions that offered food, drink, entertainment, and items for sale, all in the hope of generating income from happy visitors. The events were called ladies' fairs because women did all the work. Some of the fairs lasted for weeks and drew tens of thousands of visitors. They were new or at least more newly commercialized ways for faith communities to promote happiness. As such, they posed another set of managerial questions. Was it appropriate for this kind of festivity to happen in the same sacred space that was used for worship? Were the women who did the work supposed to enjoy themselves in the same way as the men who visited the fairs? Were there kinds of enjoyment that might put the churches in legal jeopardy? Could these events be downscaled to a manageable size that could serve as modes of entertainment in smaller congregations? I discuss these questions in Chapter 3.

The Social Gospel and other social reform movements of the late nineteenth and early twentieth centuries expanded faith communities' horizons beyond the usual worship and charity activities in which they had long been engaged by asserting that the wider society could be remade through service organizations and through useful work in the professions and other careers. Service itself was hardly a novel idea for faith communities but serving on a large scale and doing so more skillfully and responsibly was. These reform movements have been examined mostly as the kinds of service activities they organized. But they were also engaged in advancing a more forthright argument about emotional practice. That argument drew the connection between useful service and durable happiness. Useful service was to be engaged in by people of faith not simply in obedience to God but because it was a way to pursue happiness. In simplest terms, a usefully serving person was a happy person. Making this a compelling argument required reconceptualizing labor as well. The reformers hoped that doing so would reduce patronizing approaches to social service and elevate workers' sense of personal dignity. It was a tall order that mostly failed but contributed to the idea that individual persons were responsible for their own happiness. I discuss these developments in Chapter 4.

Mid-twentieth-century theologies of play added another dimension to the discussion of religion's relation to the pursuit of happiness. Although a largely forgotten theology of play had been advanced by Horace Bushnell in the early nineteenth century, the mid-twentieth versions drew from the work of Johan Huizinga and Alfred Schutz, among others, and were developed by Robert Bellah, Harvey Cox, and a few others. Play was surely an emotional practice in which those involved were expected to be happy. But theologies of play posed several problems for religious authorities: what kind of play was appropriate, could it be managed by religious authorities, and what did play have to do with theology anyway? The answers to these questions depended on depicting play as a kind of "innocent" or "childish" activity, arguing that God could be reimagined as transcendence or even as a playful being who wanted the faithful to have as much fun as possible, and proposing that worship services could be playful. Chapter 5 discusses these developments.

In recent years, the idea of working hard at one's spiritual practice and being a good church worker has further influenced how happiness is achieved, even as faith communities have maintained and adapted long traditions of celebrating the sacred. Like other religious activities, disciplined spiritual practice is expected to facilitate personal happiness or well-being, although that is generally not its stated purpose. Also, like other religious activities, spiritual practice is guided by persons with authority to do so, but spiritual practice has been guided more by spiritual directors than by clergy. It has also been furthered by new technologies of self-monitoring, thus emphasizing measurable progress, including a person's daily moods. Spiritual practice in the process offers a means of attaining happiness by engaging in hard self-examination and spiritual work. Chapter 6 discusses the hard work of finding spiritual happiness.

There have also been numerous instances in which trust in faith communities was damaged by the pursuit of illicit joy. Extramarital sexual relations, the sexual abuse of children, and sexual harassment, not to mention lying and cheating, have topped the list. These prurient ways of pursuing happiness, especially when engaged in by religious authorities, contrast with most of the other ways in which faith communities have adapted to changing emotional practices and are especially worthy of consideration for that reason. Faith communities have attempted to restore the trust that has been broken by developing trustworthy ways of responding. Some of these are composed of emotional practices in which guilt, shame, and remorse are expressed, while others involve formal hearings and legal proceedings. The fallout from these illicit pursuits of happiness is the focus of Chapter 7.

Collectively, these episodes represent major milestones in American religion's adaptation to changing secular conditions. Just as faith communities adapted to science, rising levels of education, and industrialization, so they developed accommodations to new opportunities for experiencing happiness. They found ways to shape emotional practices so that happiness could be pursued through social gatherings, festivals, play, and in other ways, not by engaging in these activities in secular venues but by doing so within the faith community itself. These were improvisations that kept religious authorities in charge while also enabling happiness to be pursued in ways resembling their expression in secular settings. People of faith were encouraged to think of happiness in its relationship to God's blessings, the value of cheerfulness in their social relationships, and the pleasures they may have enjoyed in childhood. Although these episodes were a small part of the history of American religion, they illustrate how religious institutions have dealt with the complexities of happiness in the past and suggest how faith and happiness continue to be related today.

1

Earthly and Heavenly Happiness

Dialogic Comparisons in Colonial America

In this chapter, I describe how religious authorities' depictions of heaven, the pleasures to be experienced there, and their relevance for happiness in earthly life figure as examples of the ways in which religion shapes emotional practice. I draw from the rich materials preserved in collections of sermons, tracts, testimonials, and religious periodicals produced and published in eighteenth-century America as well as the work of historians of American religion. The eighteenth century was a time not only in which much was being written about heaven but also in which ideas about its relationship to happiness in this life were changing. Longevity was increasing, child mortality was decreasing, many people were living in or near settled communities, a spiritual awakening was spreading up and down the Eastern seaboard, and a nation's identity was being forged, all of which increased the conviction that happiness could more easily be attained in the present life as well as in the life to come. Emotional practice reflected religious authorities' efforts to address these changes.[1]

Religious leaders had a great deal to say about heavenly joy. They described what heaven was like, spoke of its glory, encouraged believers to look forward to being in heaven, and told them what they had to do to get there. Although there were theological disagreements, and although a few writers disavowed the idea of heaven completely, religious authorities' training, command of scripture, leadership positions, and rhetorical skill gave them nearly unrivaled control of the discourse about heaven.[2] In using this power to explain heavenly happiness, they referred frequently to earthly happiness as well, showing how it differed from heavenly joy, how it distracted from thinking about heaven, how it could be a divine blessing, and how it sometimes prefigured heavenly happiness. In these ways, they instructed the faithful on how to think about earthly happiness by placing it in a framework that was profoundly moral as well as spiritual.[3]

Nurturing Happiness. Robert Wuthnow, Oxford University Press. © Oxford University Press 2025.
DOI: 10.1093/9780197807071.003.0002

The features of emotional practice that most clearly come into play in these changing accounts of happiness are the discursive repertoires that religious authorities employed in contrasting heaven and earth, in detailing deathbed testimonials, and in exhibiting religious claims in advice about moral living. Discursive repertoires consisting of sermons, doctrinal expositions, and creedal statements are among the most important ways in which religious communities exercise power.[4] These repertoires provide the language with which moral distinctions are drawn between proper and improper modes of action. They convey meanings about emotions as well as about doctrines and beliefs, and, in so doing, communicate moral expectations about the kinds of emotion that are considered appropriate and the kinds that are inappropriate.[5] These meanings are conveyed in idioms that attach labels to feelings, explain when and why particular feelings are appropriate, and associate the feelings with scripts about God, faith, and moral behavior.[6] Many of the discursive repertoires are expressed in narratives that depict role models whose actions dramatize choices resulting in positive or negative emotions.[7]

Dialogic comparisons that create cognitive categories are a common feature of these repertoires.[8] The comparisons establish a "discursive field" or "frame" in which the meaning of one thing is defined by contrasting it with something else.[9] The contrast illuminates certain characteristics of the topic under consideration and precludes or restricts other possibilities. When the frame is part of a hegemonic discourse, its power consists of organizing how meaning is ascribed to specific ideas and emotions. Metaphoric imagery sharpens the distinctions—us-them, up-down, in-out, and happy-sad—by personalizing the alterities, marking them with spatial distinctions, and supplementing them with positive and negative emotional valences.[10] The distinctions are nevertheless permeable, allowing the traits associated with one category to interpenetrate those of the contrasting category.[11] Heavenly glory, for example, is vastly greater than anything on earth, thereby putting earthly happiness in a subordinate position, and yet heavenly glory may be experienced in small measure in ordinary life and ordinary happiness may provide the metaphors with which heavenly glory is imagined.[12] The discursive repertoires employed in deathbed narratives add emotional intensity that is more persuasively expressed in these situations than at other times. Happiness in these otherwise grim narratives carries exceptional meaning, as the faithful are encouraged to examine their lives, pray, adhere to the Word spoken and read, and strive for eternal happiness. The discursive repertoires reinforce the power differences between religious authorities and their followers by offering authoritative accounts based on leaders' training, biblical knowledge, and homiletical expertise.

The arguments about earthly and heavenly happiness are divided broadly into three categories: denying the possibility of earthly happiness, acknowledging but diminishing the value of earthly happiness, and emphasizing the possibility of attaining earthly happiness as an inducement for virtuous living. Each of the three involved conceptions of heavenly happiness as the condition against which earthly happiness was compared. The three also implied ways of understanding human agency in the pursuit of happiness. In brief, the denial of earthly happiness identified misery, sorrow, melancholia, and gloom as emotions that were to be expected in earthly life and that were essentially given by the conditions in which people had been placed by God. The diminished value of earthly happiness granted the human desire for happiness and the possibility of pursuing and partially attaining it but showed its limitations in comparison with heavenly happiness. The idea that earthly happiness could be attained through virtuous living assumed a greater role of human agency in making moral decisions that nevertheless needed to be guided by religious authorities' teachings about heaven.

Religious authorities assumed that their guidance was essential to the public's salvation, and thus of supreme benefit, as well as advantageous to the attainment of happiness. The guidance was based on leaders' understanding of scripture, which they studied, debated, and prayed about, and for which there were rules within their traditions about how it should be interpreted. To the extent that religion was voluntary (which was truer in some locations than others), people were free to follow or not follow their leaders' guidance. The benefits of following the guidance included being a member in good standing of one's faith, having assurance of one's eternal salvation, and knowing that certain activities were right and good. But religious authorities' guidance served their own purposes as well as those of their adherents. The guidance encouraged adherents to spend time praying, studying the Bible, thinking about God, going regularly to church, and doing what they could to advance the gospel—not simply because it was their duty but because they would be happier doing so. There were emotional costs, too. When heavenly happiness was more desirable than any of the joys of earthly life, even the most innocent pursuits of happiness could be perceived as spiritual afflictions.

"Supposing we were to have no pleasure on this side of heaven," George Whitefield remarked in a 1736 letter, "yet the thoughts of being happy, and that too for all eternity hereafter, methinks should teach us to bear up under every calamity here, not only with submission, but a holy joy." Anticipating joy in heaven was enough to feel joyful—"to enjoy a little heaven upon earth"—here in the moment. "Good God! The very idea of what we are to be in glory transports me while I am writing," he declared. All that could ever have been hoped for would be fulfilled in the presence of Jesus, "attended with myriads of his holy angels, who will rejoice at our safe arrival to their happy mansions."[13] Whitefield's statement compactly illustrates the several understandings of happiness that were evident in the era's preaching and teaching: first, the emphasis on negative conditions that people have to "bear up under"; second, the possibility of feeling happy but only in comparison with heavenly joy; and third, the implied possibility of gaining control of one's happiness in this life by focusing one's thoughts in certain ways.

Obvious as it may have been that heavenly joy exceeded anything on earth, faith communities had to devote time and energy to explaining what joy in heaven might be like, telling how it compared with happiness in this life, and describing what that implied about virtuous behavior. In colonial America, it could not be taken for granted that people would be as transported as Whitefield was at the mere thought of heaven. Nor could it be assumed that heavenly joy was necessarily an appealing substitute for earthly happiness. As John Locke observed, "How many are to be found that have had lively representations set before their minds of the unspeakable joys of heaven, which they acknowledge both possible and probable too, who yet would be content to take up their happiness here?"[14]

Miseries of Earthly Life

In the writing of eighteenth-century clerics that was to shape so much of America's public theology, the superiority of heavenly joy was most evident in contrast with the miseries of earthly life. Average life expectancy in the American colonies was about forty years. One child in two died before the age of ten, and the rate was much higher among children of the enslaved. Smallpox and other epidemic diseases routinely killed a quarter of those infected. Nearly everyone who had lived long enough to marry could expect to die or be bereaved within a decade.[15] "I am the creature of a day, my body is of the dust, and returning to the dust again; I am in jeopardy every hour," the English evangelical preacher Thomas Haweis wrote in a meditation that circulated widely in colonial New England.[16] The uncertainties of earthly life were deeply emotional as well as physical and material. Sermons emphasized distress, uneasiness, discontent, and confusion. These were the conditions of life. "Among the many painful reflections that are wont to occur to the serious and benevolent mind," Haweis wrote, "there is perhaps scarcely anything more melancholy than to consider the calamitous state of this disordered world."[17] In this view, melancholia was the prevailing emotion, and it was not something that a person had much control over. It was the result of a given condition of human existence: the calamitous state of the disordered world.

Worldly woe was compounded by humanity's inescapable struggle with sinfulness, about which it was necessary to be constantly reminded. Sinfulness was by nature sufficiently subtle that a person was unlikely to be aware of it unless it was discovered through the teaching and reading of scripture. "I went to school and learned to read the scriptures in my early days," a young woman recalled, learning "that I was a sinner and must be made better or I could not go to heaven. Many times I wept on that account." As an adult, attending preaching services only deepened her despair: "[I] felt myself a condemned sinner [and] felt my sins an heavy burden intolerable for me to bear."[18] Those who believed in divine grace were rewarded with the prospect of heaven; they nevertheless were conscious of the necessity for constant vigilance against evil. "Myriads of malicious fiends walk the earth unseen, seeking whom they may destroy," the righteous were warned. "[They] must meet their adversaries with determined resolution and fight with great skill and force that they may put to flight the combined armies of aliens."[19] Heaven at last would be a place where such vigilance would no longer be required. To the extent that emotions were possible to control, the most likely consequence was becoming more aware of the miseries of the sinful world, especially in comparison with the prospect of heaven.

Jonathan Edwards described the misery that came over many of the sinners he preached to in the 1730s. "Some are from the beginning carried on with abundantly more encouragement and hope than others," he said, but many experienced serious distresses. "Some have had such a sense of the displeasure of God and the great danger they were in of damnation, that they could not sleep at nights." They were afraid to sleep because of their sinful condition, he said. And if they did sleep, they realized the frightful condition of their souls when they woke up. "They have awaked with fear, heaviness, and distress still abiding on their spirits." Some were seized suddenly with conviction, moved deeply with emotion, while others were awakened more gradually to the danger of perishing eternally.[20]

In language that would recur often in coming years, sermons argued that sinfulness was worsening. The faithful might be looking forward to eternal salvation, but they were not living as virtuously as they should. Happiness depended on virtue, and virtue depended on piety. "The primitive disciples of Christ were shining examples of virtue [whose] piety was fervent without superstition and idolatry," New York Presbyterian minister Ebenezer Pemberton asserted in 1736. "They practiced an ascetic virtue in the midst of alluring temptations and manifested a generous contempt of the world when surrounded with its most agreeable enjoyments. But where is that ancient piety and virtue?" Conditions were such now, he warned, that even professors of the Gospel were enemies of Christ.[21]

The emphasis on worldly woe was amplified by descriptions of heaven that portrayed it as the absence of worldly woe. There would be no tears in heaven, no sorrow, no suffering, no fears of death, no separation from loved ones.[22] Life would not be short, cut off, terminated, but enduring forever. People's faces would not be sad but radiant. The dwelling places would not be impoverished but thoroughly furnished with crystals and gold. It was especially in times of misery that the promise of heavenly joy was sweetest. "God loves to smile most upon his people when the world frowns most," Puritan preacher Thomas Brooks explained. "They shall hear best news from heaven when they hear worst from earth."[23]

In these comparisons, heavenly happiness symbolized the comfort of knowing that one's soul was eternally secured and that the tribulations of the present life were over. The comparisons provided a language with which to think about happiness in its purest form. The language was doctrinal, framed in terms such as "eternal" and "spiritual," but it was also sensual. There was "sweetness" about heavenly joy, compared to the "bitterness" of earthly life. Heavenly joy, one minister explained, was like "white bread," compared to the "brown loaf" of earthly life.[24]

Earthly Happiness

Much of the writing about heaven, though, contrasted heavenly joy, not with earthly misery and evil, but with earthly happiness. In this characterization, the pursuit of earthly happiness was acknowledged and yet its value was diminished with comparisons of heavenly happiness. It was in this contrast that many of the era's ideas about earthly happiness developed. The prevailing theological argument was that the joy to be experienced in heaven was true joy, rather than any joy gained from earthly pleasure. In this conception, some agency was acknowledged in how happiness was pursued, but that agency was limited by sinfulness which guided it in false directions. "I challenge all the gallants in the world out of all their merry jovial clubs to find such a company of merry cheerful creatures as the friends of God are," the noted Puritan James Janeway explained in a widely reprinted sermon titled *Heaven Upon Earth.* "Worldly ease, pleasure, health, riches"—these were nothing compared to the joy of knowing God, of experiencing the "fulness of joy and pleasure forever more." There was a hint in Janeway's argument that the redeemed could be happy in this life rather than having to wait until they died to be happy. He denied that the religious life was necessarily miserable. Yet the possibility of having a "cheerful heart" was limited to thinking about the "day of judgment" rather than expecting to find it in "jovial clubs." The religious life was not a sad, melancholic, pensive life, he said; the Christian could "think of the day of judgement with great delight and comfort" and face it "with a cheerful heart."[25]

Comparisons of earthly and heavenly happiness acknowledged the human desire for happiness. "Pray is it not happiness you are in pursuit of? Doubtless it is; for 'tis as natural for mankind to be seeking after happiness, as for the sparks to fly upwards,'" a 1768 *Letter to the Unconverted* observed. "But, my deluded friend, where are you wandering? The road you take is so far from leading to it, that it will bring you straight to misery." The letter advised the reader to recall Solomon's failed search for happiness. "Let the experience of Solomon, who kept not from his eyes anything which they desired, nor withheld from his heart any joy which it sought after, but after all, found that creature enjoyments are but vanity and vexation of spirit, together with your own experience, and the daily complainings of the most prosperous wicked, convince you."[26]

Vain pursuits generated worries about emotions that in other contexts would have been above reproach. One such emotion was the happiness a person might innocently experience from associating with a friend. The difficulty was that happiness of this kind could be deemed sinful because it elevated the friend above God. The further difficulty was that earthly happiness like this seemed beyond one's control. No matter how hard one tried to suppress it, it was there—pleasurable, to be sure, but wrong. Historian William

Scheick has described the anguish that afflicted a young Presbyterian woman named Esther Edwards Burr (1732–1758) who, in her early twenties, was friends with Sarah Prince, the daughter of a Boston minister. Burr confided to her diary how joyful she was to receive letters from Prince and how delighted she was to have Prince as a friend. Yet the joy she felt was a source of self-condemnation because she thought she should have been thinking about God. She indicted herself as "carnal, fleshly, worldly minded, and devilish."[27]

Pursuing earthly happiness apart from God was vanity because it was ultimately disappointing. "My mind was lost with different affections," David Brainerd wrote in his diary in 1742. "I was looking round in the world to see if there was not some happiness to be derived from it. God, and some objects in the world, seemed each to invite my heart; and my soul was distracted between them." As he searched for happiness, the search became a source of misery. "I have not been so beset for a long time; with relation to some objects which I thought myself most dead to. But while I was desiring to please myself with anything below, sorrow and perplexity attended the first motions of desire." The misery was resolved only when he turned to God. "I found no peace, or deliverance from this distraction, till I found access to the throne of grace; and as soon as I had any sense of God, the allurements of the world vanished. But my soul mourned over my folly, that I should desire any pleasure, but in God. God forgive my spiritual idolatry!"[28]

Addressing the affluent slaveholding planters of Tidewater Virginia, William and Mary president James Blair voiced much the same message as Brainerd. "How many are there who bend all their care and study after great estates, stately houses, rich furniture, plentiful tables, and all other things which may gratify their luxury," he asked, "and in the meantime are both strangers to the joys which rise from the exercise of virtue here and to the hopes of a blessed immortality hereafter?" The particulars of that future eternal happiness, he acknowledged, were "as yet unknown to us" but were assured to be the fullest possible source of satisfaction.[29]

"Content to take up their happiness here," as Locke phrased it, was the gravest distraction from heavenly joy. In describing the happiness of heaven, ministers had a great deal to say about happiness in the present life, inadvertently describing it in some detail, if only to show why it was inferior to heavenly happiness. An argument that later observers attributed to the period was that worldly pleasure was to be strictly avoided. Max Weber's treatise on the Protestant ethic and the spirit of capitalism famously associated the Calvinist tradition's caution about worldly pleasure with its followers' devotion to work and their success in the accumulation of material possessions.[30] There certainly were warnings about earthly pleasure both within and beyond the Puritan tradition. Clergy cautioned about the "depraved appetites of the body," the misery that "appears in the garb of pleasure," and the pleasures that "tempt to excess." The sinful person was easily led away from God by earthly pleasure. "I can't tell what will become of me after death, but I resolve to have as much as I can of the pleasures and enjoyments of this life," the English nonconformist minister John Shower wrote, panning the attitude of the unrepentant. "I'll not read the Bible or any other such books as may disturb my pleasures and disquiet my mind." The Lord would blot out that person's name from the book of heaven, said Shower.[31]

But the comparison of earthly and heavenly joy was more nuanced than simply disavowing worldly pleasure. Richard Baxter, in whose writing Weber found arguments about hard work and ascetic living, was attentive to the fact that the godly experienced certain kinds of joy in their earthly lives. While their anticipation of heavenly joy was unsurpassed, the godly took momentary delight, Baxter said, like a soldier or traveler, in looking back with relief on a narrow escape. The godly person "naturally hates sorrow and loves the most merry and joyful life," he wrote. The godly further enjoyed the happiness of earthly life in some measure because of their trust in God, unlike the ungodly who only contented themselves with earthly pleasures. It was the *spontaneous* enjoyment of earthly pleasure, Weber concluded, that the Puritans' asceticism taught them to avoid. Baxter called it "carnal mirth" and "sensual delight." These were the impulsive excesses that persons who looked forward to heavenly joy knew to avoid.[32]

Apart from carnal pleasure, would-be Christians were warned about false sources of joy even when their joy seemed to focus on God. Jonathan Edwards developed this warning in his 1746 *Treatise on Religious Affections*, which contrasted the "joy of the hypocrite" and the "joy of the true saint." The hypocrite, Edwards argued, claimed to delight in the divine and took joy in hearing the word preached, but in fact was pleased "with his own privileges, and the happiness to which he supposes he has attained, or shall attain." The true saint, in contrast, found joy in "the amiable and glorious nature of the things of God." The difference was selfish joy versus God-centered joy. The one was prideful, excitable, impulsive, and shallow; the other was passion with a foundational understanding of God's excellence, beauty, and glory. The two were similar enough that care had to be taken to avoid almost any kind of pleasure that was enjoyable for reasons other than from contemplating God.[33] Of course, the need to take care did imply that the righteous could exercise some control over how they pursued happiness.

There were also earthly pleasures of which religious authorities tacitly approved. The beauty of God's creation was to be enjoyed. Devout believers played games, socialized, laughed, and enjoyed eating and drinking in moderation.[34] Moderation meant limiting the amount of time spent on these activities and keeping them in a proper subordinate perspective. Acknowledging that these were legitimate sources of happiness enabled descriptions of heavenly happiness to take them into account while at the same time arguing that heavenly happiness was different. One of the ways in which it differed was in being so glorious as to be incomprehensible. A 1766 essay on "religious joy," acknowledging that heavenly joy was "above our highest faculties," explained that the scriptures therefore "represent the happiness of the future state by such images as are not only most intelligible but most apt to please and delight the mind of man, such as, a treasure, an inheritance, a kingdom, a region of light and glory, a life exempt from disease and death, a state of society, a perfect community, consisting only of the wise and good, free from every imperfection which attended them in this world and from all other infirmities and evils."[35] Notably, these were earthly pleasures that the author was perfectly willing to embrace. If they were humanly impossible to attain fully, they nevertheless constituted a list of what was reasonable to desire.

Although eternal bliss was incomparably better than the most pleasurable experiences of earthly life, there were aspects of heavenly joy that did not quite live up to the pleasures that people experienced in this life. Ironically, heavenly joy had to be defined in ways that better accorded with human expectations. One such difficulty was that eternity could become tedious even if it was at first enjoyable. Another was that heaven seemed static whereas earthly pleasure was often derived from new insights and experiences. Yet another was that heaven seemed to imply having to abandon all reason and desire. Like avoiding infirmities and evils, these were sufficiently understood as sources of happiness that conceptions of heaven were adapted to take them into account. "There is such a pleasant variety in the happiness of heaven that after millions of years it will be as fresh and desirable as at the first hour's enjoying," declared the Puritan preacher Thomas Watson, deferring to the popular notion that time was not suspended in heaven.[36] Similarly, although it was generally agreed that sensuous pleasure was impossible in heaven, it was arguably possible in heaven to advance over time in one's knowledge of God, formulating propositions, drawing inferences, and thereby experiencing a progressive unfolding of divine joy.[37]

Comparisons of earthly and heavenly joy dealt in some detail with what it was about earthly joy that made it inferior to heavenly joy. The comparison aimed to shed light on what was impossible for humans to fully understand about heaven by relating it to how happiness was commonly experienced. Although earthly happiness was devalued in these comparisons, the comparisons nevertheless revealed how earthly happiness was thought to be experienced. The Puritan preacher John Rowe offered one of the most thoughtful treatments of earthly happiness. The natural tendency in earthly happiness, he argued, is always to want more, whereas in heaven one's desire is fully satiated. Earthly happiness therefore was associated with desire, unstable, influenced by accidents, disappointments, and intentions gone awry. The mind, though happy, was not quieted, but was restless, worried, and confused. Earthly happiness was further limited by its relationship to the body; happiness was sensual and thus "pulls us down so much to these inferior things which are present and occur to sense that we cannot rise up in our thoughts to things that are absent and out of sight. Sensuality is like a plummet of lead that hangs upon the soul and presseth it down."[38] These were ideas that demonstrated the nuances of happiness' associations with thoughts, the senses, the body, and situations.[39]

Other descriptions of heavenly joy insisted that it was "so exquisite that it mocketh all description," yet revealed how earthly happiness was understood by using earthly metaphors to suggest what heavenly happiness might be like. "It is the peculiar felicity of heavenly pleasure that, on our entrance upon it, it shall be new to us," one writer remarked. In this respect, heavenly joy would not only exceed earthly pleasure but would be like the kind of happiness that comes from a novel experience.[40] Said another writer, "There are no frowning aspects of heaven. All faces wear the pleasing smiles of love." Whether the smiles were on the faces of angels or other saints, the implication was that heavenly joy would be like having a pleasant time with happy friends. But the godly were also warned that earthly desires could be problematic even in heaven. They were cautioned about Mammon, Milton's character, who was unable to enjoy the true happiness of heaven from being dazzled by the riches of the pavement rather than the glory of God.[41]

However, such poetic imaginings of heaven were perhaps less relevant in ordinary life than the happiness that the redeemed associated with thinking about heaven. There was a kind of inner peace, comfort, and security in contemplating this kind of heavenly presence in the moment. It contrasted with the pleasures a person experienced from food, family, and friends, and it was comforting when a person was ill or lonely. In 1772, Philip Vickers Fithian, a student at the College of New Jersey in Princeton, wrote to his mother in an introspective mood about the uncertainties of life and his desire to be with his family and friends. The time seemed long, he said, but he was convinced that "it is not the place, nor condition, neither is it the presence, nor absence of relations, and friends, though most near, and tender to us, that can give us, for any length of time, either substantial joy or grief." None of those could avail, he wrote, without the presence of Almighty God. "To him, Madam, to his grace I resign myself; of him I ask direction, in my course, and in the enjoyment of him I look for happiness."[42]

Deathbed Narratives

Deathbed narratives created special opportunities to contrast earthly and heavenly joy, connect the two, and compare the experiences of the godly and ungodly. The typical deathbed narrative depicted a person anticipating death joyfully, perhaps reporting visions of heavenly joy shortly before dying, and then dying cheerfully. In these ways, the narratives showed that heavenly joy contrasted sharply with suffering and death. Yet in some instances, the narratives also suggested that the dying person had lived a happy life and could show the living how they too could truly enjoy earthly happiness. Deathbed narratives were usually related by intimate friends or relatives of the deceased, although they sometimes included first-person testimonials and they were, on occasion, fictional accounts or loosely adapted from funeral sermons. The Reverend William Bates, who preached Richard Baxter's funeral, for example, observed that Baxter's "joy was most remarkable when, in his own apprehension, death was nearest, and his spiritual joy was, at length, consummate in eternal joy." Published in books, tracts, and religious periodicals, deathbed narratives invited readers to identify with the dying person's age, gender, and relationship to the narrator, or in other cases featured well-known persons. The narratives frequently featured children who spoke as they were dying or who looked on as a parent or grandparent died. The narratives were in these ways true to the reality of suffering and bereavement and at the same time served as important sources of moral instruction.[43]

Deathbed experiences narrated by bereaved relatives were especially compelling. In 1787, sixteen-year-old Samuel Buell died on Long Island. His father, a popular Presbyterian minister, preached the funeral sermon, which was subsequently published. In his final days, the boy was able to secure and express joy by singing or hearing sung his favorite hymns, his father said, one line of which was "Through all the changing scenes of life, in trouble and in joy, the praises of my God shall still my heart and tongue employ." The boy died, his father said, "abounding in prayer, in praise, in joy divine, with solemn cheerfulness, bidding adieu to all his earthly friends." The sermon addressed the mourners in conclusion: "Can all the powers of mere philosophy, the ignorant hero in the madness of human passion, or the deist furnish an instance of such a holy temper, joy and triumph, as we behold in this expiring youth? Surely there must be something in such a religion that is more than human!"[44]

The narrative's notable features include the fact that hymns served as a repertoire of emotional language, friends were present to witness the emotion, the joy was appropriately subdued ("solemn cheerfulness"), and the joy the dying person experienced was interpreted as evidence of religion's value. Similarly, the death of Sarah Kendall, the wife of a Baptist deacon, included an account of her speaking joyfully in the language of scripture. She anticipated the joy of being in heaven with Abraham, Isaac, and Jacob, envisioned the torment of those consigned to darkness and despair, and counseled her visitors to study the Bible. Additionally, her joy was physiologically evident. As she died, witnesses said, "joy sat on her brow and her eyes spoke the teachings of her soul, . . . and her motions gave indications of her happy frame."[45]

Funeral sermons in other instances provided the occasion for messages about happiness. When seventeen-year-old David Trumble—a Yale student—died in 1740, his family asked the Reverend Solomon Williams, pastor of the First Congregational Church in New London, Connecticut, to preach the funeral sermon. "The sorrows of life," Williams explained to the mourners, "are become fit and necessary means to recover [man] from the sink of sensuality into which he is fallen [and] to awaken in him a great concern to obtain the love of God in Christ, the pardon of sin, and the restoration of God's image and holiness, wherein lies his true perfection and happiness; to wean him from all inordinate affection to anything in this world, where all his state is attended with so much vanity as to make it impossible for him to find happiness here; to put him upon earnest striving for the holiness and happiness of heaven." Lest the message be lost on the deceased's classmates, Williams concluded, "Let our young people be persuaded to seek God in Christ as their true happiness and never be anxiously concerned about any other." Young people were at "the time of life," he warned, "when you are most apt to paint out scenes of future pleasure and to fill your minds with gay images of distant joy and worldly glory and felicity. But these are shadows and fancies only. You will find this world, if you depend on such things in it, will never yield you anything but vexation and disappointment."[46]

Fictional deathbed narratives, often written for young readers and featuring children, adolescents, or young adults, offered opportunities for lengthier and more detailed dialogue than was typically the case in actual accounts. "The Life and Death of Two Young Ladies," a story that circulated in magazines in the 1790s, portrayed Melissa, who was raised in an ungodly family, and Isabella, whose family was devout. Melissa enjoyed worldly happiness, but Isabella anticipated heavenly joy, which became evident when she fell ill and in her last days testified: "I hear the music of the new Jerusalem; it fires my soul with seraphic joy; my triumphant song of praise will never end." As she died, her countenance showed "the most lively marks of pleasure." With her dying breath, she counseled her friends and family, "Let me see none but tears of joy and gratitude in your eyes. My departure is at hand; sing praises to God, sing praises: I want words to express my joys!"[47]

Narratives of this kind took into consideration the bereaved sharing their dying loved one's rejoicing and yet being left behind, suffering emotional and material loss. Their sorrow was acknowledged, and they were encouraged to weep openly with the assurance that happier times were ahead. A favorite verse was Psalms 30:5, "Weeping may endure for a night, but joy comes in the morning." The dying person also received assurance that the loved ones being left behind would receive divine protection. Cotton Mather advised, "Let not your joy be interrupted by any fear of what may become of your friends when you shall be dead and gone. The Lord that calls you to commit your spirits into his hand, calls you at the same time to commit your widows, your orphans, and all your friends into that Omnipotent Hand: he says, Leave them all with me, and I'll take the care of them all!"[48]

It was harder to speak of divine protection when deaths occurred from accidents, natural disasters, or malicious acts and took the lives of children and young adults. Deaths of these kinds necessarily raised questions about God's goodness and inevitably reinforced the idea that God was a wrathful being who brought tragedy into people's lives as punishment. There was sparse solace in believing that these events were providential. It was possible, though, to conceive of tragedy not only as punishment but also as an indication of God's mercy. If all people, redeemed and unredeemed alike, were thoroughly sinful, as they most certainly were, then they were surely distressing to God, and it was only God's mercy that spared any of them from being punished. "When any intelligent being is really crossed and disappointed," Jonathan Edwards explained, "his pleasure and happiness is diminished." It was understandable, therefore, that God was infinitely made unhappy by the "millions and millions of instances" of sinfulness that people committed every day. It should be reason enough for rejoicing to know that God was just and forgiving.[49]

The deaths of well-known persons figured prominently in the hagiographic accounts of saints and martyrs, many of whom were the heroes of struggles between Protestants and Catholics or among competing political factions and who died joyfully while being put to death.[50] Richard Langhorne, the English barrister unjustly accused in the Popish Plot of 1679, was one such martyr. The poem he wrote as he awaited execution—"I must quit earth for heaven, my earthly prison for a liberty of joy"—circulated widely. The grisly details of martyrs' deaths made the stories compelling. Other prominent persons died ordinary deaths, and these deaths were also the occasion for commentary.[51] Except for national heroes, David Hume was one of the best-known public figures of the eighteenth century—familiar to American readers of religious periodicals as an atheist, although more accurately described as a deist, and as a critic of religion's penchant for gloom and melancholy.[52] Hume's death in 1776 became the occasion for deathbed narratives on both sides of the Atlantic. The narratives were of popular interest because, on one telling, they showed an unbeliever nevertheless going to the grave joyfully, while, on another telling, they showed just the opposite. Hume's friend, Adam Smith, published the initial deathbed narrative. In Smith's account, Hume was known for his "gayety of temper," his "constant pleasantry," and "good humor," which were never "frivolous" or "superficial" but attended by "the greatest depth of thought." In his last days, said Smith, Hume "diverted himself with books of amusement, talking with friends, and playing Whist." He died in a "happy composure of mind."[53]

Clergy took issue with Smith's characterization, regarding Hume's happiness in death as folly compared to the true joy of the devout. In a letter to Smith, the influential Anglican bishop George Horne suggested comparing Hume with Richard Hooker, who said in his last days that he was at peace with God, "From such blessed assurance I feel that inward joy, which this world can neither give, nor take from me. My conscience beareth me this witness; and this witness makes the thoughts of death joyful."[54] A few years later, New York Presbyterian minister John Mitchell Mason published a more abrasive narrative in which he ridiculed Hume and praised Samuel Finley, the Presbyterian scholar who served as the fifth president of the College of New Jersey in Princeton. Counseling readers that death was the awful dissolution of bodily existence and the separation from all that a person knows and loves, he cautioned against deathbed impressions of heaven that arose from "disturbed brains." All Hume had done, argued Mason, was to divert himself with "fictitious gayety." These were "temporal enjoyments" compared with the "exquisite meaning" of "cheerfulness," "composure," and "happiness" in the mouth of a Christian. "In Dr. Finley," said Mason, "we see a man dying not only with cheerfulness, but with ecstasy. Of his friends, his wife, his children, he takes a joyful leave: committing all that he held most dear in this world, not to the uncertainties of earthly fortune, but to the promises of his God."[55]

The more abrasive tone in which Mason wrote was indicative of the greater awareness that had developed about differing expressions of joy, even in death. The vanity of religious enthusiasts, a critic in Philadelphia wrote, persuades them to "think themselves so much more devout than all others that they obtain some special regard of heaven, and hence they expect illuminations, impulses, ecstasies, [and] revelations." These self-conceits were "contagious among weak and ill-taught minds."[56] It would be wise to remember Richard Baxter, the writer advised, who called for consideration of the Word and rational evidence against the dangerous and erroneous claims of new revelations. Another writer, testifying of the "endless felicity" he had found upon believing in God, similarly acknowledged that this language was likely to be regarded as "the ravings of a distempered imagination."[57]

Deathbed narratives and funeral sermons were intended of course to prompt readers to think about their own deaths. The impossibility of being certain about one's salvation left a thick layer of anxiety that was difficult to avoid.[58] In modeling how to die joyfully, the narratives featured scriptural and poetic imagery of heaven and sometimes included descriptions of heaven drawn from firsthand visits. A report in the *Massachusetts Baptist Missionary Magazine* of a young woman's death, for example, stated that her mother asked if she had "any remarkable views," to which the dying woman replied, "I saw the world sinking in a flood of fire, above the flood of fire there seemed to be an ark prepared, and all that were in the ark were saved, and those that were not, were swept away in the flood of fire." After that "there seemed to be a new heaven and a new earth prepared, which appeared exceedingly beautiful." Those with her reported that "she seemed to be filled with joy."[59] The narratives assured the godly not only that heaven would be joyful but also that dying could be.

Living Joyfully

How to live joyfully from day to day in the present life, though, presented believers with a dilemma. On the one hand, worldly pleasures were at best inferior to heavenly joy and at worst distractions from pursuing it. On the other hand, the pious life was to be lived joyfully, for was it not "man's chief end," as the Westminster Shorter Catechism stated, "to glorify God and enjoy him forever"? In what manner then could that joy begin in the present life? Writers devoted a great deal of attention to this question. Their arguments varied but largely agreed that happiness was desirable and indeed could be attained when properly understood and when pursued cautiously, always mindful of temptation.[60]

In a series of sermons on "man's chief end," published in 1743, Reverend Gilbert Tennent, the Presbyterian leader who played a prominent role in the Great Awakening, argued that "enjoying God" was contrary to human nature, which elevated the idolatrous pursuit of pleasure above God, and thus was only possible among the "regenerate." Being regenerate meant realizing the sinfulness of attempting to satisfy one's own desires, "warding off the evils" of one's surroundings, and "amidst the numerous disquietudes of life" turning to God for "protection and happiness." The regenerate were divinely chosen, but they were also capable of actively responding to God's grace and indeed morally responsible to do so. Enjoying God was then possible by responding to God's "divine perfection" and "adorable excellency," which was partly a way that the regenerate took responsibility for their own happiness.[61]

In similar accounts, the surest way to achieve a joyful life was to be "heavenly minded," that is, to think often about the constant presence of God as one went about one's daily activities. The Christian "runneth cheerfully," John Cotton declared, by always "looking unto Jesus."[62] Living joyfully was an indication of the godly person's awareness of and gratitude for God's grace. Divine providence was evident in the everyday blessings of life and health and the pleasures of family and friends. It was supposed to be more evident to the godly than to the ungodly because the godly willfully attempted to avoid sin and adhere to God's laws. These laws included exhibiting such virtues as benevolence, candor, and moderation, which were conducive to cheerfulness and serenity. The godly person was expected to demonstrate "cheerful submission to providence" and was supposed to take "delight in serving God."[63] The godly person was also expected to appreciate the beauty of God's handiwork and to be assured that God had a purpose for the world.[64] Moreover, godliness was conducive to the kind of happiness that showed on one's countenance. A troubled heart that succumbed to temptation was evident in a person's outward appearance, for no wicked person could truly be happy, while a person living in obedience to God's will would exhibit the effects of that inward happiness. As John Wesley observed, "Virtue, as it refines a man's heart, so it makes his very looks more cheerful and lively."[65]

Associating virtue with cheerfulness necessitated reckoning with the fact that godly people suffered, just as the ungodly did, and therefore had reason to be less than cheerful. One solution relocated true happiness from this life to the next, thereby offering the godly a reason to endure suffering in the hope of death coming soon, but other arguments dealt with the question as it pertained to earthly life. Even in suffering, the godly were expected to seek happiness and they received assurance that it could be found. The happiness to be sought and found was not cheerfulness or mirth but "unspeakable joy," "solemn joy," or "happy poverty." It was in fact elevated by enduring suffering, as the sufferer's attention shifted from the pleasures of money or health or family to the higher joy of God's infinite love that was found in the midst of suffering. "How can suffering be consistent with happiness?" Wesley asked. "Perfectly well. Many centuries ago, it was remarked by St. Chrysostom, 'The Christian has his sorrows as well as his joys, but his sorrow is sweeter than joy.' He may accidentally suffer loss, poverty, pain, but in all these things he is more than conqueror."[66]

Besides these recommendations for joyous living, the faithful were expected to experience exceptional joy in contemplating their salvation, especially at the moment of conversion but also in retrospect as they recalled their first overwhelming sense of being saved. "Puritan and nonconformist writings," historian Bernard Capp has observed, frequently showed men and women "overwhelmed by religious euphoria." There was a code of civility, Capp says, that normally demanded emotional self-control, but persons expressing euphoria about their conversion were "confident that their spiritual tears were fully approved among the devout."[67] Not only were they approved, expressions of religious euphoria were also encouraged through sermons that reminded listeners of their depraved condition prior to repentance and the joy that flooded their lives upon turning to God.

Conversion narratives amplified and defined the "euphoria" by contrasting it with other kinds of pleasurable experiences. Prior to conversion, the convert typically experienced negative emotions such as shame, guilt, and fear, which deepened the person's distress, but pleasurable emotions were also likely to have been experienced or at least sought. The author of a first-person account in the *New York Missionary Magazine,* for example, observed, "To destroy melancholy, which preyed upon my mind, I joined in the most wicked and foolish pursuits, still seeking happiness where it was not to be found, which only plunged me into deeper misery, and sometimes drove me almost to phrenzy and madness." The writer eventually had a revelatory experience in which "the scales fell from my eyes [and] everything seemed glorious."[68] In such accounts, the revelatory experience seemed to come from the outside, unbidden from God; yet the recipient was truly a penitent who played an active role in seeking conversion.

The difficulty was that actively seeking conversion put the seeker in jeopardy of not being able to sustain the happiness that was supposed to come with assurance of salvation. Joy was fleeting, and because it was, the penitent worried that sinfulness was the reason. "I solemnly devoted myself, and all I am, and have, to [God]," Elizabeth Bury, a devout woman in her seventies, wrote in her diary in 1719, "I returned with joy at the oath wherewith I had bound my soul unto God." But the joy did not last. She was "quickly seized with torpor and drowsiness again." She exclaimed, "Lord, what short sweets am I allowed here?" The cycle of joy and despair continued, even as she prayed and heard sermons encouraging her again and again to dedicate herself to God. "I was almost overwhelmed with sorrow for the sad remainders of vain and evil thoughts, pride, selfishness, etc., which damped my joy and praise," she confessed.[69]

Apart from their own salvation, the faithful were expected to find joy as they worked for the salvation of others. This joy was naturally expressed more often by preachers than by lay people. The deathbed account of nonconformist English preacher William Burkitt (1650–1703), for example, said that "the declaration of several persons by his dying bed that he had been the instrument of their conversion put him into a transport of joy."[70] Cotton

Mather wrote in his diary that if any of his efforts to bring others to Christ "led to an acknowledgment of His virtues," then the "rapture of this joy becomes unspeakable," adding "I am one arrived unto the very top of my felicity."[71] However, preachers also noted the lack of joy they felt when souls were not saved, as the Methodist leader Francis Asbury did in his journal after a disappointing week of itinerant preaching, "I feel with sorrow the spiritual death of the people; it brings on great heaviness of body and mind."[72]

Finding joy in thinking about one's own and others' salvation was couched in language that emphasized the redeemed's moral obligations. If it was possible to respond actively to God's call and to play a part in one's own redemption, as evangelical leaders like Edwards and Tennent claimed, then the redeemed were morally responsible for the choices they made about living virtuously.[73] Joy was less an involuntary emotion and more the result of actively choosing to be a righteous person—righteous, according to what their religious leaders taught. "We must stir up ourselves to lay hold on God," Tennent argued. It was "an important duty for us to use our strength in God's service." Praying casually or ritualistically was not enough. Prayer was to be done "fervently, affectionately, believingly, argumentatively, importunately," not "coldly, stupidly, presumptuously, indifferently, abruptly." It was wrong to engage in pleasurable activities instead of eagerly attending worship services. "How lively can many be in discourse, in eating and drinking, they can sit up late enough to perform these pleasant tasks; but whenever prayer comes upon the board, then their spirits lag and they are presently disposed to take a nap." Tennent had no use for "sluggish souls," preferring instead the "metaphors in scripture representing the Christian travels to the New Jerusalem"—running, wrestling, fighting, vehemently serving the Most High.[74]

It was understandable that religious authorities wanted the pursuit of heavenly happiness to serve as an inducement for a more active prayer life and greater dedication to the church. They also considered it appropriate to link the pursuit of happiness with good works. An interesting example was the 1752 funeral service for Brinley Sylvester, Esq., of Shelter Island, New York, preached by Presbyterian pastor William Throop. Sylvester was Shelter Island's most prominent citizen, an associate justice of the Court of General Sessions, slave owner, occupant of the largest house in the county, descendant of one of the community's first European settlers, known for his extravagant expenditures, and the person who had raised the funds in 1733 to build the Presbyterian church and supervised its construction. Throop's sermon focused on "mercy," by which he meant "compassion for the poor" and "liberality in supporting the gospel." The message obliquely praised Sylvester for his generosity while also calling the congregation to similar acts of generosity. The person who receives "good things as a steward accountable to God," Throop advised, "enlarges his opportunity of doing more honor to God and good to his fellow men in the world. And he finds unspeakable happiness in thus serving his generation and experiences, even here, the truth of that word, 'it is more blessed to give than to receive.'"[75]

How joy was to be publicly expressed—not only felt within one's heart but actively communicated in the presence of others—was a question to which church leaders paid increasing attention as revivalism spread in the 1740s. Revival preaching fueled controversy over the extent to which emotion could be taken as an indication of divine guidance and thus employed as a source of doctrinal authority. Joy in the Lord and fervor in expressing that joy were understood to have biblical precedent, but the "passions" and "affections" were matters of concern when they displaced rational approaches to theology. It was thus worrying to witness holy joy being displayed in unholy ways. "Some sorts of people," New England Congregationalist minister Charles Chauncy complained in a 1743 sermon, "express their religious joy by singing through the streets and ferry boats." There were instances, he said, of swooning, screaming, clapping of hands, jumping up and down, kissing, and breaking into loud laughter. All of that was disorderly. It suggested that a person's actions were guided too much by emotion and not enough by religious instruction. "Keep your passions in their proper place," he advised, "under the government of a well-informed understanding."[76]

Music was the more generally acceptable means of expressing joy. Congregational singing happened at appointed times and places in which happiness could be felt and at the same time kept under control. Music "sets all the springs of nature to work, fires the soul with divine love, and diffuses joy and gladness through the heart," the eminent New England preacher Zabdiel Adams argued in a 1771 sermon. Music was powerful, dispelled gloom, encouraged people to be more religious, and was a way to polish a person's manners, he argued. "It advances our happiness here and lays a foundation for the perfection of it hereafter."[77] Isaac Watts's hymns, including such perennial favorites as "Our God, Our Help in Ages Past," "When I Survey the Wondrous Cross," and "Joy to the World," were widely adopted between the 1710s and 1750s through the encouragement of Cotton Mather and others.[78] Music "refined into devotion," Watts wrote, "the breathings of our passions, our love, our fear, our hope, our desire, our sorrow, our wonder, and our joy."[79] It was important that the joy expressed in this way was "refined." The manner in which congregational singing was conducted, though, was often contested. As Adams observed, some "exclaim against the pitch-pipe and the motion of the hand," others contended that singing was an "introductory step to popery," and still others objected to the "harsh and grating dissonance" of congregational singing.

By the late eighteenth century, there was also a growing supply of pamphlets and guidebooks, accompanying the usual sermons and essays, explaining how happiness should be experienced in daily life. Happiness of this kind was to be cultivated deliberately rather than experienced only in moments of heavenly passion. Happiness was said to have concrete benefits for the person who experienced it and for those with whom that person was associated. Readers were advised about how not to pursue happiness through luxuries, amusements, and novels and how true happiness was to be secured through virtuous living.[80] The advice was down-to-earth, concerned with ordinary life, and it was, in a sense, utilitarian in suggesting that there were self-interested reasons to be happy. Yet, if anything, the advice added moral urgency to the pursuit of happiness. Virtue demanded taking responsibility to do the things deemed most conducive to personal happiness and the happiness of others.[81]

The joyful life was morally desirable, writers advised, because life was better when a person was cheerful. In a sermon titled "The Blessing of a Cheerful Heart," which circulated widely in the 1790s, for example, readers were advised that a cheerful heart overcomes gloom, enhances one's appreciation of nature, and is conducive to "a healthful body."[82] The English writer and abolitionist Percival Stockdale expressed a similar argument, writing that "the Christian religion, instead of exacting from us voluntary and useless austerity and rigor, allows us every pleasure, every enjoyment that is consistent with private and public good." Obedience to its laws, he wrote "naturally produces good health and good spirits [and] keeps us in good humor with ourselves and others."[83]

The benefits associated with cheerfulness supplied an additional incentive to spend time reading devotional literature. Securing greater knowledge of God by studying the Bible was a means of ensuring greater personal happiness. Scriptural descriptions of sorrow and lament included messages of forgiveness, assurance, and the joy of the Lord. Above all, scripture taught the rules of godliness and honor through which a person learned to live a virtuous life, free of anguish, and complete with "serenity of mind."[84] Besides reading the scriptures, taking notes was recommended. Writing short narratives about one's sorrows turning into joy could become a "ritual of rejoicing."[85] Diary writing, historian Alec Ryrie has observed, was a way to "pin the butterfly of spiritual experience to the page."[86]

Cheerfulness in this understanding was beneficial not only to the godly person but also to others. In Christian advice literature, it was the Christian's duty to be cheerful, especially around one's family. The writer Elizabeth Griffith who authored the widely read *Essays Addressed to Young Married Women*, for example, advised her readers that their duty as Christian wives was "to promote harmony, peace, order, and happiness in their families." This was not the sort of cheerfulness, she cautioned, that "laughs in the eye and lights up the countenance." That kind of "good humor" might come from "a lively spirit," but it was "precarious." True cheerfulness needed to result from a "designed and consistent exertion of our powers to please." It was "heart-felt" and was nurtured by prayer, following Christ's example, and by "sense, virtue, and gratitude to providence."[87] As another writer advised, cheerfulness was pleasing, unlike mirth, which was transient, because cheerfulness was "fixed and permanent."[88]

A further effect of having the joy of the Lord in one's life was the benefit it conferred on one's wider social relationships. As was understood to be true in the family, social interaction in general went more smoothly when a person was inwardly content. That was different from the kind of pleasure seeking that was sometimes termed "sensual indulgence." Inward contentment was rather being at peace with oneself, having a clear conscience, and living according to what was considered right. To be inwardly content lessened the chances of acting with malice or resentment toward others and reduced the likelihood of making a fool of one's self. Scottish author Hugh Blair in a popular essay on religious joy, for example, contrasted the "poisonous and baneful influence" of "malignant passions" with the "eye of candor and humanity" from which spring "cheerfulness and serenity." For Blair, joy was "the end towards which all rational beings tend," resembling the air we breathe, and, like air, beneficial when drawn from good sources but dangerous when derived from corrupted sources. In this important respect, virtue and joy were mutually reinforcing. The virtuous person was generous and compassionate and the person's virtuous acts were in turn the source of lively and innocent pleasure. "In purity, temperance, and self-government," Blair wrote, "there is found a satisfaction in the mind similar to what results from the enjoyment of perfect health in the body. There is nothing that gnaws his spirit, that makes him ashamed of himself or discomposes his calm and orderly enjoyment of life. His conscience testifies that he is acting honorably. He enjoys the satisfaction of being master of himself."[89]

If Hume was right about Christianity being conducive to gloom and melancholy, it was nevertheless the case, then, that preachers and Christian writers found it necessary to contemplate the meanings of joy and to guide the faithful in how to pursue it. Leaders wrote about heavenly joy, contrasted it with earthly joy, explained why it was possible to be joyful even in death, considered how godly people could enjoy the pleasures of this life, associated happiness with godly living and soul winning, encouraged believers to take joy in God's blessings and in nature, and counseled the faithful to be cheerful for their benefit and for the benefit of others. In their descriptions of earthly happiness, religious authorities encouraged their followers to pursue it by praying and thinking about God, to distinguish between a peaceful heart and frivolity, and to be self-reflective about their feelings.

Religious authorities acknowledged that people naturally desired happiness, could easily be led astray in false pursuits of happiness, and benefited from having the guidance of sermons and music for expressing happiness. There was no reason to think that the faithful followed these teachings to the letter or that religious authorities had no other ideas about happiness. But insofar as religious authority was instructive, arguments about heavenly joy were central. These were arguments against worldly pleasure, to be sure, but they were also meant as practical instruction in how godly people could be happy in their daily lives. The emphasis on these considerations of joy reflected the influence both of popular revivalism and the ideal of living a virtuous life. Joy was to be found not only in thinking about heaven but in the here and now from experiencing the pleasure of salvation and from practicing the refined, mannerly cheerfulness that naturally made for abundant living.

There was no single definition of happiness nor any simple description of how it felt to be happy. Happiness in earthly life was rather more nuanced as a practice. The most acceptable ways of being happy were to be moderate in the pursuit of happiness and to avoid extreme sensations that bordered on frivolity and giddiness. Moderation implied that happy feelings were more like cheerfulness than ecstasy. Moderation also required avoiding the pursuit of spontaneous pleasure. A devout person could find happiness in the small pleasures of food and friendship. Happiness was the tacit reward of virtuous living. Being mindful of God's blessings was a source of happiness, which could be characterized in biblical language and expressed in music. Misery was acknowledged and yet contentment in daily life could be found. Heavenly joy was understood to be unlike anything on earth. But earthly happiness could be amplified by anticipating joy in heaven. Above all, happiness was a disposition that had to be practiced; pursuing it necessitated being deliberate in seeking to live righteously and attending mindfully of God.

The ambivalence toward worldly pleasure that Weber associated with the rise of capitalism, then, was gradually being replaced by the more moderate individualistic piety that encouraged the faithful to think about joy in other ways and to cultivate happiness in their daily lives. Carnal frivolity and sensual mirth, let alone licentious pleasure, were incompatible with Christian piety, but a godly person could reasonably seek joy in contemplating God's blessings and supporting the church. In living the godly life, there was an expectation of taking delight in God's bounty as well as in the anticipation of heavenly joy. Earthly happiness was closely associated with moral living, but it was also coming to be regarded as mannerly, healthy, conducive to inner peace, and favorable to domestic tranquility.

2
Getting Happy
Revival Era Exuberance and Conviviality

Exuberance in religious settings currently evokes images of emotional guitar-and-keyboard praise services, or it possibly connotes worship in Pentecostal and Black churches, or it implies speaking in tongues. But faith communities have a long history of dealing with exuberance. Faith leaders have worked hard to encourage it while also keeping it under control. To understand these dynamics, it can be helpful to look at an earlier era when revivalism was stirring the nation in new ways and in new locations. Camp meetings are particularly interesting in this regard. They were wildly popular, but they were also especially challenging for religious authorities because people often stayed for several days, mingling with friends and neighbors, some of whom experienced rapturous indwelling of the Holy Spirit, and many who did not. The closest examples today would be summer camps and retreat centers where people come to eat and sleep as well as to worship.

Camp meetings serve as a kind of case study in what happens when faith communities manage mixed emotions—exuberance, conviviality, and worship—figuring out how to stage events to accomplish their intended purpose. Many emotional practices are like this. There are several rather than only one kind of preferred emotion. Managing what happens requires orchestrating these multiple possibilities. The shaping that camp meeting organizers employed was explicit and intentional. They discussed what to do, followed one another's examples, wrote essays about what worked and what did not, and published guidebooks. The shaping was also implicit and unintentional. The participants did what was customary and felt what they came expecting to feel. The shaping was deeply gendered and deeply racialized.

Both the exuberant happiness that participants experienced during intensely emotional revival meetings and the quieter happiness they were expected to enjoy in church fellowship halls were instances of emotional management. Happiness was experienced by different people in differing

Nurturing Happiness. Robert Wuthnow, Oxford University Press. © Oxford University Press 2025.
DOI: 10.1093/9780197807071.003.0003

ways but was guided by church leaders' plans and expectations. The meetings were carefully organized to produce the desired results. The meetings were novel enough at the start that leaders had to work out the rules governing seating arrangements, food, behind-the-scenes preparations, where the events should be held, who should speak, and how long the meetings should last. As the meetings spread, people came expecting to be uplifted, but they also came as newcomers and strangers who had no idea what to expect and who may have come only because they were curious. Managing happiness was therefore more complicated than simply forging an opportunity for everyone to experience the same emotions, as they might have done in a well-orchestrated worship service. Managing happiness necessitated dealing with multiple expectations and multiple emotions. Leaders' control of the space in which these meetings took place played a decisive role.

The idea that emotions are social practices highlights the importance of the situations in which they occur. The physical locations provide the affordances that facilitate certain kinds of emotion—an organ, for example, or simply the space for people to assemble. The situations come with built-in expectations about what kinds of emotion will be appropriate to experience and express. The expectations are likely to require improvisation based on the situations' emerging norms. The situations also generate emotions as individuals interact with one another. In nearly all situations, someone is in charge or at least has more influence over what happens than others do. The persons in charge have the capacity to set the rules that determine how the space is used and to influence the emotions that happen in that space. Camp meetings were no exception. The religious authorities who organized these events exercised their power not only to promote spiritually meaningful religious experiences, as commonly assumed, but also to stage manage the presence of people who wanted to have a good time on their own terms.[1]

Understanding the stage management that took place in these events requires taking a somewhat different perspective from the one that would, at first glance, seem most appropriate. That usual perspective would conceptualize church services, and especially the more intense activities at camp meetings, as rituals. As such, whatever emotion might be present would be induced by the ritual. It would make sense, too, to say that the ritual was organized and managed. Additionally, the standard claim in this approach is that the emotion produced is shared. Randall Collins, for example, argues that rituals be defined in terms of three ingredients: bodies that "assemble closely enough" that they perceive one another's embodied signals, attention focused "upon the same thing," and "a shared emotion."[2] But the claim that ritual participants must share—or do share—the same emotion is debatable. Spectators at a soccer game, for instance, surely are not there all sharing the same emotion, even though soccer games are one of the events that Collins identifies as ritual. Most modern rituals, after all, are complex enough that they involve a division of labor—people bring differing expectations, play different roles during the event, and these roles come with different emotions. My argument is that camp meetings were a case in point. People did not experience the same emotions. They came for varying reasons, participated in varying ways, and experienced varying feelings. Moreover, the organizers understood this and did not try to shape everyone into the same emotional mold. Their stage-managing included rules, activities, and spaces in which the varying emotions could be experienced and to a considerable extent kept separate. The organizing was interesting precisely because it managed not one but several distinct kinds of happiness.

Camp Meetings

On Sunday morning, August 9, 1807, at a farm nine miles from Alexandria, Virginia, approximately ten thousand men, women, and children gathered for a day of preaching, prayer, repentance, and praise. Gatherings of this kind—camp meetings—had been gaining popularity since the turn of the century and would continue to play an important role in American Christianity for decades to come. The scholarship on these gatherings regards them as a crucial feature of the religious revival that became known as the Second Great Awakening. They contributed to the westward spread of new churches, drawing people together and filling them with holy zeal before any resident minister or church building was in place. They established the path followed by the most prominent evangelists of later decades—Dwight L Moody, Billy Sunday, and Billy Graham. They attracted White, free Black, and enslaved people, ushered new lay leaders into the limelight, made headlines for itinerant preachers, and shaped the stories that later generations would tell of how their ancestors worshipped.

Few aspects of early nineteenth-century Christianity made as much of an impression on the public as camp meetings did. By 1820, contemporary estimates suggested that at least a thousand camp meetings were taking place annually, some with as many participants as the one near Alexandria.

The prominent persons who participated and wrote about them included Harriet Beecher Stowe, Frederick Douglass, Mark Twain, Sojourner Truth, and Jarena Lee. Nat Turner's rebellion was said to have been inspired by a camp meeting. Abolitionists hoped the meetings could arouse moral sentiment against slavery. Abraham Lincoln's early law career included defending a person accused of having committed a murder at a camp meeting.[3] Tens of thousands of advertisements, accounts, criticisms, and defenses of camp meetings appeared in newspapers and religious periodicals. For many, a camp meeting was where they had been converted and convinced to join the church. For others, camp meetings punctuated time, setting the date from which to calculate how many months it had been since their neighbor got married or another one died.

The literature on camp meetings is rich with insights into the tensions between faith communities that favored revivalism and those that opposed it. Scholars have also explored how camp meetings inflected understandings of race, gender, family relationships, and morality.[4] Camp meetings were fundamentally about sin and salvation. But they were also about happiness—the joy of salvation and the happiness simply of coming together. Happiness was not the only reason camp meetings became as popular as they did, but it is difficult to understand why people flocked by the thousands to these gatherings unless the happiness that inspired them is given sufficient consideration.[5]

As instances of emotional practice, camp meetings functioned as "emotional communities," to borrow historian Barbara Rosenwein's term, by which she means the systems of feeling that communities employ to define and assess the kinds of affective bonds that are encouraged and the manner in which emotional expression is managed.[6] The three kinds of emotion that were commonly furthered by the camp meeting organizers of the early nineteenth century were ecstatic emotion, convivial happiness, and worshipful joy. Of these, ecstatic joy has received the most attention. Historians of religion have observed the intense emotion that camp meetings typically produced. Intense emotion manifested itself in such bodily movements as falling, jerking, and dancing, and in shouts of joy as well as passionate weeping. Camp meetings were the rare places at which people who otherwise were quite restrained suddenly found themselves involuntarily expressing their emotions extravagantly in the presence of friends, neighbors, and strangers. These experiences were unusual enough that supporters and critics discussed them endlessly. However, interesting and important as they were, instances of ecstatic joy affected fewer people directly than they did indirectly. Among the bystanders, spectators, and coworshippers, convivial happiness was more common. It was the less intense but no less important happiness that affected people as they mingled for several days in proximity with other people, eating, sleeping, and conversing between meetings. Ordinary as it was, convivial happiness was heightened by the presence of others and infused with the sense of common identity that the camp produced. Besides convivial happiness, there was also worshipful joy, which was the special experience of unity with God and with one another that came during the times of preaching and singing. Worshipful joy was the intent of the camp meeting organizers, and effort was required for it to happen. Much attention was devoted to the practices that would most ensure the kind of dutiful relation to God that participants could carry with them to their homes and into their churches.

As far as emotional practice was concerned, the distinctive feature of camp meetings was that they were carefully organized. They differed from everyday life, even though participants spent several days of their lives attending them, because they were strategically planned and because every moment was managed. The managers—the clergy, lay pastors, tent monitors, guards, and police, among others—took charge of everything from setting the daily schedule to listing the rules of decorum that were meant to sustain decency and order. Understanding the emotions that happened during the camp meetings, therefore, requires paying attention to what the managers wanted the meetings to accomplish, what they did not want to happen, and what they did to guide the participants' emotions. What they wanted to happen, and what they reported having happened, did not always live up to their expectations. There were dynamics that they could guide but not control. Camp meetings, then, serve as a story about how the Christian leaders who took charge of them thought good Christians should experience joy as much as it is about what those Christians in fact experienced. Insofar as the emotional life of the typical camp meeting was orchestrated, the place to begin is with how a typical camp meeting was organized.[7]

The 1807 camp meeting nine miles from Alexandria, Virginia, is of particular interest because it was described by a firsthand witness who participated as an objective but sympathetic spectator rather than as a speaker, worshipper, or organizer. Camp meetings were new enough that newspaper readers were interested in learning about them and the *Alexandria Daily Advertiser*, founded in 1800 by seasoned newspaper printers Matthew Brown and Samuel Snowden, had established itself in the vicinity of the nation's capital as a paper of choice for information about domestic and foreign events. The land on which the meeting was held was owned by Reverend John Childs, an itinerant Methodist minister who farmed the land from 1802 until 1816 when he resumed his calling as a traveling preacher.[8] In preparation for the camp meeting, the undergrowth had been cleared, and a brush fence had been created to form an enclosure, behind which were two circles of tents. Inside the enclosure a stand had been prepared for the speakers and seats had been provided for as many as 6,000 people. The first sermon was preached on Thursday at three o'clock to an undetermined number of visitors; on Friday, the crowd was between 1,500 and 2,000; increasing to between 4,000 and 5,000 on Saturday; and to 10,000 on Sunday before diminishing to about 1,500 on Monday. The observer was especially interested in how orderly the meetings were, which owed to the fact that there was a chief manager in charge of appointing and supervising twenty guards, a vigilant magistrate who enforced rules against trespassing, and an "apparent determination of every person to observe the rules of the meeting and conduct themselves with propriety."[9]

The writer found the event novel enough to ponder why it had attracted so many people. It seemed unlikely to have been the desire for salvation alone, he thought, because no more than a hundred persons professed being converted during the week. Rather, the event seemed to be of interest because of the emotions it produced. As people participated in the services, some voiced "lamentations and cries of distress" and most expressed joy in "songs of praise and thanksgiving." During the praying and singing there was no disorder and confusion. The writer also considered how the camp meeting differed from regular church services. Those services "lose their effect" from being "long administered" in the same way, whereas those things that occur out of the common way "have a tendency to arouse the mind and occasion reflections and impressions they otherwise would not." Indeed, it seemed that at the camp meeting participants for a time seemed "to forget that they belong to this world so fully are their minds absorbed in the contemplation and enjoyment of God."[10]

The layout of other camp meetings resembled the one near Alexandria. A site was selected that was mostly flat with a stream or spring nearby and some overhanging trees. Several acres were cleared, forming a rough circle or square, around which tents were erected, the number of which ranged from a few dozen to more than a hundred at larger camp meetings. Horses were tethered and fires for cooking were placed behind the tents. Inside the enclosure, one or several platforms were erected for the speakers. Seating for the audience—men and women in separate sections—consisted of backless rough-hewn logs. Preaching services typically were held in mid-morning, mid-afternoon, and after dinner in the evening, often with an additional sermon or prayer meeting before breakfast. Spectators who did not come for worship were expected to stand or sit near the rear of the enclosure.[11]

An important feature of the layout was what a recent scholar has termed the arrangement of the "gaze."[12] The gaze was a kind of power—a crowd control mechanism—that kept the participants under the watchful eye of the speaker. As a visitor at a camp meeting in Virginia in 1834 put it, "Every one of the multitude that was convened could behold the minister, and he could look on every individual who was a hearer of what he said." This arrangement reinforced the minister's authority, as the audience looked up to the minister's elevated position on the central platform. It also enabled the minister to read the crowd, looking from person to person as the penalties of sin were explained and the joy of repentance was described, as well as to call out persons who might be talking or having fallen asleep. "So solemn was the occasion that even those of the gay and fashionable, brought here by mere curiosity," the visitor in 1834 observed, "were constrained to observe reverence, even if it was not felt, and the influence and effect that was observable on every part of the assembled congregation induced all the Lord's people to feel and think that the Lord was indeed present."[13] Other observers may have disagreed that camp meetings were "solemn," yet they would have understood that the meetings needed to be carefully organized if they were to lead people to feel that the Lord was present.

Southern camp meetings typically included a place off to one side or in back for the enslaved to stand. At the camp meeting near Alexandria, the visitor noted that a space behind the preachers' stand "was marked off for the colored people, that there might be no mixing of White and Black." Frederick Douglass described a camp meeting he attended near Baltimore in the early 1830s:

> The camp meeting continued a week; people gathered from all parts of the county and two steamboat loads came from Baltimore. The ground was happily chosen; seats were arranged; a stand erected; a rude altar fenced in, fronting the preachers' stand, with straw in it for the accommodation of mourners. This latter would hold at least one hundred persons. In front, and on the sides of the preachers' stand, and outside the long rows of seats,

> rose the first class of stately tents, each vying with the other in strength, neatness, and capacity for accommodating its inmates. Behind this first circle of tents was another, less imposing, which reached round the camp-ground to the speakers' stand. Outside this second class of tents were covered wagons, ox carts, and vehicles of every shape and size. These served as tents to their owners. Outside of these, huge fires were burning in all directions, where roasting and frying were going on for the benefit of those who were attending to their own spiritual welfare within the circle. Behind the preachers' stand, a narrow space was marked out for the use of the colored people. There were no seats provided for this class of persons; the preachers addressed them, "over the left," if they addressed them at all. After the preaching was over, at every service an invitation was given to mourners to come into the pen; and, in some cases, ministers went out to persuade men and women to come in.[14]

Although Douglass did not say, at some of the camp meetings, the enslaved came of their own accord, while at others their enslavers required their attendance.[15]

Free Black people held camp meetings of their own, such as one advertised near Baltimore in 1816 to which White ministers were invited. Jarena Lee preached at camp meetings of free Black people near Philadelphia a few years later. Sojourner Truth was the only Black person at a camp meeting in New England when she preached and sang long enough to quiet a gang that was threatening the crowd.[16] Like the predominantly White meetings, the predominantly or exclusively Black meetings varied in emotional style and intensity. Although some included intense displays of emotion, others were subdued. An account of an African American camp meeting in 1833, for example, described the event as a time in which the silence was broken only by prayer. "The effect of this meeting on my mind was great," the writer noted. "The meeting was novel to me. Oh, how little stress lay we in these times upon the simple word of God read and a prayer of faith offered up as means for the awakening of churches and securing the effusions of the spirit."[17]

Convivial Happiness

The convivial happiness that camp meetings facilitated resembled what participants were expected to experience—and presumably did experience—at regular church services but on a larger scale. Whereas church meetings met only as frequently as an itinerant circuit rider was present and often were small enough to meet in houses and barns, camp meetings were the occasion for scattered farm families to come together from far and wide. Camp meetings attracted spectators who came to mingle as well as the faithful who came for worship. "Hundreds of young and joyous people, richly and gaily dressed," a woman in Georgia recalled, "could be seen moving in all directions, or standing in small groups beneath the shade of some wide spreading tree."[18] There were opportunities for all to socialize, to see and be seen, and to engage in amiable conversations—all of which were consistent with church leaders' encouragement of Christian fellowship. Such opportunities were perhaps especially valued in sparsely settled districts, such as at Cane Ridge, Kentucky, where contemporary estimates (that were likely exaggerated) claimed that some 20,000 people in 1801 gravitated from miles around for an encampment of preaching and spiritual revival. A letter from Reverend George Baxter to fellow Presbyterian Dr. Archibald Alexander described the meeting as a serious time but said it promoted an "amiable" and "friendly temper" that contributed to "temporal happiness."[19]

A perceptive essay in 1825 by a writer—who was critical of camp meetings—emphasized their friendly, almost carnival-like atmosphere: "It has got to be as fashionable among many Methodists to go to a camp meeting or two, yearly, as it is for more fashionable people to go to the Springs or seashore." There were of course participants wrought by prayer and supplication with a "pitch of enthusiasm," the writer said, but there was another class of participants who "attend the preaching, eat, drink, and sleep at regular hours, receive their friends and visit them, while their conversation is often bordering on the light and worldly."[20] Something similar appears to have been the case among the enslaved, who, according to historian Albert Raboteau, sometimes eagerly anticipated camp meetings as "big times," when, as one participant recalled, they would have a "jolly time" visiting, singing, and "making friends."[21]

The camp meeting Harriet Beecher Stowe described in her 1856 novel *Dred* was a scene for piety and reverence but also of conviviality and laughter. Two of her characters, Nina and Uncle John, stood at their tent door "laughing heartily." Nina explained to a third character, Anne, who wasn't laughing, "The distance between laughing and praying isn't so very wide in my mind as it is in some people's." A moment later, the trio noticed a man they did not know "shaking hands among the company with a free and jovial air." When the meeting broke for lunch after the morning worship service, "there was an abundance of chatting, visiting, eating, and drinking." Stowe's characters continued to circulate throughout the day, talking among themselves and overhearing conversations among strangers. Although their mood was happy, Stowe emphasized, they were also party to a heated conversation about slavery.[22]

In Stowe's story, the characters mostly interacted with the one or two other characters with whom they were related, which was likely to have been the pattern at camp meetings where people came as families and spent their nights in family tents. However, wider social networks were likely to have been involved as well, playing a role in how people heard about camp meetings, how they secured transportation, and who they interacted with during the meetings. An interesting example of such networks was evident in the 1833 trial of Reverend Ephraim Avery for the murder of a young woman named Sarah Cornell. Camp meetings figured in the trial because Sarah was reported to have attended one or more camp meetings and may have had contact there with Reverend Avery. One witness reported having spoken with Sarah about three months before Sarah was found dead and learned that Sarah intended to attend an upcoming camp meeting. A second witness reported that Sarah had discussed the possibility of securing a tent at the camp meeting. A third witness reported giving her a ride to the camp meeting. That witness said there had been a great deal of talk at the shop where he worked about the upcoming camp meeting. Another witness reported seeing her at the camp meeting with a young man and was reported to have "behaved well." The young man in question reported that he had been there with her. She was also seen at the meeting, dining at the ladies' common table and conversing with members of the Methodist church. At another camp meeting two weeks later, two women discussed having seen her at the earlier camp meeting and discussed a rumor that Rev. Avery had expelled Sarah from his congregation. One of the women, upon hearing that Sarah had been expelled, sought out Rev. Avery and asked him about it. Another witness denied that she had been expelled and was a member in good standing. But another witness testified of overhearing a tense exchange between Sarah and Rev. Avery.[23] In this example, then, camp meetings were sites at which people participated who knew one another through diverse connections and who became the objects of discussion among people with whom they were only casually acquainted.[24]

Leaders were cautious about casual socializing and the convivial emotion that might result. On the one hand, they hoped for a "harmony of feeling" to be present during the camp meetings as believers interacted with other believers. "Little alienations of feeling," as one writer explained, should be set aside. Coming together was to be an antidote for feeling downcast. "Having passed through a long, dark, cheerless winter night of stupidity during which everything wore a discouraging aspect," the writer observed, made it all the more enjoyable to come together.[25] On the other hand, leaders warned participants against lighthearted, frivolous socializing that would detract from the meetings' holy purpose. One leader, for example, complained that "the crowd talked freely and walked from place to place during the services [while] several preachers and recruits from the laity performed simultaneously [and] as many as six hymns were sung at once."[26] To prevent that from happening, most organizers established strict rules and used trusted volunteers to maintain order. The leaders of a camp meeting at Martha's Vineyard, for example, took pride in reporting that "No undue levity, no smile of contempt, no gatherings for fruitless discussion were observed during the meeting."[27] Organizers worried especially about people coming to the meetings for the wrong reasons. "It is well known that the greatest difficulty connected with these camp meetings," said one, "is the rude and indecorous conduct of a rabble who are apt to attend them."[28] Another wrote of her experiences at several camp meetings in Rhode Island where an army of "local louts in search of entertainment" threatened to turn the events into an atmosphere of "uncivil amusement."[29]

The rules that leaders imposed on the participants in the hope of keeping conviviality from becoming boisterous were enforced in two ways. One was through the camp managers, monitors, and guards who walked among the participants and whose presence was enough to serve as a reminder of the rules. The other was the spatial organization of the meetings, which kept strangers, hawkers, and suppliers outside, and which set aside spaces in the rear of the encampment for casual visiting. The spatial arrangement of the seating further separated bystanders from penitents, men from women, and the enslaved or free Blacks from the White participants. While the meetings were sometimes described in pious accounts as profoundly holy times happening on a biblical scale in sacred space, the events, therefore, were not entirely understandable in those terms. They were spaces in which convivial happiness was also organized.[30]

Few of those who organized camp meetings would likely have agreed with many of the arguments advanced by William Ellery Channing—the prominent New England preacher and writer who vehemently opposed narrow Christian teachings. Yet they likely would have agreed that Channing's view of "innocent pleasures" could aptly describe the kind of convivial enjoyment that camp meeting organizers hoped to evoke. Innocent pleasures, Channing said, produced a "cheerful frame of mind, not boisterous mirth." They invigorated the body and spirit, occurred in the presence of "respectable friends," and were favorable to "grateful piety." They were accompanied by the "consciousness that life has a higher end than to be amused."[31]

Extravagant Emotions

Amid the conviviality that participants reported, camp meetings also inspired the extraordinary emotions that observers witnessed variously as falling down, jerking, crying out, weeping, and shouting, and that participants described simply as "getting happy."[32] Camp meetings of course were not the only places in which such expressions of extravagant emotions happened. The revivals of the 1740s sometimes became so lively that order was difficult to maintain; for example, George Whitefield's preaching, it was said, roused the crowds with such shouting that the meetings sometimes had to be terminated. Nor was exuberant emotion the typical response of most camp meeting participants. The most glowing accounts usually acknowledged that only forty to a hundred out of several thousand participants experienced something like a dramatic conversion. Camp meetings nevertheless became known for uncontrollable outbursts of weeping and joy.

At a camp meeting in Georgia in late July 1803, eight thousand Methodists and Presbyterians participated for five days in prayer and worship led by a team of thirty preachers. An account of the event that circulated widely in denominational newspapers reported that many of the participants "became the happy subjects of awakening and regenerating grace, attended by falling to the ground with cries for mercy, and acclamations of joy."[33] In March 1804, near Bedford, Virginia, the itinerant evangelist Lorenzo Dow and eighteen local preachers led a five-day camp meeting of some three thousand participants. It was reported to have been a "devout and joyful" gathering with penitent sinners exchanging lamentations for "glad songs of praise and salvation."[34] A few years later, Methodists at a three-day camp meeting in Georgia "[broke] forth into shouts and acclamations of joy while others appeared to be lost in wonder, love, and praise."[35]

The exceptional emotion experienced at some of the camp meetings was more subdued at others. Many of Lorenzo Dow's camp meetings, judging from his extensive notes, were occasions at which decorum presided, and the few participants who were saved mostly experienced peace and contentment of mind. Dow more often described his own emotions as "happy" than as exceptionally joyful.[36] At Cane Ridge, Reverend Baxter observed people falling down but rarely shouting or experiencing anything he considered ecstatic. Of those who fell down, some were unable to speak but when they recovered were able to converse "with calmness and composure." Baxter considered the meeting to have been of positive value but was eager to distance revivals of this sort from the charge that they promoted enthusiasm. "Enthusiasm is a vain, self-righteous spirit, swelled with self-sufficiency, and disposed to glory in its religious attainments," he wrote. "If this be a good definition, there has been, perhaps, as little enthusiasm in the Kentucky revival as in any other. Never have I seen more genuine marks of that humility which disclaims the merit of its own duties and looks to the Lord Jesus Christ as the only way of acceptance with God."[37]

But at other camp meetings, exceptional bodily movements—especially falling down, jerking, shouting, and dancing—were observed. A visitor at a camp meeting of some 2,500 people near Bank's Chapel, North Carolina, in 1807, reported that some of the several dozen converts jerked, danced, and even barked. After exhorting and singing, the jerking convert would be seized with "violent fits of jerking" followed by shouting and praising God. Dancing converts—sometimes dancing with a dozen other dancers—would extend their hands over their heads while dancing and sometimes fall to the ground where they would lie lifeless for nearly an hour.[38]

In 1826, the *New York Telescope* published a summary of what had become widely known as "the jerks." The jerks, as such, consisted of violently moving the head toward one shoulder, then the other, and then backward and forward—remarkably without sustaining physical injury. The jerks were sometimes accompanied by a rolling exercise in which the person appeared to be forcibly thrown down, rolling over and over like a dog, often through mud and dirt, and sometimes with the added effect of barking. "In this exercise both men and women personated and took the position of a dog, moved about in a horizontal posture upon their hands and feet, growled, snapped their teeth, and barked as if they were affected with the hydrophobia."

Whether the persons so affected were behaving involuntarily or voluntarily was uncertain. This writer thought they were sometimes entranced as if by a "contagious distemper," loudly vociferating their feelings, but perhaps were also acting voluntarily in the hope of making converts. "They sang, shouted, clapped their hands, and leaped for joy" while they also exhorted their "careless friends" to repent and forsake their sins.[39]

Among the accounts reported by those who personally experienced an ecstatic experience of some kind at a camp meeting, one that eloquently put into words what she experienced was penned by Zilpha Elaw, a free Black woman who lived near Philadelphia and preached at open-air meetings. "Whether I was in the body or whether I was out of the body on that auspicious day, I cannot say," she wrote. "I became so overpowered with the presence of God that I sank down upon the ground and laid there for a considerable time." As she lay there, her spirit "seemed to ascend up into the clear circle of the sun's disc." She was unsure if what she experienced was a "trance or ecstasy." She only knew that "God was so powerfully near to me for the space of several hours [that] I appeared not to be on earth but far above all earthly things."[40]

Ecstatic joy posed an interesting question for the camp meeting leaders whose job it was both to encourage and restrain it and to counsel their followers about how to interpret it. It was so common and such a memorable aspect of many camp meetings that implicit rules and explicit responses were put in place to guide how it happened and to inform how it was understood. The implicit rules consisted of expectations that spread by word of mouth and in newspapers almost as quickly as camp meetings became popular. The expectation at Methodist camp meetings was that displays of extravagant emotion were acceptable, while at Presbyterian events they were less likely to be encouraged. In either context, extravagant emotion was understood as an involuntary eruption driven by the Holy Spirit rather than having been induced by the crowd. As a writer in South Carolina noted in explaining why unusual outbursts happened even at normally restrained Presbyterian meetings, "I have seen a few of our strongest men compelled to cry out, right or wrong. They made every exertion to avoid it. They tried every posture of body but all in vain, their joy was too full. They were happy beyond expression and their cups ran over."[41]

The explicit practices with which displays of extravagant emotion were managed dealt mainly with keeping order. Falling, shouting, and jerking might be the kind of emotional display that signaled the Holy Spirit's presence, but it was nevertheless disruptive of the preaching and singing that was supposed to be taking place. The disruptive persons were quieted or physically removed. Historian Ann Taves describes several incidents at camp meetings where the persons who were shouting and in mournful or rapturous emotion either came to order immediately when the horn was sounded for preaching to begin or were escorted to another part of the encampment where they could pray under the guidance of one of the pastors. The stage managing also protected persons from harming themselves and then guided their recovery. Camp meeting organizers typically supplied ample amounts of straw to cushion those who fell. Leaders were designated in advance to stand or sit near and assist those who might be in danger of harming themselves. Separating worshippers from the "rabble" and prohibiting the sale of alcoholic beverages was meant to ensure the purity of any ecstatic displays.[42]

Managing the outbreaks of extravagant emotion was crucial to the camp meetings' success not only because of some religious leaders' criticisms of such displays but also because these practices disrupted the norms governing ordinary social interaction. Especially the norms that neatly separated men and women were violated. "The structuring of the setting was completely broken down as mourners, saints, and preachers entered the pen [place reserved for conversions] together," historian Dickson Bruce observed in his study of Southern camp meetings. "The original structure was actually turned upside down, for not only did everyone enter the pen, but people who were ordinarily assigned a subordinate place in Southern life, the women and children, actually assumed leadership of the activities." They did so as exhorters, calling on their wayward husbands and brothers to repent, and as converts filled with spiritual power.[43]

As camp meetings spread, proponents understood that it was as important to regulate how extravagant emotions were interpreted as it was to manage how they were experienced. Tracts, hymn books, and short essays in religious newspapers played an increasing role in shaping how extravagant emotion was to be understood. Reverend Barlow Weed Gorham's *Camp Meeting Manual: A Practical Book for the Camp Ground, in Two Parts,* which circulated widely in the 1850s, was an influential guidebook. It consisted of a dialogue between two characters—a novice who asked questions and a minister who answered the questions. The dialogue included a question about instances of emotional "extravagance." The minister responded, "Some persons are inclined to make unnecessary ado anywhere and about any matter. Such persons, among others, attend camp meetings; and they are there what they are at home—excitable, headlong and vociferous." These persons, he suggested, "have sometimes been allowed undue prominence." He nevertheless offered a defense of "extravagant" emotion, arguing that "when rightly viewed," it was a "proper and scriptural instance of religious zeal," backing up this claim with several examples from the Bible.[44]

In these accounts, leaders took credit for—or were credited with—inspiring extravagant emotion. Dynamic preaching was properly understood as the means through which the Holy Spirit worked, which meant that extravagant emotion was driven by God rather than the preaching. It was less clear if camp meeting organizers considered it appropriate to credit anything about the crowd, the heat, standing or sitting for long hours, or sleepless nights as having a role. There was at least some acknowledgment that being outdoors and away from daily routines were contributing features. "Saturday morning the light of a fair and pleasant day dawned," a participant at a camp meeting in New Hampshire wrote, "and while the bright sun beamed from the eastern sky upon our encampment we could not but think of that glorious Son of Righteousness that shone with so much glory and splendor upon the darkness of our moral world. There is scarcely anything in nature that strikes the mind with more sublimity than the pleasant morning scene of a camp meeting."[45]

During the 1840s, the ecstatic experiences reported at camp meetings were also being interpreted in light of criticism about spiritualism, Millerism, and news of occasional murders, fires, and cases of insanity that were associated with camp meeting and protracted meeting participants.[46] It was dangerous, one writer observed, for clergy to "raise a whirlwind which they cannot control."[47] The excessive emotion, as critics described it, prompted religious leaders to call for closer supervision of the meetings. At a Baptist ministerial conference in Illinois in 1843, for example, the assembled delegates endorsed "revivals" but asserted, "That, as the tendency of the age is to extremes in everything, it is the duty of ministers to conduct such meetings with great circumspection and care . . . lest Satan by his devices obtain an advantage."[48] Although the concerns generally focused on decorum and order, greater emphasis was also placed on the effects simply of people who otherwise lived quiet lives meeting in large numbers. "It is plainly impossible, among hundreds and thousands, of all ages, and sexes, and characters, dwelling in the woods, night and day, for a whole week together, and crowded under tents which afford but a partial accommodation for retirement or repose," wrote one critic, "that there should be observed all the duties, and restraints, and proprieties, and delicacies of ordinary life." The result, the writer suggested, was a kind of unreality—"a new state of existence"—that lowered the individual's ordinary sense of reserve. In the worst scenario, the individual would be "insensibly affected by the scene [and the] many influences adapted to excite conflicting feelings" or to "mislead and corrupt."[49]

Exuberant emotion, then, was perplexing enough that it had to be managed—and perhaps even discouraged. While there were accounts of upward of a thousand "converts" being made at protracted revival meetings, the numbers at camp meetings were much smaller, despite large numbers having attended. The organizers could handle several dozen people jerking, dancing, and falling on the ground, but would have been overwhelmed had a thousand done so. Even the smaller numbers were a mixed blessing. Spiritual indwelling was a power different from the organizers' authority. When a person suddenly blessed with the spirit decided to proclaim with divine authority, that was challenging indeed.[50]

Worshipful Joy

Worshipful joy was the more tempered sense of harmony, inner peace, and happiness that participants were expected to experience during the time devoted to preaching, singing, and corporate prayer. It was in these times, more than during moments of ecstasy, that participants were supposed to feel the presence of God in ways that were reassuring, comforting, and yet demanding of attention and obedience. In this respect, worship services at camp meetings were no different from regular Sunday church services. There was, however, an intensity to worshipping among a large gathering of worshippers in a special place and doing so three or four times a day for several days in a row that could not be duplicated on ordinary Sundays in ordinary churches. The most fervent preaching was expected to facilitate the intensity, usually with an emphasis on guilt, obstinacy of the heart, backsliding, and faithless prayers—hanging a "gloomy drapery" over the scene, as one leader acknowledged, more than evoking a spirit of joy.[51] It was more often when the assembled crowd engaged in singing favorite hymns that a sense of rejoicing occurred. "A marked feature of those meetings," a prominent Methodist leader recalled, "was the singing." He remembered many years later how the multitude of voices blending caused "the air to quiver as with pulsings of joy. The power and effect of those inspiring melodies resounding in the wilderness were indescribable."[52] The hymn books and hymn singing facilitated the expression of joy but also shaped the meaning of joy by associating it with memorable lyrics about God, scripture, and the church.[53] Those connections were important enough that religious leaders knew the significance of selecting the right kind of music. "Cold singing" was deadly, leaders were advised. "Instead of your slow, cold psalmody, give us your warm, lively revival songs. Have a good singer or two take the lead."[54]

What most clearly differentiated worshipful joy from ecstatic joy was the call for worshippers to exercise agency, or, as it was called, "spiritual industry"—in other words, to integrate a sense of Christian duty and moral responsibility into the emotions they were experiencing. Ecstatic joy was assumed mostly to be involuntary, a feeling so powerful that it evoked an outburst of jumping, shouting, or falling over which the person had no control. Worshipful joy, in contrast, was an act of will, a voluntary decision. In his *Lectures on Revivals of Religion*, Charles Finney described it as "determination to act out duty and to obey the will of God, by which a Christian should always be governed." Principle, meaning doing that which was right, was to take precedence over feelings: "Whether he feels any lively religious emotion at the time or not, he will do his duty cheerfully, and readily, and heartily, whatever may be the state of his feelings."[55]

Worshipful joy was sometimes a means of backing away from the extravagant emotions with which camp meetings were so popularly associated. "How many Christians there are who seem never to enjoy themselves much, unless they are in a lively prayer meeting, class meeting, or camp meeting, where the exercises are such as to induce strong excitement of the mind," a writer complained in the *Christian Intelligencer*.[56] Yet it was possible to have both ecstasy and worshipful joy and many camp meetings found ways to combine the two. The more disruptive expressions of ecstatic joy were kept within bounds, restricted to the few who fell under the deepest conviction, while the focus on decorum and order contributed to the spoken message about discipline, duty, and devotion to God, whether intense feelings were present or not. "The question with every disciple therefore should not be, how shall I be happy," a leader explained, "but how shall I be and do that which is right in the sight of God." A person could be suffering from "unbroken gloom," the writer argued, but that person should nevertheless obey God "because it is right and not simply in pursuit of happiness."[57]

By the 1850s, camp meetings were transitioning from the "bush and basket" style that had previously animated them and moving toward a more settled pattern of institutionalized practices. Camp meetings were more often under the sponsorship of denominational authorities, held in conjunction with church conferences, and located closer to towns and transportation routes. In the vicinity of populated communities, "protracted meetings" increasingly took the place of camp meetings. Protracted meetings typically ran for at least four days—sometimes longer—and included three or four sermons a day with prayer times and meals in between, but participants lived close enough that they could return home at night. Protracted meetings emphasized order and decorum and were often described as serious events, although there were also the more dramatic shedding of tears and expressions of joy.

Camp meetings continued, as they had in the past, to offer the same opportunities for repentance, salvation, and emotional exuberance but more often were organized as regularly scheduled annual or quarterly events on campgrounds owned or leased by camp meeting organizations. More of the meetings were managed by camp meeting committees that constructed permanent buildings for worship services; stored tents and other equipment; appointed tent masters and mistresses to administer decency and order; hired agents to purchase straw; had their own police officers; and supplied food, water, and baked goods for a fee. Denominational committees took charge of further developing the meetings, sending speakers to new locations, and using the meetings to start new congregations in the Midwest and West.[58] The ever-present concern that meetings should be conducted in an orderly fashion was institutionalized as well, in many cases as published rules and regulations. One list of rules and regulations, for example, specified that "There shall be no walking to and fro or gathering together in companies for conversation of any kind during public worship at the stand." The rules further stated that "There shall be a Superintendent appointed by each tent's company. His duty it shall be to preserve order in his tent in accordance with the regulations of the meeting." The regulations also stipulated that all talking should cease at 10 p.m. and indicated in which direction men and women should walk when needing to relieve themselves.[59]

Camp meeting proponents also defended their continuing importance with new arguments. Meeting in the open air or in pavilions on campgrounds was said to be economical, effective, morally instructive, and a way for religious groups to compete with the increasing number of large rallies held by political parties and other secular organizations.[60] Among other things, the camp meeting experience was said to be healthful:

> The purity and constant freshness of the atmosphere at camp meeting is in strong contrast with the confined air of the church or lecture room. The lungs usually get a freer, larger exercise there than elsewhere. And then, there is something in the novelty of the scenery and the occasion well adapted to banish enwei and hypochondria, and to produce a healthful flow of the animal spirits, while the purest and most elevated aspirations of the soul evoked by the services of the occasion react powerfully and happily upon the body.

Legacies

Historical accounts emphasize several of camp meetings' lasting contributions. Among these was the significant role they played in the growth of Methodism, accounting by some estimates for at least half its growth in the early decades of the nineteenth century. This growth—the "progress of the church"—was itself a reason to rejoice. Individually, Methodists and other Christians could rejoice that their sins were forgiven—as one camp meeting participant observed, "The flame of religious feeling rose very high, nor did it cease with our brethren after returning to their respective homes."[61] Collectively, they could rejoice that the gospel was spreading. The "prosperity of Zion" was a cause for "holy joy." A great revival was happening. Men were being called to the ministry. The church was flourishing almost in biblical proportions: "The wilderness and solitary places shall be glad, and the deserts rejoice and blossom as the rose," a minister in Tennessee declared. "Let our ministry be humble, holy and zealous, and the pleasure of the Lord will most assuredly prosper in their hands."[62]

Along with Bible societies, temperance societies, and tract societies, camp meetings contributed to the conviction that America was becoming a Christian nation. There was truth in the perception that the ideals advanced in these movements contributed to an understanding of commonsense morality, individualism, and democracy. The distinctive role that the camp meetings played was in bringing people together. Spending several days together, living in proximity with one another day and night, and taking their meals together at common tables engaged people physically and emotionally in ways that differed from merely reading and thinking about biblical themes. Participants experienced in their bodies the sensations of being together in a large crowd, feeling that they were in the presence of God, and witnessing themselves or others being moved with extravagant emotions.

As more of the population lived in the vicinity of established congregations with buildings of their own, the convivial joy that camp meetings nourished happened more often in church parlors and at church picnics. Church leaders recognized that creating opportunities for their members to enjoy themselves in ways other than simply coming for worship would be beneficial. To that end, they invented the idea of the "church sociable"—a "new measure," as they described it—for mingling with neighbors, meeting newcomers, and enjoying a meal together. But church sociables, like camp meetings, required careful management if they were in fact to be happy occasions. Mixing pleasure and religion was novel enough that many church leaders considered them totally inappropriate. The women who prepared the food needed to be happy enough about doing it, the strangers who were supposed to be welcomed had to be made to feel at home, and there were thorny questions about where these events should be held.[63]

Although camp meetings' contributions to longer term considerations about happiness are harder to assess, the evidence suggests several possibilities. Historians of literature have noted that camp meetings, perhaps most evidently in the wide readership that Harriet Beecher Stowe's work attained, created a template that legitimated and modeled expressions of public emotion in the work of other writers. Although reason was supposed to be valued more highly than emotion, the kind of emotion displayed in camp meetings could be considered as an appropriate display of deeply felt inward feelings in a public setting. The conversation about feelings edged into the open in ways that challenged notions about extreme joy being expressed only at the moment of death.[64]

In his work on slave religion, Albert Raboteau observed that camp meetings became the focus of conflicting interpretations of racial differences in American religion. Melville Herskovits, writing in the 1950s, for example, argued that White participants' emotional arousal at camp meetings was influenced by Black participants' practices of shouting, dancing, and having ecstatic experiences at the meetings. Erika Bourguignon, writing in the 1960s, saw the exuberant expressions of emotion at Black camp meetings as a means through which the ritual heritage of Afro-Caribbean spirit possession was preserved. Both interpretations contrasted with those of White preachers in the early 1800s who disapproved of any emotional extravagance, but who were more critical of it when it occurred among Blacks than among Whites. Raboteau cited other scholars who attached less emphasis on spirit possession and more on the traditions of dancing, shouting, and singing through which African Americans expressed the joys and sorrows of religion.

Raboteau's own interpretation emphasized the differences between Black and White religious emotional practice that continued to be evident over the years but also noted two important similarities. One was the role that intense emotion played in the revivals that spread a kind of individualistic or personalized popular Christianity among both Blacks and Whites during the nineteenth century. The other was the simple pleasure of getting together that attracted Blacks and Whites to the camp meetings, which was similar but also different. "Although religious slaves enjoyed the fellowship and excitement of church services and revival meetings, their enjoyment was marred by the shadow of White control." It was this, as much as anything else, Raboteau argued, that led the enslaved and formerly enslaved to prefer worshipping in their own places. Whether the enslavers imagined, as some did, that the enslaved's presence at camp meetings was evidence that the enslaved were happy, there was little evidence that the enslavers thought in broader terms about the pursuit of happiness being a universal right to which all persons were entitled.[65]

Among faith communities, ecstatic joy continued to be an important aspect of divisions along denominational, racial, and regional lines. In England, where Methodism was less identified with emotionalism than in America, a split developed between mainstream Methodists and smaller groups that favored emotionalism. In America, the mutual participation by Presbyterians and Methodists in early camp meetings diminished as Presbyterians increasingly distanced themselves from the "enthusiasm" they considered excessive among Methodists. Denominational diversity that included holiness practices and the eventual emergence of Pentecostalism preserved the more ecstatic experiences evident in camp meetings. The racial boundaries that enslavement and segregation imposed facilitated the continuation in Black churches of an expressive style reflected in camp meetings and drawn from African traditions. Camp meetings were set apart from ordinary church services such that a person could be transported emotionally in those special places without necessarily being embarrassed or feeling the need to express emotion in the same ways at other times.

Camp meetings demonstrated the significant extent to which faith communities directly and indirectly sought to set the rules for expressing emotions and for interpreting those expressions. Besides the sermons they heard and the guidance they may have received from books, Christians who participated in camp meetings learned something that went beyond lessons in godly joy. Camp meeting participants lived for several days under the watchful supervision of camp meeting organizers who managed the times and spaces in which exuberant, convivial, and worshipful joy took place. The meetings served during these few set-apart days not only as a time to hear preaching but also as an experiment in Christian living. Participants' lives were coordinated into a kind of ritualized experience in which the distinctions between the redeemed and unredeemed, the engaged participants and the bystanders, the leaders and all the others were dramatized. Not only words and actions but also emotions were displayed. What participants may have heard said about feelings in other contexts, they now experienced firsthand as preachers and tent managers monitored their conversations, encouraged them to interact happily and harmoniously, cautioned them against frivolity and mirth, explained how God was present, and interpreted the meaning of emotionally intense moments. The leaders, too, learned that setting the rules for feelings was easier to do than achieving strict conformity to those rules.

3

Festive Emotion

Fairs, Gender, and Identity in the Age of Industrialization

It seems safe to say that festivity has always been complicated for faith communities. On the one hand, faith communities' leaders have condemned festivity's tendencies toward licentious pleasure; on the other hand, faith communities have regularly incorporated festivity into their own services and celebrations. Clearly, festivity is conducive to a kind of joy, an escape from the humdrum of ordinary life, and for faith communities, festivity has scriptural warrant. Festivals are special occasions set apart for rejoicing in divine blessings and for reveling in praise and thanksgiving. But festivity is also fraught with moral danger. For festivity to be morally acceptable in faith communities, it must be either carefully managed or, in the extreme, suppressed.

In 1585, the Puritan pamphleteer Philip Stubbs offered a memorable description of the May Day festivities that spread across rural England each spring: "Every parish, town, and village, assemble themselves together, both men, women, and children, old and young, even all indifferently, and either going all together, or dividing themselves into companies, they go some to the woods and groves, somc to thc hills and mountains, some to one place, some to another, where they spend all the night in pastimes, and in the morning they return, bringing with them birch bows and branches of trees to deck their assemblies withal." Stubbs then remarked, "I have heard it credibly reported (and that *viva voce*) by men of great gravity, credit, and reputation, that of forty, threescore, or a hundred maids going to the wood overnight, there have scarcely the third part of them returned home again undefiled."

This account was one of the hundreds compiled and published by English antiquarian John Brand and subsequent editors as *Observations on Popular Antiquities, Chiefly Illustrating the Origin of Our Vulgar Customs, Ceremonies, and Superstitions,* a massive three-volume work totaling more than fifteen hundred pages. Covering topics as varied as wakes, exorcisms,

Nurturing Happiness. Robert Wuthnow, Oxford University Press. © Oxford University Press 2025.
DOI: 10.1093/9780197807071.003.0004

sheep-shearing festivals, Shrovetide, Valentine's Day, and May Day, the volumes surveyed the variety of customs involved, drawing on sources from Great Britain but also from Europe and North America. Edited, revised, and expanded by Brand until his death in 1806 and then by fellow antiquarians over the rest of the nineteenth century, the volumes were widely read, excerpts made their way into sermons and essays, and the work was credited with having formed much of the basis for the emerging field of folklore studies.[1] Max Weber might have had criticisms of the May Day festivities in mind when he wrote, "Asceticism descended like a frost on the life of 'merrie old England.' And not only worldly merriment felt its effect. The Puritan's ferocious hatred of everything which smacked of superstition, of all survivals of magical or sacramental salvation, applied to the Christian festivities and the May Pole and all spontaneous religious art."[2]

As American Christianity became more ethnically, racially, and denominationally diverse, festivity played an important part in defining the distinctive identities that set the various communities apart. Festive times were enacted in holiday festivals, parades, and at special events honoring patron saints, heroes, and major triumphs. The standard way in which these events have been treated in the social sciences is as rituals. Rituals have power because they symbolically enact the community's meaning and because they convey something about the sacred. That much is well established. Less attention has been given to festivity as a source of joy. There can be little doubt that festivity is attractive because it facilitates happiness among those who participate. Yet there are many interesting questions about how this happens and what it means.

Early in the nineteenth century, Catholic and Protestant churches in East Coast cities began experimenting with church fairs. The idea was not exactly new, reminiscent of medieval fairs held in churchyards on religious holidays, but the nineteenth-century fairs represented another departure from the usual ways in which faith communities had tried to promote happiness and to manage how it was expressed. Church fairs were large-scale events that took months of preparation, were considered successful when they raised sufficient cash, and depended on being described in newspapers and by word of mouth as special occasions for having a good time. They were in these respects novel emotional practices that religious leaders initiated and managed for innovative purposes. Like other festivals, their success required leaders' care in orchestrating the boundaries separating the kinds of emotion that were appropriate in houses of worship from those usually experienced in secular venues. In the process, church fairs evolved, communities initiated folk festivals that competed with religious events, and religious authorities faced new questions about how to adapt.

Fairs and festivals are emotional practices in which happiness is expected—the pleasure of time away from work and out of the home, socializing with friends, and being entertained with music, games, and food. But they are not designed only to provide pleasure. They serve other such purposes as well, such as fundraising, promoting ethnic identity, furthering children's education, and solidifying community relationships. When religion is involved, the lines separating sacred enjoyment from secular fun are problematic enough that the events' activities and participants must be monitored. Careful monitoring is also required when gender norms and racial and ethnic identities are changing. Fairs and festivals are examples of social practices in which regulated improvisation is a prominent feature. The fairs and festivals that religious organizations sponsored in the nineteenth century demonstrated the ways in which regulated improvisation mattered. Expectations about gender roles and ethnic identities were modified, as leaders and participants became more accustomed to the events' functions in their communities. The modifications were guided by religious authorities but illustrated the limits of those leaders' influence.[3]

The contribution that this consideration of church fairs and festivals makes to the study of emotional practice is threefold: first, the authority that influences how emotions are experienced and expressed, these examples suggest, is rarely singular or centralized (although it has often been studied as if it was), more often being dispersed among several entities that have informal as well as formal authority; second, dispersed authority of this kind varies in the extent to which it is coordinated or contested; and third, this dispersion of authority opens possibilities for multiple emotions to be expressed and at the same time necessitates improvisation in the norms governing those modes of expression. Church fairs and folk festivals were emotional practices that, in differing ways, were managed not only by religious authorities but also by lay women's organizations and community groups. These influences were relatively more coordinated by religious authorities in the case of church fairs than for folk festivals; yet, for both, the events were widely publicized in newspapers, which helped to attract participants, but which also meant that emotional practices were being interpreted increasingly by journalists rather than by religious authorities even when churches were hosting the events. The improvisations that took place dealt significantly with gendered norms of emotional practice and with emotional practices that symbolized ethnic identities. Fairs and festivals were used increasingly to promote civic pride, philanthropy, abolition, education, machinery, and consumer goods—all in ways that symbolized changing connections with religion. These improvisations, moreover, were contested, happening through advocacy for new understandings of authority, new causes, new ways of bridging denominational differences, and new opportunities for emotional expression.[4] But the fairs and festivals were interesting in themselves, too, rather than only as examples of theoretical abstractions. For the thousands of women who spent countless hours planning them, and for the thousands of visitors who participated in them, it was the details of what happened, where, and with whom that mattered most.

Ladies' Fairs

On October 20, 1878, a spectacular church fair opened at St. Patrick's Cathedral in New York City. It was the largest of its kind that anyone in the city had ever attended—and it was arguably the grandest church fair anybody in America would experience in their lifetimes. Most church fairs lasted for a few days or a week at most; this one lasted six weeks. Most church fairs convened in church basements, outdoors, or in rented halls; this one occupied the entire worship space of the massive cathedral itself. Single congregations usually hosted a church fair; this one's organizers included parishes all over the city. The usual fair's offerings were an assemblage of homemade crafts, baked goods, inexpensive donated items, and perhaps a humble meal; this fair auctioned everything from baby cribs to billiard tables. The revenue from most church fairs was meager; the proceeds from this one were huge in comparison. The one thing this fair and nearly all church fairs had in common was that they were organized and staffed by women.

A visitor even today might wonder how it was that St. Patrick's Cathedral was once the venue for a fair—a fair where fancy goods were sold, where raffle tickets were exchanged, and where thousands of people came to spend time consuming refreshments and having fun. The fair poses interesting questions about the time and place where it happened. How did the planners come up with the idea that people who ordinarily went to church on somber occasions and for sacred purposes would visit the same location to be entertained? Why did it seem likely that organizing a fair could be a

In advertisements, testimonials, and fictional accounts, the fairs' most appealing attraction was the allure of "pretty ladies." Pretty ladies who staffed the tables beckoned beguilingly to the eager bachelors who populated the fairs, tempted the willing males with beautiful tresses and smiles, teased the innocent visitors with coquettish looks, and stopped just short of outright seduction. A young man might bargain for a kiss while considering an article for sale and then ask to escort one of the damsels to her home. These were delights a male visitor might have expected at a party; finding them at a church was all the more alluring.

The origins of ladies' fairs are sufficiently obscure to depend mostly on speculation. A plausible theory suggests that English settlers in the American colonies inherited the idea from ancestors who celebrated midsummer "church ales" at which minstrels played and home-brew was sold to supplement parish coffers. An alternative theory traces the idea to Dutch colonists in New York and New Jersey who celebrated Pentecost (*Pinksteren* in Dutch) with a several-day gathering for baptisms, spiritual renewal, and merriment. Pinkster seems to have grown in popularity along the Hudson River to the point that by the mid-1700s, Pinkster festivities were popular in Black settlements as well. Another theory suggests that ladies' fairs were offshoots of colonial-era men-only festivals. Freemasons, for example, celebrated midsummer St. John the Baptist festivals, which legends said came from Druid ceremonies or dated to holy feasts at Solomon's Temple in Jerusalem. Men who were not freemasons invented other festivities. One such invention was an at-first obscure and then widely dispersed festival organized each spring by the Sons of King Tammany in honor of an ancient Lenni Lenape leader named Tamanend. No less obscure was Pope's Day, the American anti-Catholic equivalent of the British Guy Fawkes Night festivities commemorating the November 5, 1605, Gunpowder Plot. There were precedents in patriotic festivals as well. John Adams, for example, wrote to Abigail the day he signed the Declaration of Independence that the new nation should have an annual festival with "Shews, Games, Sports, Guns, Bells, Bonfires, and Illuminations." Village fairs and festivals by the end of the eighteenth century were traditions that villagers felt obligated to celebrate and—however, faintly they may have understood their origins and purpose—to imagine as fanciful moments when time was set aside for joy. "For here is pleasure's happy round, ye undisturb'd may share," a poet rhapsodized in 1806, "Delight, unmix'd with woe, is found, to grace our Village Fair."[6]

The best theory of ladies' fairs' origins traces them to female prayer groups and charitable associations, the earliest of which were organized in the late eighteenth century in New England and the Mid-Atlantic states. Many of these groups began as prayer meetings, female reading societies, and missionary associations, which besides praying and discussing the Bible collected money for relief funds, charity schools, and temperance organizations. By the first decade of the nineteenth century, female benevolent societies had been founded in African Methodist, Baptist, Congregational, Episcopal, interdenominational, Jewish, and Presbyterian congregations. The groups' by-laws typically excluded men from participating, although in one notable exception, the Female Benevolent Society in Washington, DC, called on Francis Scott Key—he, having the year before composed the poem that became "The Star-Spangled Banner"—to help in soliciting contributions. Many of the groups initiated something akin to church fairs by organizing fundraising events at which audiences were treated to guest lectures, charity sermons, and musical performances. The groups supplemented these efforts by producing handcrafted knitting and needlework items, which the members gave directly to relief organizations or sold at cooperating business establishments or at auction houses. Sewing circles—the contemporary equivalent of medieval women's spinning and weaving guilds—produced many of the items. These groups tended to multiply as one congregation's women mimicked another. Historian Carolyn Lawes who traced six early nineteenth-century sewing circles in Worcester, Massachusetts, for example, found their zeal for good works was matched only by each group's desire to outdo the other groups.[7]

Sewing circles were understood to be their own sources of enjoyment for the women who participated in them. A writer intimately familiar with sewing circles in Philadelphia described how they typically met once a fortnight at four o'clock at one of the members' houses, took tea together, commenced sewing while one of the group's members read something useful of a "religious character," and disbanded promptly at eight o'clock after a prayer. The meetings, the writer said, "promoted precisely that kind of social fullness and cheerfulness in friendly feeling which is indeed of great value." It was "a cheerfulness without waste of spirits in levity or of time in idleness, a friendly feeling beyond suspicion formed by the union of kindred minds in a common cause, cherished and strengthened in the enjoyments of a company, the pleasure of which suffers no interruption by the introduction of praise and prayer to God."[8]

Furthered by these sewing circles, a veritable explosion of causes to which women's charitable efforts were devoted occurred in the 1820s. Besides assisting widows and orphans, benevolent groups helped victims of fires and floods, charity day schools and boarding establishments were established in growing numbers, and criminal justice reformers created houses of refuge as alternatives to prisons. Churches were built in increasing numbers—most with mortgage payments that came due with stunning regularity and thus depended on effective ways of stoking contributions. New seminaries, academies, and church colleges needed financial assistance. Foreign mission boards established ladies' auxiliaries to support a growing corps of international evangelists while domestic mission board members started schools for Native American children. The decade also saw a commanding growth in Bible and tract societies, Sabbath schools, and temperance associations. "Benevolent societies are springing up in every quarter," one church leader observed.[9]

The growth of benevolent societies was matched by creativity in soliciting funds. Creativity was necessary because simply increasing members' dues threatened—or was perceived to threaten—giving to congregations. Tapping new congregations on the expanding frontier was promising, but many of these congregations needed assistance rather than having assistance to give. One creative idea was asking men and women of means to become lifetime members of benevolent societies. Another solution was asking sewing circles to step up their output. Yet another was tasking the recipients of benevolence with fund-producing labor. Charity schools' directors, for example, put their young charges to work plaiting straw bonnets and making fancy baskets. Foreign mission groups, finding they could make up in used clothing for what they lacked in cash, solicited donations of second-hand shirts, stockings, suspenders, pantaloons, shoes, gloves, pillowcases, bedding, and quilts. Thespian troops were enlisted to put on ticketed charitable performances at village festivals. Community orchestras and choirs were invited to give sacred music concerts sometimes accompanied by sumptuous dinners. And the most sought-after itinerant preachers traveled wider circuits giving well-publicized charity sermons after which offerings were taken.

Few of these fundraisers offered much that counted as festivity. This changed in 1826 when planners realized that charitable appeals could be linked to the fiftieth anniversary celebration of the Declaration of Independence. One of the benevolent groups that saw the potential in the upcoming anniversary was the Society for the Colonization of Free People of Color of America. Founded in 1816 in the hope of promoting the manumission of the enslaved and the settlement of free Blacks in West Africa, the organization attracted wide interest among churches from which it sought to raise funds to pay for purchasing and freeing the enslaved, covering the cost of their passage, and assisting in their settlement. There was no better place to host an event in support of the organization than the recently consecrated St. Paul's Episcopal Church in Alexandria, Virginia, designed by none other than the architect of the US Capitol, Benjamin Latrobe. The church's leaders, still rebuilding the denomination's reputation in the aftermath of its disestablishment, were eager to lend their support to an event geared so obviously toward making the connection between benevolence, freedom, patriotism, and the church. To that end, they hosted a widely attended Fourth of July festival in celebration of the "Grand Jubilee of our National Independence" to which members of all the churches in the area were invited.[10]

Fairs as Fundraisers

The year ladies' fairs showed that they would be a staple attraction for decades to come was 1827. Fairs that year in the vicinity of Baltimore and Washington, DC, were organized in April, October, and December. The kickoff event in April differed from most everything that followed because it was not sponsored by a church, not held at a church, and was not convened to benefit a church. The Grand Lodge of Maryland held the fair at its recently constructed building in Baltimore to support families displaced by the Greek War of Independence, which had taken thousands of lives since 1821. The women who organized the fair set up tables in the lodge, sold handmade crafts and donated articles, and provided refreshments. "The collection of saleables," a visitor wrote, "comprised an infinite variety of articles calculated for ornament or utility and met with purchasers readily." Two thousand people attended, earning the fair's organizers $1,500. The visitor wrote, "Many a Grecian mother as she sees herself and darling little ones snatched from famine by their timely aid will pray for blessings on the daughters of America."[11]

The April fair's success led to plans for a ladies' fair in October to coincide with the annual Cattle Show when farmers' wives and daughters could seek relief from the cow pens and horse stalls by purchasing from an exhibition of domestic fabrics, wines, butter, and fancy work for the benefit of orphaned girls at the city's Charity School. The fair's tables were supplied and staffed by the St. Paul's Episcopal Parish Female Benevolent Society whose members—an advertisement for the fair said—"vie with each other in ingenuity, taste, and generosity."[12] The Baltimore fair attracted such interest that the ladies in charge of the Washington Orphan Asylum organized a three-day event for its benefit during the week between Christmas and New Year's. To an extent even greater than in Baltimore, the Washington fair's organizers appealed to the city's charitable instinct. The orphans would someday themselves be mothers and thus would have benefited from the fair in becoming useful members of society, it was hoped, "instead of spreading the contagion of vice around them."[13]

Interest in ladies' fairs spilled into the following year as word spread up and down the East Coast that the Washington fair had netted more than $3,000. Everything from baby caps to fire screens had found buyers who relished their purchases while enjoying homemade cake and ice cream. Rumor had it that members of Congress and foreign ministers had participated, that President John Quincy Adams had helped publicize the event, and that Mrs. Adams contributed two hundred pairs of garters "knit by her own hands." Soon, writers' descriptions focused decidedly on the idea that ladies' fairs were pleasurable. The fairs were "delightful," the crowd was "lighthearted," and the mood was "good humored." There were above all the pleasures of encountering the ladies. "I never saw young ladies more lovely—more truly interesting or more attractive than those appeared who were engaged in this most praiseworthy exertion," a writer observed, "Whether it was the result of their surpassing loveliness and grace of manners or the very simple and natural effect of seeing beauty engaged in the service of charity and religion, I know not."[14]

A ladies' fair in 1829—organized that fall in Baltimore to raise funds for the Colonization Society—showed how clearly the idea of turning these events into entertaining festivals had caught on. The hall where the fair was held was decorated with roses and geraniums, there were cakes and confectionary delights, the vendors were "women of beauty" and there were girls "just blushing into womanhood," a band played at intervals, and the tables were filled with dolls, cradles, silver plate, lamps, paintings, gloves, slippers, and knickknacks. The write-up in the *Baltimore Republican* assured readers that the fair's purpose was benevolent but made abundantly clear that nothing had been spared to make the occasion an irresistible pleasure.[15] "Wend ye to the Ladies' Fair?" a poem that circulated widely that year asked. By all means, the poet advised, "Bid adieu a while to Care, Haste where Pleasure's torch is burning." There were "nymphs and graces," "scattered treasure," "art and charms," "pearls and pearlings," "silks and laces," "sweet-faced damsels," and "belles arrayed in beauty bright"—something for doctors, merchants, tradesmen, farmers, every sex, and every age. "Sparkling eyes and smiling faces call the gay and gallant out." Would you be happy? Then "Hasten, hasten to the Fair."[16]

No sooner had they begun than the fairs evoked concerns from cautious religious leaders. Was it proper to locate the buying and selling of goods in a place of worship? Was it appropriate to mingle pleasure with charitable service? "We should not consider it proper to introduce public prayer at any place of public sale; at the Fair, the shop, or the market," one writer advised. "There is a time and season for everything, but our Saviour condemns making a house of prayer one of merchandise." If the "ladies who direct" the fairs are "consistent Christians," the writer further advised, "we do not think a spirit of levity will characterize them."[17] Another writer—most likely a woman—agreed that nothing should be done that would "endanger the propriety of the whole by the coming in of a promiscuous and noisy throng." She thought it best if those who came to purchase were members of the same congregation, acquainted with the sellers. "While there is cheerfulness, sobriety and order [must be] observed throughout."[18]

Critics also objected to women's involvement in the fairs—neglecting their domestic duties, exhausting themselves, selling homemade goods, appearing at the fairs too finely dressed, and demeaning the sacredness of charitable work. Rebutting these criticisms, a writer supplied an anonymous response in the *Boston Recorder*. The homemade articles, she said, "do great honor" [to the] head, hands, and heart" of the benevolent women who make them: "Never is woman so lovely as when a ministering angel." The idea that women should only work at home was "so narrow and selfish a spirit [as] to be inconsistent with Christianity." Should women shrink from the effort? "Rather shall we not esteem it a privilege to be in labors more abundant—and to be allowed to realize, by our own delightful experience, that it is more blessed to give than receive!"[19]

The 1830s, when Alexis de Tocqueville made his famous tour of America, commenting approvingly on the voluntary associations he observed, saw an impressive increase in the geographic spread and sponsorship of ladies' fairs. Within a few years of the events in Baltimore and Washington, women were organizing fairs as far south as Georgia and the Carolinas, north in New England, and in newly settled communities on the western frontier. Women in Savannah organized a fair to support the construction of a new Baptist church. A fair in Cumberland, Maryland, brought the struggling community's residents together to establish a nondenominational church. The first ladies' fair in Wisconsin—an interdenominational event—preceded the state's admission to the Union by more than a decade. The ladies' fair in Nashville helped fund a new Episcopal church. The one in Rahway, New Jersey, supported the town's Sabbath School. The one in Albany, New York, raised money for the Society for the Relief of Orphan and Destitute Children. The fair's organizers "exceeded the expectations of the most sanguine," Orissa Heely, the society's founder, wrote to a friend; "they would have realized some hundred dollars more if they had had twice as much room."[20]

The fairs reflected the widening diversity of American religion. The women who organized them were African Methodists, Baptists, Catholics, Congregationalists, Episcopalians, Jews, Methodists, Presbyterians, and Unitarians. They worked through congregations and in community-wide organizations. There were "German ladies' fairs," "South-end ladies' fairs," "young ladies' fairs," and "rural ladies' fairs," as well as fairs for female beneficent societies, seamen's organizations, schools, orphanages, hospitals for the insane, and institutions for the blind. The women timed the fairs to coincide with church festivals, holidays, harvests, fruit-picking, agricultural exhibits, graduation ceremonies, and visits from touring dignitaries. William Henry Seward, campaigning for the New York governorship in 1839, for example, recalled arriving at a small town near the Vermont border where a ladies' fair was under way. It was "a scene of wild and glad merriment," he wrote.[21]

The ladies' fairs also reflected the growth in popularity of other kinds of charitable fairs and trade exhibitions. These events were organized by skilled artisans, trades people, and manufacturing companies to display goods such as glassware, silver-plated dinner ware, furniture, and other items marketed as newly patented "mechanical" devices. The fairs supplemented printed advertisements in newspapers and magazines by assembling thousands of items for display at a convenient urban location to which middle-class householders could be enticed. Like the church fairs, these fairs added charity as an incentive to attract wider participation. The first such fair was organized in 1837 in Boston by the Massachusetts Charitable Mechanic Association, displaying some fifteen thousand items and attracting more than seventy thousand visitors.[22]

Staging Festivity

The key to a successful ladies' fair was combining a biblical understanding of benevolence with festivity. Visitors applauded the ladies' fairs' organizers for "true charity" and the fairs' "sacred ends" while describing the enjoyment of evenings spent eating strawberries and ice cream, drinking lemonade, consuming the newly invented drink called "soda water," purchasing cakes and jewelry, and (though less often) dancing. The fairs' dual purpose was symbolized in the items purveyed being advertised as both "useful" and "fancy." The same was true of visitors' remarks about the women in charge of the fairs who were at once philanthropic in spirit and ingenious in putting "the squeeze" on male patrons with "bright eyes and blooming cheeks."[23]

The ladies' fair that out-classed all the smaller fairs preceding it was the Monument Fair organized by Sarah Josepha Hale in 1840. Hale was one of the most accomplished writers, editors, and entrepreneurs of her day. Hired in 1828 by Episcopal pastor Reverend John Lauris Blake to edit the *Ladies' Magazine*, which she did until 1836, and serving as editor of the popular *Godey's Lady's Book*, Hale founded the Seaman's Aid Society in 1833, was credited with being the author of the nursery rhyme "Mary Had a Little Lamb," and would later play a pivotal role in persuading Abraham Lincoln to make Thanksgiving a national holiday. The Monument Fair raised $25,000 toward the completion of the Bunker Hill Monument—the 221-foot obelisk that had been commissioned in 1825 in commemoration of the Battle of Bunker Hill. The fair featured a daily newspaper edited by Hale, replicas of the monument, refreshments, a post office, and tables piled with aprons, bags, belts, dolls, toys, and baskets—"everything to delight the eye and please the taste."[24] Hale's success in organizing the fair reflected one well-established principle of ladies' fairs and two innovations. The well-established principle relied on the preexistence of numerous women's groups in the Boston area with experience in organizing fairs. One of the two innovations was Hale's ability to publicize and solicit donations through her publishing—an innovation that would prove useful for the publishers and readers of other religious periodicals as well. The other innovation was drawing on and coordinating the involvement of dozens of churches and women's societies in the Boston area and as far away as New York City.

The Monument Fair was so well publicized that ladies' fairs appeared with increasing regularity in fictional accounts exploring the relationships between pleasure and morality, amusement and religion, and between men and women. Timothy Shay Arthur was one of the writers who shared the pages of *Godey's Lady's Book* with Sarah Josepha Hale. Arthur's most popular work was the temperance novel, *Ten Nights in a Bar-Room and What I Saw There*, published in 1854, the theme of which—resisting temptation—was already present in an 1842 story. The story was set at a ladies' fair in Philadelphia where the lead character, James Irvin, succumbs to temptation. Anticipating the "beautiful girls [all] so full of life and good humor" he expects to see at the fair, James encounters one "lovely creature" after another who persuades him to betray his "religious principles" and part with all his money. Coming increasingly to the realization that he is a person of weak character, James eventually meets a woman whose husband narrates the moral of the story: "How great danger there is of our being carried away with these fashionable movements got up in the name of charity." James vows never to attend a fair again, but the reader is left wondering if he will keep the vow.[25]

The fairs' popularity evoked the same concerns that had been expressed a decade earlier. It was still concerning to some essayists in religious periodicals to see women engaging in the kinds of public roles that the fairs required. "The rough business of public selling belongs properly to man," an essay in the *Weekly Messenger* contended. "When a woman assumes it even for a day, she steps out of her appropriate sphere. No matter how delicate may be the wares she exposes, it is the publicity which makes it out of place." It struck the writer that evil was being allowed on the excuse that good was being done, which was no better than promoting theaters in the hope of encouraging benevolence.[26]

From 1840 to 1860, most ladies' fairs remained small-scale events that hosted visitors at churches or community halls for several days and earned a few hundred dollars for the church or a benevolent cause. The fairs offered "useful and fancy" articles for purchase, served strawberries and ice cream, and competed with one another to earn the most glowing accounts. An 1858 essay in the *New York Herald* described nine concurrent fairs, prompting the writer to declare that the fairs were "decidedly an institution in the Northern and Eastern states." Months of preparation were of course required as the sewing circles were "busy as bees," but these were surely times of "amusement" for the ladies themselves, the writer concluded. As in the past, visitors remarked about the "bright eyed" and "lovely ladies" presiding over the festivities.[27]

However, there were several interesting innovations. One of the more novel ideas was implemented in 1854 when the women in charge of the ladies' fair in Springfield, Massachusetts—apparently inspired by the growing popularity of horse and cattle shows at agricultural fairs—staged an exhibit at which half a dozen human babies were displayed, judged as to their apparent flourishing, and awarded prizes. The baby show drew criticisms from scandalized commentators throughout New England. "This is certainly the most ridiculous farce that I ever saw perpetrated by a church," a reader in Rhode Island observed, "I had thought that any female capable of being a mother must have an irresistible constitutional delicacy and semi-physical abhorrence of such . . . that would drive her from such a scene to hide her head in shame."[28] But P. T. Barnum, always on the lookout for a dollar, seized the opportunity. The following year, Barnum organized a four-day baby show in New York City with more than a hundred babies on display for more than ten thousand ticket-purchasing visitors.[29]

The baby shows were controversial enough that few ladies' fairs included them until the end of the nineteenth century when baby exhibits gained new interest from eugenics proponents. The innovation that did catch on—despite criticism—was raffles. Raffles added new opportunities for earning money from donated items and for lucky pleasure seekers who might take home a $20 silver bowl or gold-headed cane by investing no more than 50 cents or a dollar on a raffle ticket. Raffles were "a method of raising the wind that would have shocked our great grandmothers," a visitor at a fair in San Francisco observed shortly before they became illegal there, "but in these days I believe it is allowed that the end justifies the means no matter what they may be."[30] Raising the wind this way was increasingly popular at Catholic fairs and soon proved attractive at Protestant fairs as well, earning severe condemnation from Protestants troubled by "Romish" influences. "It is customary here in Gotham about the time of the Christmas and New Year holidays for the grog shops, barrooms, and cheap groceries to have what are termed raffles at night for poultry and such other commodities as are in demand at that season," a writer distraught about the fair at a Methodist church in New York complained. "It is hard to believe that the church has resorted to such villainy to extort money from the simple and vicious for religious purposes."[31]

The innovation with the farthest-reaching effects was organizing ladies' fairs to benefit anti-slavery societies. Women initiated anti-slavery fairs soon after the first anti-slavery societies were formed in Boston and Philadelphia. The first such fair was held on December 16, 1834, in a modest second-floor room above a bookshop in Boston. Black and White women worked together to organize the fair for the New England Anti-Slavery Society, netting proceeds of approximately $300. The fair differed from the typical ladies' fair in several ways: first, it was uncommon for Black and White women to work together; second, the fair's visitors remarked about its lack of "frivolity," which contrasted with the city's "vanity" fairs; and third, the articles the fair offered were labeled to remind visitors who purchased them of the anti-slavery cause, such as a sugar bowl for "sugar not made by slaves" and a flag bearing the words "stripes on the banner none on the back," as well as biblical inscriptions such as "let the oppressed go free" and "the truth shall make us free."[32]

The fair became an annual event, moving from one venue to another, and facing criticism from moderate leaders who considered the anti-slavery movement too extreme. A visitor from England who attended the fair in 1841, for example, recalled some years later, "I was much struck—in the distinguished and agreeable companies which I had the good fortune to frequent with a few honorable exceptions—at the tone of disparagement, contempt, and anger with which the abolitionists were mentioned, just as any very patrician company in this country would talk of a socialist."[33] Disparagement notwithstanding, the fair grew as the abolitionist movement gained wider support. The fair's most significant expansion occurred in 1845 as controversy over the annexation of Texas deepened support for abolition. The 1845 fair was advertised as the National Anti-Slavery Bazaar and was organized by abolitionist Maria Weston Chapman with a board of thirty distinguished women with abolitionist credentials and from leading Boston families. The organizing committee secured Faneuil Hall which not only provided 4,000 square feet of space but also carried symbolic value as the "cradle of liberty." Donations of clothing, books, paintings, and tapestries flowed in from Scotland and Europe and from England where Frederick Douglass popularized the fair.[34]

The annual National Anti-Slavery Bazaar continued in Boston until 1858 when it was discontinued and relocated to Philadelphia. The fair's success, annually raising more than $3,000, showed the value of such fairs but also the challenges the organizers faced. The challenges escalated with the passage of the Fugitive Slave Act in 1850, which put several of the organizers in danger for having assisted fugitive slaves and deterred others from participating. The Boston aldermen who each year granted the use of Faneuil Hall refused the request in 1851, forcing the bazaar to be held in a hall near the Worcester Railroad depot and to relocate again the following year. Adversity continued in 1854 from inflation in the money market, which dampened donations and attendance, and, among the least expected of circumstances, the Crimean War which held up boxes of donations from England at Liverpool by Cunard steamers being needed to transport troops.[35]

The challenges facing the anti-slavery bazaar seem not to have been experienced by many of the small-scale ladies' fairs that flourished in parish halls and church basements. Visitors at church fairs and at newly established fairs for fire companies, temperance organizations, and the YMCA reported favorably about the festivity they experienced. In 1859, shortly after John Brown's raid on Harper's Ferry, a correspondent from nearby Centerville, Virginia, observed that the annual horse race had come off successfully and the ladies' fair had been liberally patronized, which he hoped provided enough excitement that there would be no need for "shooting, stabbing, or hanging."[36] A writer from San Francisco said the visitor "at once feels the spirit of festivity" at the fair. A visitor at a fair in New York wrote an account suggesting the event's main purpose was "to give the ladies an opportunity to show their new clothes and to talk with a multitude of unknown gentlemen without any preliminary introduction."[37] A man in Ohio wrote half in jest that ever since the fair at his church he was living off his friends' charity: "I found myself so bewitched with the siren voices and dazzling eyes of so many rare beauties that after having exhausted my ready cash and not willing to deny any such appeals to my generosity and charity I immediately applied to a friend for an advance of several dollars."[38]

The Civil War dramatically affected the fairs held from 1861 to 1865. After an initial drop in numbers and popularity, the fairs continued but with no pretense of providing amusement or distraction other than perhaps in small ways cheering the soldiers. The fairs did what they could to assist wounded soldiers and support the widows and orphans of fallen men. A few days after the devastating battle at Antietam on September 17, 1862, for example, the Soldiers' Aid Society in Norwich, Connecticut, organized a ladies' fair selling fruit, poultry, butter, and cream to assist the sick and wounded soldiers. Simultaneously, a fruit fair was organized in Providence by the Ladies' Relief Association, and a few weeks later fairs were held in Philadelphia and Buffalo for the benefit of citizens' volunteer hospitals. Fairs were also organized to support sick and wounded Confederate soldiers and their families. An 1863 ladies' fair in Aiken, South Carolina, that raised $653, for example, drew praise from a correspondent in Charleston who wrote, "With such women to inspirit and cheer them, the men of the South cannot fail to prove invincible and win the noble prize of Southern independence."[39]

But nothing compared with the mobilization of women's groups that took place on the Union side under the US Sanitary Commission. Created by federal legislation in 1861, the commission raised money and provided in-kind contributions to support sick and wounded soldiers in the Union Army. The commission relied heavily on sewing circles, female benevolent societies, ladies' auxiliaries, and other women's organizations to collect donations, knit sweaters and socks, and provide nursing care. Fairs became one of the most effective means of raising funds and soliciting volunteers. Borrowing nearly every aspect of the Monument Fair that Sarah Josepha Hale and her committee organized in Boston in 1840, and the National Anti-Slavery Bazaars held there in the 1840s and 1850s, the sanitary fairs were organized by women's committees, held in spacious venues in large cities, publicized in newspapers and churches, provided refreshments, and featured home goods and donated articles for sale. The largest fairs were held in Chicago, New York City, Philadelphia, Boston, Cincinnati, and St. Louis. The fair in New York included a daily newspaper, dramatic performances of selections from comedy and opera, and a raffle that featured donated furniture and art. More than three hundred women served on the forty-six committees that staffed the fair. The fair in Chicago included a military parade and an original hymn composed by Oliver Wendell Holmes and displayed the latest advances in washing machines and agricultural implements as well as the usual offerings of toys, handcrafted articles, and food. The fair in Philadelphia—where Presbyterian, Jewish, Episcopal, and Quaker women formed organizing committees—offered everything from children's articles and lingerie to demonstrations of a steam glass blower and a horseshoe machine.[40]

Mary Elizabeth Wilson Sherwood served as secretary of the New York fair. In her memoirs, she recalled sitting night after night during the months prior to the fair writing more than two thousand letters soliciting donations, articles, dignitaries' autographs, and anything that could be sold at the fair. "People took down their old silver, their choice editions of valuable books, their heirlooms," she said. Celebrities like Frederick Law Olmstead and Sarah Josepha Hale sent their autographs to be included among the articles raffled. "The whole countryside became a sewing circle," Sherwood recalled, "everyone was knitting woolen stockings." The mood was a "carmagnole"—a rallying spirit of frenetic work. "Everybody would give away his or her most treasured possession to be sold for the soldiers." The fair sent a check for $1,183,506 to the Sanitary Commission. "But it killed a great many women," she said. She meant this both literally and figuratively. Two of the women she knew personally died—one died from heat and overwork while cooking, and the other dropped dead on the floor of the crowded fair one warm evening.[41]

When the war was over, ladies' fairs resumed providing fairgoers with evenings of festivity to raise funds for church construction and benevolent associations. New attractions at some of the fairs included a telegraph for fairgoers to send "messages of love" and "Rebecca's Well" lemonade stands where a thirsty "way-fair-er" could be tempted. Meeting the competition from secular entertainment, more of the fairs advertised themselves as "festivals" and emphasized the inclusion of "enchantments," music and art, and "ingenious and amusing devices." Freedmen's associations were the new cause to which some of the fairs' organizers turned—enlisting the support of ladies' church societies and relief organizations to attract visitors with refreshments and entertainment similar to the ones offered before the war. The fair at New Brighton, Pennsylvania, organized by three women for the North Shore Freedmen's Aid Society in 1866, was typical of the smaller fairs. "It was successful in more than one sense," the society's secretary wrote, "for it was a great and genuine social pleasure as well as a pecuniary advantage." She noted that "a few sensitive souls were deterred from attending a fair whose object was to help their sable fellow countrymen, but their absence was atoned for by the good manners and cheerful contributions of those who did come."[42] A large Freedmen's fair in Chicago supplemented the usual attractions with spent shells, swords, sashes, and other battlefield relics. The one at Philharmonic Hall in St. Louis advertised that General Grant would visit but when the visit fell through settled for a display of portraits of Grant, John Brown, and Frederick Douglass.[43] The decorations at the Freedmen's fair in New York, a visitor recalled, "were in excellent taste and so were the young ladies." At the candy table, he "hesitated a long time before deciding which I would rather eat, the delicacies that were sold or the charming creatures who sold them."[44]

Many of the fairs in the decade after the war honored veterans and raised funds for the widows and orphans of deceased soldiers. The Grand Army of the Republic organized fairs of its own and coordinated appearances and lectures by decorated veterans at other fairs. The patriotism that inspired these events influenced other patriotic associations to sponsor similar events. One such cause was the Cuban revolt against Spain in 1868 which—despite

US neutrality—aroused sympathy from anti-slavery, religious, and women's relief societies. As word spread that thousands of Cuban women and children were suffering from lack of clothing and shelter, a force of some fifteen hundred veterans of the American Civil War volunteered for the short lived, never-dispatched "First New York Cavalry Cuban Liberators" while, more effectively, a women's organization called the Cuban Ladies' Relief Association formed, mobilized donations, held concerts, and organized a large fair to support the sick and wounded of the patriot army in Cuba.[45]

The Franco-Prussian War drew a similar response from relief organizations in 1870. Relief concerts and fairs were held by supporters of both sides. The most popular French fairs were held in and around New York and sought to attract supporters of Ireland as well as France. The largest of the "German Ladies' Fairs" were held in Cincinnati, St. Louis, and New York. In the hope of attracting wider participation than only from German neighborhoods, the organizers posted announcements in English-language newspapers and asked clergy of all denominations to encourage attendance. Alleviating German soldiers' and their families' suffering was the fairs' objective, but the fairs' announcements emphasized festivity. The account in the *Missouri Republican* of the fair in St. Louis, for example, described it as a "lively sight" with a "good humored" purpose where "German jollity" was on full display. There were many fine articles and decorations, a fish pond, a witches' tent, an eu de cologne fountain, and "all the variety of sweets that Germans delight in." The fair netted $11,000.[46]

To the doubters, the fairs' proliferation seemed excessive. "About this time every year there is a great cropping out of fairs," one critic complained. "We always manage to have excellent reasons for holding them. This time they are for the benefit of the 'French sufferers' and 'German sufferers.' Last year it was the 'Cretan sufferers.' The one before it was the 'sanitary' dodge and our own sufferers." It struck the writer that the fairs were all hawking the same useless merchandise—"impracticable pincushions and impossible penwipers." Unhappy men were being swindled. "Why don't ladies make up some nice shirts?" he wondered.[47]

But doubts of that sort did not deter plans for an even grander fair from moving ahead. The fair that became known as the Centennial Exposition—held in Philadelphia in 1876—was of a magnitude that belied any comparison with the modest ladies' fairs that preceded it. The Centennial Exposition was of a different order even than the largest sanitary commission fairs. The exposition opened on May 10 and remained open for six months. Nearly ten million visitors attended it. Fourteen thousand businesses and representatives from thirty-five countries took part. There was one way, however, in which the exposition imitated the ladies' fairs that women had been organizing for decades. That was the role women played at the exposition. A small committee of women mobilized approximately a thousand women to raise upward of $70,000, create a women's pavilion at the fair, organize daily entertainment and refreshments, and showcase women's accomplishments in employment, education, philanthropy, and literature.

St. Patrick's Fair

The St. Patrick's Cathedral Fair of 1878 was the apogee of half a century of ladies' fairs and church festivals—events that started small and mostly remained small but also evolved over the years into larger endeavors addressing diverse objectives under diverse sponsorship. A few (perhaps many) of the women who organized the St. Patrick's fair had attended the Centennial Exposition in 1876 or one of the Sanitary Commission fairs in the 1860s. Some of them in fact had helped organize an 1875 ladies' fair at St. Francis Xavier Church, which was one of the parishes that participated in the St. Patrick's fair. And many would have remembered the "Great Catholic Fair of '67" which netted over $100,000 for the New York Catholic Protectory to construct a four-story building at 86th Street and 2nd Avenue to accommodate three hundred destitute girls. There were plenty of models to emulate, therefore, and from which to gain confidence that the St. Patrick's fair would be a success.

The reason for the fair was to raise money to pay off the debt incurred in constructing the cathedral. The planning to construct St. Patrick's Cathedral in New York City on Fifth Avenue between 50th and 51st streets began in 1850 under the direction of Bishop John Joseph Hughes who saw the need for the city's growing Catholic population to have a large cathedral to replace the older cathedral in Lower Manhattan. The plans were finalized in 1858, and the cornerstone was laid the same year. The plan was an ambitious design that would give the cathedral an unrivaled presence in the city and indeed in the nation.[48] After two years, work on the cathedral was suspended because of the Civil War and did not resume until 1866. The building was finished in 1878 except for the spires which were completed in 1888. Funding for the cathedral was secured through subscriptions from individual donors and annual assessments averaging $2,000 each from the nearly four dozen constituent churches of the archdiocese. The final cost was $1.9 million, of which $400,000 was a mortgage loan borrowed at 7 percent interest. The fair attracted more than a quarter of a million visitors and earned the cathedral the handsome sum of $172,625.48.

Handsome as it was, that sum fell short of the organizers' expectations by nearly $30,000. The fair opened while the city's economy was still suffering from the financial crisis of 1872, which would not be fully recovered until 1879. Wages that had risen during the Civil War were 25 to 30 percent lower than in 1872 and the New York newspapers were filled with arguments that wages should be lower still. The cathedral was already under attack from critics who viewed it as an ostentatious display of wealth. The fair had to be explained if it was going to succeed at all. Reverend William J. McClure, Rector of the Church of the Immaculate Conception of the Blessed Virgin, took up the challenge. In a lengthy statement printed in the fair's daily newspaper, McClure acknowledged that church fairs were "substantially a modern means of acquiring funds for religious purposes where their regular sources of church revenue fail and especially [for] the redemption of churches from debt." In the present instance, the fair was necessary, he said, because there were no wealthy endowments, by which he implied the endowments on which the city's most notable Episcopal churches depended. Were it not for the fair, the burden would fall heavily upon "the poorer class." Responding to Protestant criticisms of church raffles, he contended that the fair's success depended on lotteries of this kind and that there should be no anxiety about expending money in this way for the "general good." He invited the public to visit the fair's attractively laden tables.[49]

The fair featured forty five tables, each of which was thirteen feet in length and included shelving up to five feet in height. The cathedral's 87,000-square-foot sanctuary provided ample space for the tables and the aisles between them, although the space was hardly sufficient for the seven to ten thousand visitors who crowded the cathedral most evenings. Each table was the responsibility of one of the forty-five churches in the archdiocese. The tables were "tastefully" and "judiciously" decorated with velvet, silk, or lace tablecloths and drapes and were festooned with canopies, pedestals, sculptures, and flags. Each table was stocked with fifty to a hundred donated articles that visitors could buy or win by purchasing 25-cent raffle tickets. The articles included many high-end items that had been donated by wealthy families and the city's elite jewelry and general merchandise stores, including Tiffany's and R. H. Macy's. The least expensive items included pickle dishes, napkin rings, pillow shams, books, inkstands, embroidered chair coverings, lap blankets, silver card baskets, gold-headed canes, sofa cushions, opera cloaks, silk screens, and French dolls. Among the more expensive items were a diamond bracelet, a set of bedroom furniture, a billiard table, a Steinway piano, a horse-drawn touring vehicle, a rail trip to San Francisco, and a first-class steam liner voyage to Europe. There was also a wide selection of distinctly Catholic items, including Bibles, crucifixes, vestments, candles, sculptures, and pictures of Pope Pius IX. Each week, as items were sold and raffled, new items were added—including such oddities as five hundred boxes of laundry soap, two barrels of apples, an 1847 letter written by Stonewall Jackson, the King of Spain's autograph, and a cactus. Were that not enough to attract visitors, there were also concerts, glass blowers, and miniature steam engines.

The first evening of the fair "was marked by an air of metropolitan festivity," a reporter for the *New York Herald* wrote. "There was nothing of the rural donation party or the ordinary church fair type about it. The cathedral itself seemed to have extended its dimensions." The tables and booths were "ablaze with temptations to benevolence, filled with toys, with books, with shawls, with silver, with works of art." He marveled at the architectural beauty of the space. "The vistas of wealth and worth, property and people . . . were gay and full of exhilarating cheer."[50] The *Irish American Weekly*'s report was far less effusive, instead reproducing the texts of the speeches given by Cardinal John McCloskey and Mayor Smith Ely Jr. and detailing the items displayed on many of the tables but emphasized that the thousands of people at the fair were pleasantly jostling against one another and playfully submitting to the fair's temptations.[51]

Among the challenges the organizers of any fair faced was providing enough lighting for fairgoers to see the items being offered clearly enough to know what they were purchasing or hoped to win. This challenge was more daunting at St. Patrick's because of the cathedral's 180-foot ceilings and its vast space. Fairs and worship services at most churches as well as gatherings at theaters and music halls were illuminated by kerosene lamps and candles, but these were dangerous and sometimes deadly—as happened in 1876 when fire broke out, resulting in three hundred deaths during a performance at the Brooklyn Theatre. Edison's electric lights would not be widely displayed until the following year. The solution at St. Patrick's was 2,000 gas lights, each providing 25 watts of illumination, and a newly patented pneumatic apparatus enabling them to be turned on and off simultaneously. The system, one visitor observed, made it possible to read even small print distinctly.[52] Simply seeing the lights was one of the fair's attractions—as another visitor exclaimed, "the softness, brilliancy, and purity of the light is not surpassed in the world."[53]

True to form, the reports filed in the city's newspapers emphasized the "lovely ladies" gentlemen could enjoy at the fair. A reporter for the *New York Tribune* was beguiled with all the ladies "wearing coquettish little caps." He mused, "Hardened indeed must be the man who can run the gauntlet of appealing eyes and beseeching tones, which urge him to take a chance in articles sufficient to start an old curiosity shop. The only way to escape is to drift with the current of the crowd down the center of the aisles midway from the sirens on either side."[54] The *New York Herald* described the "gay and festive damsels who provide all manner of cheer" and the "bevy of vivacious young ladies" selling cigars and cigarettes. Another account claimed to be an interview with a man who frequently "haunted church fairs to feast his eyes" on beautiful girls. "I've been to no end of fairs," he said, "but I never knew of one where a fellow could enjoy himself as much as in this place."[55]

Women's perceptions were rather different from the reports about festive damsels. Organizing a fair was like fielding an army. There were thousands of articles to be accepted, displayed, and their donors properly thanked; raffle tickets and receipts properly recorded; and thousands of visitors to be persuaded to attend, spend money, be entertained, and be united with their purchases and winnings. The schedules of nearly a thousand women had to be coordinated to ensure the tables were staffed and refreshments were served. Once in place, the women staffing the tables were on their feet for hours. On several occasions, fistfights had to be broken up. Even bathroom breaks were challenging since there were no public toilets in the building. Whatever joy there was, it was the satisfaction of a job well done in the service of a worthy cause.

Mary A. Sadlier was one of the women in charge of the fair. Sadlier was the author of some twenty books and numerous magazine articles, many of which were set in Ireland or featured Irish Americans, and she held salons at her homes in Manhattan and on Long Island, convened meetings among popular writers, and was a central figure in the Catholic community. With her daughter Anna T. Sadlier, she was among the women who worked tirelessly staffing and advertising the fair. As the fair opened, she published an essay anticipating what to expect. "The work in which we are engaged dear associates and fellow workers—this grand fair for a grand and noble project—is one that demands all our energies, all our zeal, with no small amount of patience and self-sacrifice." She cautioned that it would be "a work of several weeks duration and will require constant and wearying attention and ceaseless activity to make it the great success which it is confidently expected to be." She reminded her fellow workers of the exertions of their predecessors, their humble beginnings, and their accomplishments. They now had the opportunity to work with one heart for the cathedral that would stand as "a fitting monument of your faith, your charity, [and] your love and gratitude."[56]

There was a strong connection between the women who staffed the fair and the women who visited it. Although the fair offered items for men, most items were meant to attract women—and women were in fact the winners of two-thirds of the items raffled. The fair's success depended on the social networks through which women were acquainted in their parishes and neighborhoods. The reason each parish was expected to provide at least twenty women to serve as volunteers was to widen the social networks with whom they could publicize the fair as much as it was to supply sufficient coverage for the work required. Without these personal contacts, persuading visitors to spend money was harder. As one of the women staffing the tables remarked, "A good many come in the afternoon, but, you know, they're ladies and they're so fussy and a dollar to them looms up as large as a harvest moon. You can't get them to take more than a twenty-five cent [item]; if you mention a dollar, they think you are wild."[57]

Of one category of women who may have been present in large numbers at the fair hardly anything is known. They were the servant girls, many of them Irish, who made up a large share of the female working population in New York and other cities. Two articles in the *New York Times* suggested that servant girls were an important constituency of the city's ladies' fairs. An article published a few months after the St. Patrick's fair (almost certainly written with that event in mind but without mentioning it by name) observed that "the effect of raffles at church fairs, particularly in entertainments of this kind gotten up by Roman Catholics, has been to make this species of almsgiving exceedingly popular among the lower classes in our large cities." The article advised, "Those who will take the trouble to question their servants, either Irish or German, will learn that they have almost daily calls made upon them to take a chance in this or that raffle, the result of which is to put a little ready money into the pocket of some more or less deserving person, for as a rule there is a coloring of charity given to these enterprises to meet moral objections which might otherwise be raised." The other article, published in 1868, observed that "the most profitable patrons of Catholic fairs are servant girls, who are very profuse and often spend a month's wages in an evening."[58]

It was true that 25-cent raffle tickets were cheap enough that young poorly paid working women might have purchased them in the hope of winning a $20 silver platter or necklace. It was plausible that domestic laborers populated the fairs in the 1860s in Union Square—closer to where they lived and worked—but less likely that many would have made their way to Midtown Manhattan in 1878 where an entry ticket alone was worth two or three days' wages. It was likely, though, that newspaper stories were tinged by a dismissive attitude toward Irish servant girls who readers routinely referred to generically as "Bridget" and derided for foolishness, laziness, indolence, ignorance, wastefulness, and immorality.[59]

The fair ended in December, and St. Patrick's Cathedral was dedicated on Sunday, May 25, 1879, with more than forty prelates and two hundred priests presiding over the five-hour service. The ceremony merged the solemnity required of the occasion with an acknowledgment of a different kind of festivity—the solemn joy—that was appropriate on such an occasion. The Right Reverend Patrick J. Ryan, Coadjutor Bishop of the Archdiocese of St. Louis, delivered the sermon. "Joy, holy and exultant, fills our heart today as we come into this glorious house of the Lord," he said. "The joy is universal."[60]

Church fairs remained popular through the end of the century but rarely with the enthusiasm of the 1870s. Facing stiffer competition from theaters, carnivals, and sporting events, they adapted by turning one-off events into annual endeavors, relying on the growing cadre of middle-class women who populated the larger and more numerous churches in cities, and providing familiar entertainments while adding new attractions. The typical fair included refreshments, music, and tables lavishly stocked with dolls, aprons, candy, packaged goods, and handicrafts. Newer attractions included grab bags, races, drill teams, children's events, smoking rooms, catered dinners, and exhibitions of electrical appliances. A modest repeat of the St. Patrick's fair in 1894 included an exhibition of girls' calisthenics skills. A church fair in Jersey City treated visitors to a working X-ray machine. It was not uncommon for fifty or sixty women to be listed by name in news stories describing the fairs and for five to ten times that number having visited the fair. Raffles were common at Catholic fairs—and still were often the bane of Baptists, Methodists, Episcopalians, Presbyterians, and the public officials who shared their concerns. Many churches hosted strawberry festivals and potluck dinners but realized was it easier to take up a special offering than organize a fair.

By the end of the century, church fairs' popularity was waning in lieu of rummage sales ("a new experiment," as one writer remarked) that were easier to organize, smaller, less often concerned with "fancy" items and more commonly stocked with used clothing and toys, but still devoted to charitable causes and still publicized as festive occasions. Like church fairs, rummage sales were events that reflected how middle-class Americans spent their time, now including time devoted to shopping for no-longer-wanted lines of merchandise ("rummage") during special sales days at department stores. Church rummage sales were guided by the diverse interests and needs of their congregations. Some were organized by ladies' aid societies, others by Sunday school teachers, and still others by youth groups. A good rummage sale could be considered a success if it earned fifty or sixty dollars. The sales took work and yet were simpler than church fairs—simple enough that even boys and girls could organize them, as a writer in Montgomery, Alabama, advised: "Have you ever heard of a rummage sale? Do you know what one is? No, it isn't a sale of something in which you have to rummage all over town to find buyers." A rummage sale only required going through the attic for discarded items, the writer said, and "then, after it has all be brought down and carefully dusted, selling it to whoever will buy, and giving the proceeds to some good cause."[61] Rummage sales were sufficiently lacking in controversy—no raffles, no dancing, no liquor, no seduction—that even Baptists and Methodists felt comfortable organizing them. However, they were not entirely free of controversy. A Methodist rummage sale in Chicago offered such bargains that two hundred men and women crowded the church to get first pick of the items, broke down the door, and shattered a plate glass window before the police were called to restore order.[62]

Folk festivals increasingly took the place of church fairs as well. The festivals were happy occasions, set apart from working life as times for revelry, the ritual commemoration of folk traditions, and the renewal of ethnic identities. Religion was usually included but folk festivals were in more important ways a potential threat to religion because they were organized by other community groups. The most important groups were playground associations that worked in cooperation with settlement houses to provide spaces and events of pedagogic value for urban children. The organizers considered it important for children to learn that fun and education went together and that diverse ethnic identities could be celebrated as an important feature of being "American." The festivals built on the church fairs' legacy in managing expectations about happiness. Careful planning was of course necessary, but festivity also came to have moral meaning. It was pleasure for a purpose.[63]

The church fairs had established to a considerable degree that religion could be fun—enjoyed for purposes other than praise and fellowship. There was a season for rejoicing within a consecrated space that was not a religious holiday or a day for worship. The fairs amplified the usual conviviality of Sunday greetings as an occasion set apart for the buying and selling of pleasurable articles and entertainment. There was to be cheer in the house of God—cheer of a specified kind. It was to be different from secular amusement. The articles displayed were to be tastefully and judiciously selected. The fleeting passion one might experience in the crowd was not to be sustained for long. There was to be the serious joy of furthering a worthy cause. If there was mirth, it was to be restrained. If there was joy, it was to be in the service of a charitable purpose.

The fairs, then, were an important—though overlooked in later years—chapter in faith communities' nurturing of happiness. The fairs were an emotional practice, oriented toward generating happiness in a novel way that was nevertheless under the auspices of religious authorities. The organizers, the staff, and many of the visitors were women. For religious authorities, the challenge was two-fold: how to facilitate and yet manage the novel experiences the fairs promoted, and how much to modify the traditional patriarchal authority of religious institutions to ensure that women who knew best how to organize the fairs had the authority to do so. Hosting the fairs in sanctified buildings required clearly distinguishing the timing and purpose of the fairs from the usual calendar of religious services. The distinction was impossible to make without some ambiguity but generally set a precedent for religious buildings to be used increasingly for parties, banquets, sports events, and fundraisers as well as for worship. The "institutional" church, as it was called, became a multipurpose organization where fun could be had if it conformed to moral standards. How gender roles were reassigned took years to be negotiated. For the most part, women contributed to the happiness that churchly events provided by shouldering most of the work.

4
Durable Happiness

Progressive Era Constructions of Work and Service

An audience of some five thousand clergy, religion scholars, lay people, and interested members of the community assembled in 1911 at the open-air Greek Theatre in Berkeley, California, to hear Theodore Roosevelt deliver five lectures sponsored by the Pacific School of Religion. Roosevelt took advantage of the opportunity to address moral and ethical issues of interest to the assembled clergy and lay leaders, avoiding the major policy debates of the day. His embrace of the strenuous life was on full display, challenging his listeners to adhere courageously to the ideals of their faith and to connect their "Sunday conscience" with their "weekday conscience," thus better relating what they did in their private lives to their responsibilities as public servants. He spoke about happiness in the second lecture. Cautioning against the pursuit of raw pleasure, he talked of decency, virtue, responsibility, and service. He called the crowd's attention to the Civil War soldiers, some of whom were in the audience, who had sacrificed their days of ease, put duty before pleasure, and gladly risked everything. "In the long run no man or woman can really be happy unless he or she is doing service," he advised. "Happiness springing exclusively from some other cause crumbles in your hands."[1]

If happiness is an emotional practice that people manage for themselves (or is managed for them), then one of the most important management tasks is to identify and pursue the kind of happiness that does not "crumble in your hands." The crumbling kind was ephemeral, an elevated mood experienced momentarily during an enjoyable event. The exuberant moods that church leaders promoted at camp meetings and the joy they hoped people would experience at fairs and festivals were of this kind—worthy but short lived. Church leaders wanted the faithful to experience a more permanent kind of happiness. That was more the purpose of religious devotion, after all, than providing pleasurable moments. Church tradition termed it faith, the assurance of salvation, and hope. Theodore Roosevelt linked it to service.

Nurturing Happiness. Robert Wuthnow, Oxford University Press. © Oxford University Press 2025.
DOI: 10.1093/9780197807071.003.0005

Rousseau called it durable happiness.[2] What they had in mind was a stable, meaningful form of happiness that people could depend on through the ups and downs of life. Serving God and serving others were part of the story, but what that meant and how it related to happiness changed as people faced new challenges and experienced new opportunities.

In this chapter, I describe how useful service—productive work, charitable activity, social reform, and simple acts of kindness—came in the first years of the twentieth century to be emphasized in enlarged ways by prominent religious authorities as the means of attaining durable happiness. The connection was made partly through straightforward appeals like Roosevelt's. The connection was just as importantly forged through habits, aphorisms, and routine activities that reinforced it in daily life. Happiness was durable not only because people were somehow inclined to believe that it was, but because of the practices in which they could regularly engage and through which they could be reassured that the quiet contentment they experienced was truly the most enduring kind of happiness.[3] Happiness was in these ways nurtured and managed by defining it as quiet contentment and by locating it in situations such as work and service that were routinely available to everyone. Religious authorities took a risk in advocating that happiness could be found in these ways. If it was available in ordinary situations, most of those were not under the direct control of church leaders. Religious authority, therefore, had to rely on moral persuasion if it was to shape how people pursued happiness. Moral persuasion took form in teachings that stressed religion's responsibilities toward the society, rather than only toward individual souls, and that conceived of these responsibilities as being fulfilled through useful service, which in turn was conducive to happiness.

The arguments about service and happiness were mostly that—arguments put forward by leading preachers, theologians, and seminary professors in sermons, lectures, essays, and books. The arguments were meant to instruct frontline pastors and parishioners in ways to think about the wider world in which they lived. There was optimism that people of faith could make the world better through acts of service. There were also groups—fellowships, mission programs, settlement houses, and civic organizations—that put the ideas into practice. The connection with happiness was usually described as a side benefit. Service work was to be done for its own sake, not as a way of achieving happiness, but a person engaged in useful service could expect to experience durable happiness as a result. The idea illustrated a way in which religious authorities could shape emotional practice, not by stage managing it but by guiding its meaning. Happiness in these new progressive understandings could be found in the world, in worldly careers that usefully served others, in work, and in other ways of serving God. Happiness could be durable because it consisted of quiet inward contentment that could include—but did not necessitate—intense emotion. It was durable because people were constantly reminded that it was by what they heard in their places of worship and by what they knew about it as they went about the routine tasks of serving their families, doing their work, and serving others. As time went on, these were messages communicated in popular culture as well as in the churches through advice columns in newspapers, in films, and at public events.

An Enlarged Horizon

The early years of the twentieth century posed new challenges for faith communities and offered wider opportunities for service than ever before. The period from about 1897 to 1920, the Progressive Era, included the Social Gospel movement, Prohibition, muckraking, anti-trust legislation, and the campaign for women's suffrage. No single movement or idea defined the period; it was also known for Jim Crow laws and lynchings. The Social Gospel was one of many developments in religion, among which were fundamentalism, the holiness movement, Christian socialism, new domestic and foreign missionary agencies, the settlement house movement, an expansion in the number of private religiously sponsored schools and hospitals, and the formation of specialized ministries such as the Salvation Army, YMCA, and YWCA.[4]

The change that broadly characterized these developments in religion was an expansion of its social horizons. All of these developments in one way or another represented an expansion of the frameworks in which local churches typically operated, whether through the kinds of multistate networks that linked fundamentalists with one another, the locations in which Pentecostalism grew, the federations that bonded mainline Protestant denominations with one another, the labor ministries of the Catholic church following the social encyclical of *Rerum Novarum* (1891), or the parachurch organizations that organized social services and advanced social reform efforts. Theological conceptions that focused on individuals' relationship to God continued to do so but also placed greater emphasis on social transformation. Ministries that churches had practiced within local congregations were now enlarged to include wider and more diverse populations. This expansion encouraged new thinking about how service activities could be useful, emphasized the value of useful work in general, and tightened the connection between ideas about useful service and happiness. There was nothing new in the idea that serving others could be a source of happiness, but these early-twentieth-century years demonstrated in yet another context how faith communities interpreted and sought to manage the meanings of happiness, particularly by associating it with useful service to the wider society and by condemning pleasurable self-indulgence.

The programs that ministered to larger and more diverse populations through individual congregations consisted of Sunday schools, youth programs, revival meetings, and charities. Located in New York, Chicago, Philadelphia, Saint Louis, and other large cities, these programs expanded the outreach of congregations beyond their immediate memberships. The Menard Street Mission in St. Louis under the leadership of Reverend Charles Stelzle, for example, launched a Sunday school program that attracted an estimated 1,500 pupils from working-class families and was said to be the largest of its kind west of the Mississippi.[5] Across the country and in a variety of denominational traditions, other congregations developed similarly expansive ministries. The Institutional Church and Social Settlement founded by African Methodist Episcopal pastor Reverdy Ransom in Chicago provided men's and women's clubs, a dining room, gymnasium, kindergarten, childcare, and concerts.[6] Fort Worth's First Baptist Church led by controversial evangelical pastor Reverend J. Frank Norris grew in the 1910s from a congregation of a thousand to as many as five thousand; was active in campaigns against prostitution; and coordinated ministries for youth, working women, and the poor throughout the metropolitan area.[7] The African American congregations that W.E.B. Du Bois described in *The Philadelphia Negro* ministered broadly to the educational, health, charitable relief, and spiritual needs of the city's Seventh Ward.[8] The Berean Baptist Church in New York City expanded successfully under the leadership of Reverend Edward Judson, constructed a new sanctuary with support from John D. Rockefeller, and launched new community-wide educational and healthcare ministries. The church's expanding reach into the city's lower-income population, Judson said, was like a "creature of the sea that stretches out on every side to explore the dim element in which it swims."[9]

Denominationally sponsored efforts to enlarge ministries were evident in the Methodist Federation for Social Service, which aimed to arouse churches' sense of responsibility for social needs; the Presbyterian Department of Church and Labor, which Stelzle played a role in initiating; the Society of Saint Vincent de Paul, which originated in France and was active in the United States by the 1840s; the interdenominational Open and Institutional Church League, formed in 1894; the New York Federation of Churches and Christian Workers, founded in 1896; and the Federal Council of Churches, founded in 1908.[10] Social service organizations that broadened faith communities' work included Hull House, founded by Jane Addams in 1889; the Salvation Army, originating in London in 1865 and active in the United States by 1880; the Catholic Home Bureau, organized in 1898 to support the placing-out work of children's agencies; the Deaconess Movement of the 1880s and 1890s; and lesser-known efforts, such as an Episcopal program in Virginia that trained Appalachian girls for domestic service, and the Tennessee Town kindergarten established by Reverend Charles Monroe Sheldon in Topeka, Kansas.[11]

Social reform efforts with links to faith communities varied from prohibition advocacy to women's suffrage, restrictions on child labor, the anti-lynching movement, the pacifist Fellowship of Reconciliation, and the National Association for the Advancement of Colored People.[12] Faith communities' horizons were enlarged through the meetings, conversations, preaching, and publications of leading scholars in theology and related fields. They popularized the idea that new opportunities were available for service and social reform and provided a biblical rationale for more expansive and diverse ministries. The Brotherhood of the Kingdom, founded in 1892 by Walter Rauschenbusch, professor of church history at Rochester Baptist Seminary, and Leighton Williams, pastor of the Amity Baptist Church in New York City, for example, formulated the central ideas of the Social Gospel movement.[13]

The social circumstances that facilitated these enlarged ministries and toward which many of them were addressed reflected the expanding urban environment of the late nineteenth- and early twentieth centuries. Between 1890 and 1910, New York City's population grew from 2.5 million to 4.8 million; Chicago's from 1.1 million to 2.2 million; and Philadelphia's from 1.0 million to 1.5 million. The population doubled in smaller cities, including Atlanta, Cleveland, Dallas, Denver, Fort Worth, Houston, Indianapolis, Kansas City, Los Angeles, Portland, and Seattle. Immigration peaked in 1907 when

1.29 million people entered the United States. Population density increased in major cities, especially in crowded lower-income neighborhoods composed of recent immigrants.[14] Public and private transportation increased, retailing and advertising expanded, and the number of persons working in the professions and other service occupations grew.[15] The last decades of the nineteenth century also witnessed significant growth in the number and size of hospitals, insane asylums, schools for the blind and deaf, orphanages, and other social service institutions.[16] These organizations created opportunities for reform-minded people to serve in venues other than local congregations. There was also an expanding network of media—some 2,000 newspapers—through which to communicate information about social conditions and in which sermons, essays, and advice columns appeared with increasing regularity.[17]

The reformers, social gospel advocates, and early social scientists who discussed the social changes through which they were living sketched a map of the expanding social horizon's crucial features. The prevailing feature, made clear by industrialization, was that people who earned their living in one kind of activity depended on people who earned their living in different pursuits. The division of labor was evident not only in the traditional exchanges that took place between bakers and millers or farmers and shopkeepers but also between more finely differentiated occupations, such as machinists and welders. "Human society tends to become constantly more interdependent," Rauschenbusch observed. "It used to be like a colony of mollusks; it is becoming like the body of a man. We live by faith in one another. We have to trust our health officers to test our water supply and the milk brought into the city, for we cannot do it. We have to trust our newspapers to report the facts correctly to us."[18] This division of labor's implication was that obligations—and trust—extended beyond those with whom one was intimately acquainted. The community of relevant others was distant as well as nearby. The further implication was that each person, group, or trade had a responsibility to do its part, for the welfare of all required the diverse contributions of all.

Stark inequality separating the rich and poor was another feature of the social horizon. For those in the middle, to whom the reformers usually directed their messages, the implication was that Christian responsibility required doing something to ameliorate the situation. Were it only that some families were disadvantaged and others were not, charitable activity within congregations could be sufficient. However, the argument for reform identified special interests, monopolistic business practices, trusts, corruption in government, and racism as problems contributing beyond industrialization to the gap between rich and poor. The impediments hindering qualified people, especially African Americans, from finding useful work, Du Bois wrote in his study of Philadelphia, was "a disgrace to the city—disgrace to its Christianity, to its spirit of justice, to its common sense."[19]

Among the features that writers also emphasized was the striking anonymity that pervaded urban life. Unlike in small towns where neighbors interacted socially, city residents were transient, away from their families, worked in deafening factories where conversation was impossible or were restricted from talking at work, and often did not speak the same language as their closest neighbors. Courtship was less often chaperoned and churches' efforts to promote "sociables" had proven less effective among working-class people than had been hoped.[20] Anonymity implied that virtue was left to the individual who lived in "moral isolation," as Jane Addams put it.[21] To be morally isolated was to live free of the constraints previously imposed by the watchful eyes of family, friends, and neighbors. Without this constant monitoring, an internal compass was needed. The individualism of the era in this respect went hand in hand with an understanding of society as impersonal and yet interdependent. Its impersonality put the responsibility for virtuous action squarely on the individual, yet the interdependence of society's parts implied that cutting corners would catch up with those who shirked their responsibilities. Whatever was done to address social conditions, therefore, also had to be concerned with the individual's moral development.

It was not hard for Christian writers to reconcile these views with classic biblical teachings. Followers of Jesus could learn from the gospel about sacrificial love and care for the needy. The novelty lay in rediscovering theological conceptions that emphasized the redemption of society—"social salvation"—rather than only the redemption of individuals.[22] For Rauschenbusch's Brotherhood of the Kingdom, the central idea was in fact "the kingdom," which meant emphasizing the kingdom of God on earth. That kingdom was composed of "such real things," Brotherhood of the Kingdom member Samuel Zane Batten argued in his influential book *The New Citizenship: Christian Character in Its Biblical Ideals, Sources, and Relations*, "as homes and stores, factories, and counting rooms; with such real relationships as buying and selling, marrying and giving in marriage, voting and working."[23]

Service as Useful Work

In emphasizing the realities of everyday life, writers like Batten argued that useful endeavors, especially work, were the way to have a purpose in life and to benefit oneself, one's family, and the society in which one lived. People "want to be useful," Batten argued, "they want to serve their fellows according to the will of God."[24] Being useful applied to men and women in the labor force but also to their household activities and church participation. Work was usually difficult and for many, it was a struggle for existence. There was no getting around the fact that working in mines and mills, digging ditches, laboring around dangerous engines, and breathing dangerous chemicals were undignified and degrading. Nothing said about it could make it any less so. Yet it was the nature of humanity to seek ways to be useful and to find meaning in making useful contributions.

Effort that had the character of "general utility," the Connecticut pastor Reverend A. W. Stevens declared in an essay on the social aspect of labor, was work that "inures to the benefit of the whole community." Effort of this kind was a moral obligation. "The capacity and the willingness to do some useful work of some kind, for the benefit of all," he argued, "is the highest grade of social morality to which any man can attain." Engaging in useful work therefore was to be applauded regardless of the occupation in which it was done. "I pay my highest respect and praise to the man who is an honest and faithful worker, whether he worked with his brawn in a coal mine or with his brain in the professor's chair." Useful labor, he added, was not only morally commendable but also the key to a good society. "In our great social experiment we must stand shoulder to shoulder and link hand in hand if we would succeed in anything but miserable failure."[25]

The complexity of urban, industrial life persuaded writers that useful effort of all kinds was more urgent than ever before. "It is no small task to take care of a world full of people, feed them, clothe them, house them, fetch and carry them where they want to go, preserve their health, minister to their spiritual needs, educate them, settle the difficulties which must needs arise among them, organize them industrially, capitalize their activities, amuse them, relieve their poverty, [and] augment their wealth," a 1910 essay in the *Dallas Morning News* explained. "The real needs of such a world are so many and so exacting that it keeps the whole world busy, something doing every minute." The challenge therefore was to be usefully engaged. "The very essence of the spirit of Christ is service, useful service."[26]

The value of useful effort contrasted with idleness, which could be seen among both the idle poor and the idle rich. Rauschenbusch grounded much of his condemnation of the wealthy in their propensity for idleness and their failure to engage usefully in the general welfare. "The resistance of the upper classes has again and again blocked and frustrated hopeful upward movements, kept useful classes of people in poverty and degradation, and punished the lovers of humanity with martyrdom of body or soul," he declared. "Insofar as profit is only another name for the fair reward which society owes for useful labor and service, it has a sound moral basis and we have no quarrel with it." But when profit was gained without productive labor, "a Christian man is under no obligation whatever to feel moral respect for it." Little wonder, then, that resentment was felt when the wealthy turned to useless luxury.[27]

Reverend Stevens castigated the "social shirk" who "habitually ignores or disowns his social responsibility to assist in providing for others or even for himself, but who is willing to be a drone in the great hive of human industry and gorge himself on wealth and the production of which he has taken no part." The shirk was as bad as the "shark" who preys on others, benefiting from others' work. Stevens believed there should be no "leisure class" and no "lazy, shiftless" people who ignored their responsibilities to the society. He hoped that "we are rapidly approaching the time when the idlers and dodgers, the drones and do nots, the sharks and shirks of society will be abolished, root and branch."[28] Other writers argued that being idle instead of being engaged in useful activity was a temptation that everyone should guard against. "According to the law of God in the Old Testament and in the New," Batten argued, "it is as wrong for a man to be idle as for him to be dishonest, or impure, or covetous. Idleness is an immoral thing; an idle man is not a good man."[29]

If useful work was an individual's moral responsibility to society, society in turn was deemed to have a responsibility to the individual. The clearest proponent of this side of the argument was the noted Catholic moral theologian John A. Ryan. In *A Living Wage*, Ryan described the obligations of employers, laborers, capitalists, and the state, arguing that each had a responsibility to one another and to the society. It was not enough, in his view, to say that workers of all kinds, rich and poor, had an obligation to do useful work. Rather, society also had an obligation to provide even the least skilled worker with a living wage. There was thus an incentive for social reform to be directed at society—especially to those in power—to ensure that a living wage was possible.[30]

Besides arguing that useful work was a duty to God, some writers suggested that work itself was sacred. They argued that work was not especially godly when it was performed on behalf of the church. Nor was work the profane activity in which people had to engage only to earn a living, while their true relationship with God was expressed in prayer and at worship. Rather, work of all kinds, as long as it was done honestly and usefully, was sacred. "If life is from God," Hubbard asserted, "all useful effort is divine, and to work is the highest form of religion."[31] Helping God do his work in the world was thus how to truly serve God. Batten, reflecting on the division of labor necessary in a complex society, described work as the essential contributions of all workers, whether in farming, grinding flour, making shoes, or trading in goods and services. When "rightly done," work of every kind was a service to human welfare. Therefore, the best advice to follow when thinking about one's work is to remain in one's calling and be useful in that calling. "If God's work is sacred, high and glorious," he wrote, "man's work is likewise."[32]

Although work of all kinds was deemed a service to humanity, effort that directly served persons in need was special. Helping the needy implied visiting the sick, welcoming the stranger, and giving cheerfully to all the ways in which congregations engaged in charitable work.[33] Helping the needy further implied that clergy and church members should rethink their priorities, spending less time on "filling the pews" and more time on charitable work.[34] Charitable work, moreover, would in the best instances sensitize those doing it to the need for more effective methods of addressing social ills. Rauschenbusch regarded charitable work as the pride of Christian ministry because it was a response to suffering, but also as Christianity's shame because so much more needed to be done. "Those who have had contact with the work," he wrote, "feel that they are beating back a swelling tide with feeble hands."[35]

Social gospel promoters argued that congregations' charitable activities should be enlarged to address the social arrangements in which poverty, corruption, greed, vice, and other problems were rooted. Christians' duty was not only to be Good Samaritans by assisting the suffering traveler who has been set upon by robbers, a Social Gospel leader in Michigan argued, "but to capture the robbers, get them reformed if possible and make the road safe." The church "should champion good causes," he said. "It should know its times, its neighborhood. It should build upright social conceptions. It should urge a sense of social responsibility." There were indications that the churches were moving in these directions. He enumerated a few of the ones that made him hopeful: the Men and Religion movement under the direction of Charles Stelzle, the Methodist Federation for Social Service led by Harry F. Ward, Presbyterian and Episcopal service agencies, the work of some 1,600 licensed deaconesses making house calls, and new courses on social service in seminaries and Christian colleges.[36]

The Pursuit of Happiness

The pursuit of happiness in these discussions retained its historic meanings but took on new interpretations. One of its perennial meanings was that cheerfulness, whether it was an authentic feeling or the happy face that a person wore on certain occasions, was godly. "Cheerful service and kindly words befit the Christian and bespeak his companionship with Jesus," one Social Gospel writer observed. "Gentleness in dealing with others, thoughtful consideration of their feelings—these are evidence that the golden rule has found its way to the heart and that Christ is enthroned within."[37] Cheerfulness was thus a trait that should set Christians apart. "God wants a ministry of gladness," another writer observed. "The hungry world and the half-starved church are attracted only by radiant faces and overflowing hearts." It was better to be a happy Christian "than a learned professor or a liberal millionaire." The joy of the Lord was in fact something that could be displayed almost like a cheerful face used in business. "We must show people something better than they have and we must carry the advertisement with us and be living samples ourselves of a gladness that rises superior to all circumstances."[38]

A related argument held that being joyful was a duty to God and that God's blessings were in turn sufficient reason to be joyful. "God does not intend his creatures to be unhappy," a Methodist preacher explained. "He puts joy into human hearts, and laughter on to human lips. The old notion that it is sinful to be happy was never God's notion. The Puritan notion that every pleasurable sensation was necessarily sinful is no longer believed to be a Christian notion."[39] It was thus incumbent on an obedient Christian to enjoy the pleasures God had planned for his children. "The Christian life is one of obedience and of service, but the unconverted who imagine it to be joyless and constrained are radically mistaken," an essayist writing in the *Northern Christian Advocate* explained. "The Christian life is one of freedom. It is as joyous as it is loyal." To be an obedient Christian meant taking delight in following Jesus, much like an artist is pleased to pursue beauty and a scientist enjoys making a discovery. "Those who follow Jesus," the author said, "have sunshine around them and sunshine within them." The Christian's joy "is as natural as fragrance to the flower or song to the bird."[40]

Although biblical and poetic expressions of happiness frequented the popular literature, there was growing interest in thinking about happiness in new ways. Psychology, medical research, and marketing were contributing new perspectives. Psychologist G. Stanley Hall wrote about "religious emotion" being chiefly composed of fear and anger. William James's treatment of "healthy-minded" and "sick-soul" religion dealt with the emotional aspects of each. The study of "scientific joy" described the role of specific facial muscles in expressing happiness and grief. A branch of phrenology claimed that facial expressions among children revealed underlying propensities toward mirthfulness or seriousness. There were discussions of differences between women and men in the kinds of emotion that were normally expressed and about how emotions were expressed in home decorations. Trade journals increasingly advanced ideas about happiness, too, suggesting that cheerfulness was of "high market value," an "asset to the traveling salesman," a virtue that should be "carefully cultivated," a "mark of a gracious employer," and a "secret of success."[41]

The argument that appeared more widely than any of the others held that working and happiness went together. "People long for idleness in order that they may be happy, whereas happiness lies not in sitting with folded hands in the sun but in busy, useful activity," an editorial that circulated widely in 1905 stated. "It is in work that most of the happiness of all classes of people is found, and those who seek to live without it drop into a miserable existence in most all instances." Having work to do therefore was a blessing, especially when it was useful work. "The greatest promoter of real happiness, next to spiritual influences, is the opportunity to perform some useful work with regularity." To be working was to have a clear conscience. To be working was to be of benefit to society. "It is a privilege to be one of the workers—one of the great army of happy, contented people who perform their daily tasks with light hearts, turn for an occasional hour to some simple diversion, and thus move along in their walks of life without fear of the future and with no reproach of conscience to torment them."[42]

"The chance to do work, the duty to do work is not a penalty; it is a privilege," Theodore Roosevelt said at a conference in 1903. "It is so constituted that the man or woman who has not got some responsibility is thereby deprived of the deepest happiness that can come to mankind." It was an "inestimable privilege [to be] doing the Lord's work in this world." Working was what everyone did from day to day. This was where happiness was found. "Each and every one of us, if he or she is fit to live in the world, must be conscious that such responsibility rests on him or on her—the responsibility of duty toward those dependent on us; toward our families, toward our friends, toward our fellow citizens, the responsibility of duty to wife and child, to the state, to the church."[43]

Other leaders similarly stressed the idea that to be happy a person must have something useful and important to do in their various "walks of life." It was up to the person who had the opportunity to do so to "find their niche" in the world. In filling their niche, they would find happiness. Authors pointed to Thomas Edison who had found happiness working sixteen-hour days in his laboratory and Jane Addams doing useful service at Hull House as examples.[44] "Happiness," Hubbard wrote, "is only attainable through useful effort," and in another essay elaborated, "When you have reached a point where your work gives you a great, quiet joy, and through this joy and interest, you concentrate, then comes self-confidence. The joy and satisfaction of successful effort—overcoming obstacles, getting lessons, mastering details which we once thought difficult—evolves into a habit and gives concentration, industry and concentration and self-confidence spell mastership."[45]

There were likely to be times, as Hubbard suggested, when one's work generated special feelings of intense joy, perhaps from finishing a difficult task or overcoming a period of depression. However, the value of working was that it was something a person could do from day to day and from which an ongoing sense of happiness could be attained. "Happiness and joy come in the most normal exercise of one's power," Simmons College president Henry LeFavour told a gathering of teachers. "It is not the dramatic service rendered in a crisis that counts so much as the everyday and every hour service; the repeated monotony of a program; the contribution made to the lives around one. The rendering of useful service makes life a very simple matter and enables one to live in harmony and happiness."[46]

It was the routine—the regularity of being able to devote oneself to a meaningful task—that enabled a person to experience lasting happiness. "On looking round we find those men and women, who surrender themselves to the accomplishment of some definite object in life, do, unless some abnormal circumstance intervenes, attain that inward peace, which in desirability surpasses every other form of human happiness," British suffragist

Lily Montagu explained. It was the "self-forgetting" that came from this kind of dedication that resulted in true happiness. Idlers, she said, seemed "to float on the sea of circumstance like froth" instead of finding "permanent joy."[47]

Like the idea of doing useful work, these arguments implied that happiness was ultimately up to the individual. The argument in simplest terms was that an individual had a moral responsibility to do useful work and thus was responsible for his or her own happiness. But the idea that society had a responsibility to the individual was important, too. From that perspective, happiness—or at least the pursuit of happiness—was a right. It was among the rights to life, liberty, and the pursuit of happiness described in the Declaration of Independence—unalienable rights endowed by the Creator. Like he was on the right to a living wage, John Ryan was also clearest on this point. If the right to happiness was conferred only by society, he argued, then those who were capable of doing useful work had a right to happiness while those who for no fault of their own were idle or engaged in less useful work did not have this right. That view, he wrote, implied "that the lives of those who are less useful to society are essentially inferior to the lives of those who are more useful." It was quite different, he argued, to acknowledge that rights derived from God, not from society, that all human lives are sacred and thus have intrinsic worth. Individuals' right to happiness was from God, Ryan argued, and therefore was among the natural rights that applied to everyone. In this formulation, he asserted, "the individual has a right to all things that are essential to the reasonable development of [that individual's] personality, consistently with the rights of others and the complete observance of the moral law. Where this rule is enforced the rights of all individuals, and of society as well, are amply and reasonably protected."[48]

How the right to happiness was pursued in practice reflected the choices individuals made about their lives, the norms guiding them, and the opportunities that were available to them. Although working was a source of happiness, it was not the only one. Religious leaders suggested that pleasure in moderation was essential and that joy could appropriately be found in such activities as swimming, kite flying, playing lawn tennis, and gardening. "There are certain pleasures which elevate and ennoble the soul—music, art, poetry, natural science," as well as playing games and spending time in nature, wrote Batten. He characterized these as "diversions" from working—the idea being that work was naturally a service to humanity and to God, while time spent not working was essential, too, but had to be monitored carefully to ensure that it was "lawful and expedient."[49] Pleasures that were ennobling avoided excessive displays of emotion, evoked gratitude to God, passed the test of a strict conscience, and happened in the spaces that defined what was appropriate to do. A Methodist pastor affiliated with the Epworth League expressed these views, calling pleasurable activities a "diversion," and cautioning about the temptations drawing working people toward questionable kinds of pleasure: "In these days of intense pleasure seeking it is well to take only such diversions as may be employed in the name of the Lord Jesus. Earnest people have little time for mere pleasure and such as they do indulge in will be innocent and harmless."[50]

The reference to innocent and harmless pleasure was a warning against partying, carousing at dance halls and roadhouses, and especially against drunkenness, which was the concern that directed many of the social reformers to be active in the Prohibition movement. Intoxication was the certain path to self-indulgent, useless dissipation, and sorrow. "Wherever the devil has a young man or a young woman he wants to ruin, and to damn for time and eternity," the popular California Baptist pastor Dr. James Whitcomb Brougher warned in a sermon that typified prohibitionist arguments, "he first gets them to take the step by indulging in the intoxicating cup."[51] There were many reasons to be wary of drinking, but the temptation to enjoy a moment of pleasure that one would regret for a lifetime was high on the list.

The most dangerous kind of happiness was pleasure pursued for its own sake. Religious leaders cautioned against the idea they associated with utilitarianism that attaining happiness was the ultimate purpose of life. If that were true, people would likely be disappointed. Lasting happiness depended on living a principled life. Without that, only custom would prevail. "Pleasure! Pleasure! Pleasure! That is the end of life," Lyman Abbott complained, those were the ideas that were "undermining the moral life of America."[52]

Worldly pleasure served the important rhetorical function of identifying by way of contrast that which did not lead to lasting happiness. "Wealth, honor, position, pleasure, fame are some of the leading enjoyments of the so-called heaven on earth," evangelist R. A. Torrey told the tent meeting crowds who gathered to hear him preach. "Gaining the world means gaining the things that are desirable in the world? [But] does the theater satisfy? Does dancing satisfy? Does the opera satisfy? Does the card table satisfy? How about Monte Carlo?" All of these, he granted, were popular places to seek happiness. "But do the excitements there obtained bring lasting happiness? Not a bit of it."[53] Permanent happiness was instead the result of performing one's duties, obeying the fundamental rules of society, and having the benefit of a clear conscience.

News stories of the day also supplied readers with ideas about the kinds of joy they should avoid by characterizing its expression among "alien" groups in exotic ways. Spanish speakers, for example, were described as going wild with joy during celebrations. Chinese American residents were said to be loud and boisterous on holidays. Italian Americans enjoyed their food too much. Young unmarried women were prime examples of the kinds of people who were led into shame by the desire for pleasure. "They crave for the clothing, the trinkets, the pleasures that glitter about them," Rauschenbusch wrote. The temporary joy they attained contrasted with the commendable pleasure of the "happy home" and "happy family."[54] There were also tales of people dying from becoming excessively joyful. The implied message was that earnest people found happiness and expressed it in more appropriate ways. The message reflected norms governing the control of emotions more generally.

Working-class people and immigrants were often depicted as prone to excessive displays of emotion while cultured people were more controlled in how they expressed emotion. These were norms of middle-class respectability that social reformers understood and tried to uphold in how they dealt with those they served. The reformers may not have been excessively joyful, but they were passionate about their work, which implied a hearty emotional investment in what they did. Passion bordered on excess when it challenged expectations about what was reasonable to do, such as making a difference in how laws dealt with corruption and greed. Jane Addams felt that she had to walk a fine line between the norms of business as usual and the fanatical passion of radicals and utopians. The settlement movement was to be a "place for enthusiasms" between the two.[55]

The social gospel reformers also walked a fine line when using pleasure to promote their ministries. Although their focus was on service and reform, they wanted people in working-class communities to come to their meetings, spend time at church, and thereby learn to "better themselves." But that was difficult when more compelling attractions were available. "The spiritual nature," Rauschenbusch observed, "is but slenderly developed even in the best of us, compared with the powerful instincts of hunger, sex, and pleasure."[56] It might be necessary to employ a few of these enticements, some of the reformers believed. According to historian Susan Curtis, entertainment was in fact one of the principal means through which the reformers advanced their work. The idea that worship services should be festive rather than dreary became more widely accepted. Large urban churches that helped the poor also provided gyms, swimming parties, game nights, drill clubs, drum corps, plays, concerts, lectures, and films. Washington Gladden's approval of church dances was one of many such examples. Hull House events were both educational and entertaining. Stelzle studied the methods of vaudeville, motion pictures, and advertising to make his programs more appealing. It seemed, Curtis argued, as if the churches' authority depended on living up to the standards of an increasingly consumer-oriented culture.[57]

The entertainment that religious groups organized was meant both to reward the volunteers who participated and to attract newcomers who could benefit from becoming more involved in religious activities. The Salvation Army's festive brass band parades accomplished both—giving volunteers something exciting to do and making the movements' mission to the poor better known. As historian Diane Winston observed, "Using the celebratory aspects of popular culture to enliven its message, the Army successfully competed with the commercial aesthetic by offering adherents a religious experience that was fun."[58] Sunday school parades accomplished something similar. Having begun in the 1820s, Sunday school parades became immensely popular in the 1910s. Following the pattern established in Brooklyn, where a Sunday school parade had been held almost every year since 1829, parades were organized in large cities such as Cleveland, Dallas, and New Orleans and in smaller communities such as Augusta, Georgia; Beaumont, Texas; Gulfport, Mississippi; and Wilkes-Barre, Pennsylvania. The parades typically occurred at the end of the school year, included children from many Protestant denominations, were organized by ministerial associations and business leaders, and in the case of Wilkes-Barre included many of the community's mineworkers as well as temperance leaders. Floats, banners, and bands added to the parades' festivity and children were invited to their respective churches after the parades for cake, ice cream, candy, and apples.[59]

Among the kinds of work that contributed to happiness, serving others was in a special category. The New Testament taught that the beloved community was to find joy in being of assistance to one another, in ministering daily to the needs of the needy, and in sharing the gospel of good news and redemption to a sinful world. These were ideals that American colonists brought with them, dependent as they were on the mutual aid of other colonists. Yet it was only gradually that happiness as a chief motivation for service came to be emphasized. It made greater sense to regard serving others as a duty, which in the best understanding was a contribution to one's own self-interest and survival. Happiness, as feeling good about oneself, became more of a motivation for serving when mutual self-interest was less obvious as communities became larger and as charitable efforts sought to reach in wider directions. Helping others was harder, more difficult to motivate through sheer willpower alone, when those being helped were strangers, and when they were being assisted at a distance through charitable organizations. There had to be an "inward satisfaction" as well. Inward satisfaction came from witnessing the smile of relief that was shown on the face of the recipient when the help was given in person. Inward satisfaction could also be derived at a distance from reading stories about grateful recipients and from imagining that Jesus was pleased.[60]

Happiness from serving others was the kind that depended less on momentary enjoyment than on sustained commitment. It was the reward that came from knowing that service was valued. There was satisfaction in believing that one's service—at work, in the family, through a faith community, as a volunteer—was a beneficial contribution. Service was a practice in which one engaged as a matter of routine, and through which one acquired an identity as a serving person. There were some activities, Rauschenbusch wrote, that were "in the main dominated by the Christian conceptions of solidarity and service." These were the sources of joy that aroused admiration. Washington Gladden hoped for the day when the "spirit of social service" would inspire "men and women who are able to put the common welfare above personal gain or pleasure, and to work for the common good."[61]

Happiness that endured differed from the kind of enjoyment that came simply from taking pride in one's work. For Rauschenbusch, happiness was more a condition of life than a feeling. He wrote about "happy conditions for all," conditions that "make us all good, wise, and happy," and activities that make people "healthy, intelligent, happy, and good." Happiness was a state of being that depended on the commitment to the higher Christian principles of mercy, justice, and love. "Love with Jesus was not a flickering and wayward emotion," Rauschenbusch wrote, "but the highest and most steadfast energy of a will bent on creating fellowship." Flickering and wayward emotion was the kind Rauschenbusch associated with religious revivals that inspired a kind of "superstitious panic" filled with deep joy or sorrow that encouraged people to indulge their "passing emotions." "Christianity is more than a fine emotion," he wrote.[62]

Ambiguities and tensions were inevitably present in arguments that attempted both to encourage workers to find happiness in their work and to reform the conditions that impeded work from being a source of satisfaction. The reformers who called attention to social conditions and who challenged the churches to promote social service activities emphasized the moral responsibility of individuals to look out for themselves. Happiness was to be found both in serving others and in helping oneself. It was not the exuberant joy that might be experienced at a festival but was more than a vague sense of well-being. Happiness was the enduring sense of satisfaction that came from contributing to the common good. It was a slender reed that depended on writers, activists, and the leaders of faith communities to explain what it was and to provide assurance that it could indeed be the result of expending effort in these ways.

Linking happiness as strongly as they did with doing useful work was the opening for reform programs that tried to control how those being served enjoyed themselves. These programs functioned not only as services for the sick and hungry but also as sources of ideas about social reform. They also drew a firm line between the kinds of entertainment they thought working women, men, and children should avoid and the kinds they considered appropriate. People of all social classes, especially the poor, were frail creatures prone to "low delights," "self-indulgence," "idleness," and "sinful pleasure." Surrounded as they were by commercial entertainment, they were tempted to waste their time doing nothing of value and their money on alcohol and gambling. Providing gyms, concerts, game nights, and lectures at churches and offering educational meetings and book discussions at settlement houses were meant to guide working people toward more useful forms of entertainment.

The reform movements that defined much of what the Progressive Era represented ceased to attract as much interest after World War I as they had during the previous two decades, but ideas from those decades about useful service and happiness continued to be expressed.[63] They did so through the messages of religious leaders who argued that being a person of faith meant doing something regularly—praying, witnessing, helping, working as a responsible employee, and being a diligent parent—as the truest source of enduring happiness. The same messages were increasingly expressed in films, popular literature, and especially in newspaper advice columns as well.

While religious leaders spoke with the authority of the churches they represented and social reformers advanced claims based on the movements they founded, advice columnists' authority rested on their ability to reach communities with compact observations about daily life that readers could repeat to themselves and discuss with their families and friends. Advice books and advice columns in newspapers had risen in popularity during the nineteenth century and by the early twentieth century were regularly appearing under the names and pseudonyms of syndicated columnists whose columns appeared in household, family, and women's sections of major newspapers. Written especially for women and featuring emotional practices that arose in conjunction with families, many of the columns' authors were women. Two of the most popular columnists were Antoinette Donnelly, who wrote as Doris Blake from 1919 to 1962, and Elizabeth Meriwether Gilmer, who began writing in 1923 under the name of Dorothy Dix (later as Muriel Nissen) and whose columns continued after her death in 1951.[64]

Advice columnists encouraged readers to find happiness in everyday life. The columns offered practical suggestions about dating, flirting, petting, falling in love, dealing with cranky husbands and stepmothers, disciplining children, stretching family finances, cooking nutritious meals, treating minor illnesses, and tackling similar household problems. "Your husband's happiness depends on your not worrying," a typical 1920s column advised. "If he sees you cheerful and untroubled, he will catch your spirit by reflection and have clearer judgment for his work and a surer instinct in guiding his business."[65] There were also suggestions about how to think about happiness. Doris Blake said it was the same thing as inner contentment. "Most of us are happier than we think we are," she wrote.[66] "The longer we live in the world," another columnist explained, "the more do we find that happiness comes to us just in proportion to the pleasure we extract out of little things." She wrote, "If we wait for great occasions of joy or thankfulness, we shall long, perhaps always, wait in vain; while if we rejoice in the little deeds of sweet temper and sunny faith, we can get much delight out of almost nothing."[67]

Readers were encouraged to develop happiness habits: spend a few minutes every day counting one's blessings, read a few verses from the Bible, pray, lend someone a helping hand. "Almost any one among us can have [happiness] for a little thinking and planning, for a sane adjustment to our situation, for an effort to work well and serve generously, for the price of square dealing and fair play," one columnist wrote.[68] Many of the columns suggested that "self-forgetting" through serving others was the best habit to cultivate. Other columns supplied a Bible verse, a quote from a famous person, or a short poem that could be memorized and recited. The simplest suggestion was to acknowledge that happiness is derived from the small things in life. "When all is said, happiness does not consist in any particular environment or condition of life, or any one thing that happens to us," Dorothy Dix wrote. "It lies in little everyday things that the poorest and the humblest may have as well as the rich and great."[69] In another column, she wrote, "As for my own recipe for happiness, I can condense it into one word—work."[70] This advice resembled the preachers' and reformers' messages. Lasting happiness was to be found in working, helping, serving, parenting, and managing one's thoughts—in the simple things that any person could do.

In retrospect, then, the emphasis on "useful service" in Progressive Era sermons, advice columns, and popular culture represented an important chapter in American thinking about happiness. The happiness at issue differed from the kind that religious leaders promoted at camp meetings and ladies' fairs or during festivals and holiday celebrations. Those were important because they lifted the spirit in special experiences of the divine. The life of service in contrast was routine, daily, habitual, even monotonous, and in that constancy was the source of a deeper, more enduring kind of happiness. It was possible to understand this durable happiness as faith—as an unspoken, deeply held conviction that God was in charge and life was good. An understanding of culture as underlying systems of value would conceive of durable happiness this way. But that view pays insufficient attention to what happens from day to day. Durable happiness is an emotional practice that happens from day to day as well as an outlook on life in general.

The day-to-day reinforcement of durable happiness in Progressive Era practices consisted of routine activities in which everyone participated in their own ways—work, family responsibilities, service, self-care, and caring for others—activities that were identified as sources of enduring happiness. The identifiers were aphorisms articulated in the sermons people heard at church, the stories they read in religious periodicals, the anecdotes they told their children and neighbors, the advice columns in their newspapers, and eventually what they heard on the radio or saw on film. Enduring happiness came from being useful, working hard, doing one's best, showing mercy, having a clear conscience, bearing one's load, and serving God in small acts of kindness. The aphorisms reminded people that the truest happiness was found in ordinary activities. The aphorisms explained why these activities were understandable as instances of enduring happiness. True happiness depended both on what a person did and on that person grasping its significance. Genuine happiness was inner, quiet, and peaceful. It differed from thrills, excitement, and worldly pleasures that were at best temporary and at worst emotionally exhausting. These emotional stabilizers promoted durable happiness by encouraging people to do small things that would even out the fluctuating feelings associated with the usual ups and downs of life. A person could make it a habit of doing things that would help a neighbor or simply say reassuring things to oneself. Encouragement to pursue a great cause in life was framed in advice about doing something useful from day to day. The same was true of arguments about happiness resulting from virtue, which meant being a person who not only believed in goodness but also behaved accordingly.

Understood and stabilized in these ways, durable happiness was an adaptation to cultural conditions that for many middle-class Americans facilitated their attainment of relatively secure working conditions and family lives. It allowed for adjustments during personal crises and national trauma. The aphorisms that encouraged happiness in small acts of service advised that better times were coming and that true happiness was possible despite living in a sorrowful world. To be of useful service implied self-forgetting and self-sacrifice as a way of life. In bad times, happiness was to be found in helping those who were suffering the most. In good times, happiness derived from feeling that what one was doing was useful. These means of attaining durable happiness in ordinary life were in a sense empowering for individuals. People could be confident that what they were doing was right, and they could imagine that God was working alongside them, supporting them, and asking them to serve others. A God like this was imminent in these respects, operative in commonsense moral terms, and strengthening individuals in their daily lives as they labored in their respective callings. There was, though, a different way of thinking about God that dealt with imminence in less commonplace terms. For some, this way of thinking shifted attention from work as a source of happiness to play as a source of transcendence.

5

Transcendent Play

Searching for Wholeness in the 1960s and Beyond

Should faith communities encourage people to pursue happiness by spending time playing? Or does playing imply something secular that at best distracts people from serving God and at worst leads people astray morally? The questions have rarely been addressed in terms quite this simple, but the answers have generally acknowledged both the relevance of play for faith communities and the degree to which it can be problematic. There are many good reasons for people of faith to play, especially to relax, escape from the drudgery of working, and enjoy God's blessings. There are dangers to be avoided, too. But an interesting argument has also been put forward from time to time about play as a special way of relating to God. In this view, play was both a pleasurable activity and a practice through which a person could attain self-transcendence.

Play was "looked upon as an evil necessary but incident to childhood and youth [and] in adults, play—childish, useless play—was not only foolish; it was sinful," a writer in the *American Journal of Sociology* declared in 1914. But that view was changing, the writer argued, even among religious leaders who were coming to a greater appreciation of the pleasurable activities—pageants, holiday festivals, fairs, and other playful activities—all "joyous occasions" that were part of religion itself.[1] The relationship of play and religion, others observed, reflected changing views about society, social obligations, and how emotions should be experienced and expressed. In one view, emotion was a natural feature of human existence that needed to be freely and openly expressed if it was to be a healthy part of adult life, which meant that play was emotionally beneficial and should be encouraged through such activities as sports, dancing, theatrical performances, and casual entertainment. "All life is cadenced between work and play, striving and recreation, failure and success, defeats and victories," psychologist G. Stanley Hall wrote, "and the great soul hungers for both, loves risks and hardships as well as enjoyments."[2] In another view, play was a commendable activity

Nurturing Happiness. Robert Wuthnow, Oxford University Press. © Oxford University Press 2025.
DOI: 10.1093/9780197807071.003.0006

but subject to the corrupting influences of commercialism and the entertainment industry. Others called for closer consideration of what play was, after all, and how it was shaped by custom, sociability, symbolism, and such important social distinctions as race, gender, and social class.[3] The differing views implied that whatever religion might do to encourage play, it had to be done carefully. Certainly, religion could benefit its place in society and its participants by providing more entertainment than it had in the past, but religion's place could be undermined if it went too far toward embracing secular entertainment.

The options religious leaders had at their disposal for managing how people engaged in play included their institutions' control of physical and cultural space. Fellowship halls, auditoriums affiliated with parochial schools, and the gymnasiums that larger churches constructed were places in which certain kinds of play could be organized and from which other kinds could be excluded. Additionally, religious leaders could use their wider influence in local communities to rent auditoriums, sponsor amateur athletic clubs, and propose laws against motion pictures and dancing, among other things.[4] Religious leaders could also import popular culture into their activities, such as illustrating sermons with clips from movies and hosting themed parties that combined stories from popular literature with biblical instruction. As ideas about spirituality were increasingly influenced by popular culture, though, spirituality and play came together in ways that were harder for religious leaders to control, such as through movies and television, popular music, and fan clubs.

Against this background, the idea that play could be a means of attaining transcendence gained attention among a handful of influential mid-twentieth-century writers who recognized, on the one hand, that traditional conceptions of God were being questioned and, on the other hand, that there were interesting possibilities for thinking about transcendence in new ways. This was a novel idea that had been hinted at in earlier discussions of play but that acquired new significance in the context of changing beliefs about religion and spirituality. Understanding the connection, I suggest, depends on grasping the distinctive way in which play was conceptualized as an emotional practice. It was, to be sure, an activity that took time and energy, differed from work, and generally was enjoyable. But the writers who associated it with transcendence also conceived of it as a culturally situated emotional practice, located in a way that added to its symbolic significance. As they described it, play was voluntary, intentional, innocent, spontaneous, and uplifting. It differed not only from work but also from the taken-for-granted reality of everyday life and was conducive to a sense of wonder that could be felt emotionally but impossible (or only with difficulty) to be expressed in propositional language. It was in these respects "spiritual" and therefore possible to be understood as a source of transcendent experience.

This chapter traces the connections with transcendence that developed within these understandings of play as an emotional practice. I describe how mid-twentieth-century scholars of religion came to focus on transcendence, how earlier writers had hinted at the connection between play and transcendence, and how the more recent writers picked up and developed those threads. I then discuss how faith leaders attempted to gain control over the more entertaining aspects of play by importing selected aspects of popular culture into their communities' activities. I suggest how the kind of transcendence that play represented was an adaptation to popular culture that expanded the ways in which spirituality was experienced. Transcendent play was in these respects a kind of happiness that was hard for religious authorities to manage. However, they did eventually carve out a niche in the happiness market, I suggest, by rediscovering teachings about happiness in their own traditions and by rebranding the church as a place to play.

The Quest for Transcendence

Among the several paths that led to these developments, one of the clearest was articulated in the early writing of the prominent sociologist Robert Bellah.[5] In a 1968 essay, Bellah argued that transcendence in the modern era should be examined not in terms of a divine being who exists outside the world but as an experience that changes how a person thinks about the world. "It is not now so much the substance of that which it is claimed is transcendent," he wrote, "as the function of the claim itself that is of interest." From poet Wallace Stevens, Saint Augustine, psychologist Abraham Maslow, and others, Bellah pieced together what that function might be. Stevens considered it the insistence found in both religion and art on "a reality that forces itself upon our consciousness and refuses to be managed and mastered." Augustine, Bellah suggested, underscored the "vast inner regions" that for many people were more real than external things. Maslow's interest in "peak experiences" suggested that transcendence offered a solution to the "unsatisfied desires and longings that overwhelm all men at certain times."[6]

Bellah was among the generation of post–World War II social scientists, philosophers, and theologians who challenged the received wisdom of mainstream American Christianity. These scholars included Paul Tillich, Thomas Altizer, Michael Novak, Suzanne Langer, Harvey Cox, Thomas Merton, Dorothy Day, Jürgen Moltmann, Peter Berger, and Thomas Luckmann, among others. Transcendence became the stand-in for the God-talk that had become problematic through criticism of anthropomorphic conceptions of the supernatural. In response to writers who declared the "death of God," a new line of interpretation sought to retain something of the meaning and mystery of the transcendent through such nonanthropomorphic conceptions as "ultimate concern," "totally other," and "cosmic wholeness." Greater attention to nontheistic religions, especially Buddhism, also motivated an interest in functional conceptions of transcendence. Had they been only of intellectual interest, these discussions would have been less important for religious practice, but they developed amid the period's wider political and cultural ferment and at a time when faith communities were adapting to new uncertainties. The discussion about transcendence posed questions about how it should be understood and about how it could be experienced in an increasingly secular world. These questions, in turn, prompted a renewed interest in play as a source of transcendence, which opened for consideration of new ideas about the relationships among religion, play, and the pursuit of happiness. Bellah's essay on transcendence served as one of several windows into these developments.[7]

As in much of his subsequent work, Bellah did not rest his case on arguments about transcendence filling personal deficits. A fuller account of transcendence, he observed, required understanding the social arrangements in which the search for transcendence occurred. The conditioning of social arrangements was two-fold: on the one hand, society was, as Durkheim had emphasized, an externality that connoted how power was conceived and from which individuals often felt estranged; and on the other hand, social arrangements included supportive communities that reinforced individuals' conceptions of how transcendence should be understood. Additionally, transcendent experience was always mediated through symbols, rituals, and language; indeed, it was for Bellah chiefly the symbols—such as Being, Nothingness, God, and Life—that transcended the individual to grasp reality as a whole.

The self—the individual's quest for identity, meaning, and fulfillment—was at the center of this conception of transcendence. Although Bellah would in much of his work write critically of American individualism, he did so as a scholar deeply concerned with the fate of the modern individual—a concern evident not only in his references to Stevens, Augustine, and Maslow but also in the tradition of Emerson, Whitman, and Tillich with which he identified. The concern was amplified by the counterculture, political turmoil, and new religious movements of the 1960s and by the coming-of-age challenges of the baby boom generation. To speak of transcendence as experience, function, and consciousness was to emphasize the self's relationship to transcendence.

The quest for personal wholeness was a prevailing motif in the scholarly literature on religion at the time Bellah was writing and would continue to be for the remainder of the twentieth century. Bellah found the quest for individual wholeness expressed in Durkheim's work on anomie and collective solidarity and in Weber's emphasis on the loss of meaning under the iron cage of modern rationality. Wholeness, in the sense of an all-encompassing framework of meaning in life, was grounded in an understanding of individuals' lived experiences. The starting place for Bellah and especially for his contemporaries, Peter Berger and Thomas Luckmann, was the phenomenological conception of the "here and now," which constituted an everyday reality fragmented into zones of relevance that required language and social interaction capable of forging a greater sense of cohesion.[8] Other conceptions dealt with questions of personal integration, alienation, the role of autobiographical narratives in providing meaning and motivation, and the feelings of wholeness described by persons having deeply memorable religious experiences.[9] Observers of the circumstances in which the quest for wholeness was located related it to the commercialism and materialism of the modern era and to the associated collapse of claims about traditional religion. Wilfred Cantwell Smith aptly described the modern skeptic of traditional religion as a person "for whom life consists of a congeries of disparate items among which they find no coherence."[10]

In much of the literature, wholeness referred to divine revelations, all-encompassing philosophical ideas, and wide-ranging cultural movements operating in the grand sweep of history. Transcendence referred to the cosmic order, to that which broke through the taken-for-granted realm of nature and inspired thoughts of what could be the reality beyond reality. Transcendence was thus a way of viewing the universe that reflected an entire epoch in human development. Bellah's own work, culminating in his *Religion in Human Evolution*, regarded the emergence of transcendence itself as the result of an evolutionary process involving "an almost unbearable tension threatening to break up the fabric of society, and the resolution of the tension . . . by creating a transcendental realm and then finding a soteriological bridge between the mundane world and the transcendental."[11] There was in this evolutionary epoch not only a profoundly important emergence of the idea of a transcendent realm but also the possibility of a kind of joy expressed in play, "mythospeculation," mastery, and even renunciation.[12]

Although the discussion of wholeness emphasized ideas and beliefs, wholeness was not meant to be understood only as an intellectual quest of the kind that could be framed in propositional language. Bellah drew on Jean Piaget's developmental psychology to suggest that something less philosophical, rational, intellectual, or logical—something playful, artistic, metaphoric, intuitive, experiential—was better suited to the quest for wholeness. Other treatments associated the quest for wholeness with faith, myth, ritual, and exceptional moments of bafflement. It was the nature of wholeness to be mysterious, ineffable, beyond belief, and beyond reason. Wholeness could be sought but not fully grasped.

That was true intellectually, the argument suggested, placing wholeness in the realm of art and music more than in the domain of theology and philosophy. It was less clear what this view of wholeness implied for the emotional aspect of transcendent experience. Surely a person experiencing a sense of unity with the universe should feel something in the way of gratitude, awe, comfort, release, and relief. But was that fundamentally beyond description? Could it be described as joy? And if so, how was it experienced differently?

The theoretical literature on wholeness suggested that transcendence is experienced in ways that reflect the distinct functions from which the quest for wholeness arises. These functions, the literature suggested, are deeply existential. They arise in the posttraditional cultural milieu in which the existence of God is no longer assured and thus are ultimately concerned with the meanings of life and death. A sense of having grasped something of the mystery of life, therefore, is infused with both gratitude that life is meaningful at all and despair in being unable to fully understand or appreciate what that meaning is. It is little wonder that experiences of transcendence are sometimes resisted as much as they are sought.

The idea put forth by theologian James Sellers, about the same time as Bellah's essay, that most of us are content with "a mosaic of tidbits, small morsels of meaning" rather than with truly seeking transcendence offered an appealing way of thinking about wholeness.[13] If transcendence is too big, too overwhelming, too existentially frightening to be comfortably experienced, then modest pursuits are understandably compelling. It was correct, in this respect, to say that transcendence was imperiled by the secularity of a culture in which a two-tiered universe composed of gods and humans had collapsed. But that did not necessitate taking a diminished view of the smaller ways in which moments of something like transcendence may be experienced.

The assumption in discussions of wholeness as different as Bellah's and Sellers's was that an individual person's quest for wholeness was intimately related to ideas about cosmic wholeness of the universe. But this relationship was understood to be problematic. The modern person clung uncertainly to traditional beliefs about the existence of a supernatural realm that transcended life on earth. That uncertainty was thus tenuously resolved by the individual having a deeply moving transcendent experience of feeling in touch with cosmic transcendence and experiencing a sense of personal wholeness as a result. Or the person could avoid thinking about cosmic wholeness and attempt to experience wholeness in the small meanings of everyday life.

The difficulty with this way of thinking about transcendence was that it limited the idea of transcendence to understandings of cosmic transcendence while acknowledging that these were for many people hard to grasp and rarely experienced. The wholeness found in everyday life was problematic as well since small morsels of meaning were considered likely to remain devoid of an overarching sense of meaning. A work-around that proved to be of considerable popular as well as scholarly interest was to pay closer attention to how individual meaning was found in everyday life. In other words, instead of starting with considerations of cosmic transcendence and declaring them problematic, focus first on everyday life and ask how something special—call it "the sacred," "holiness," "spirituality," or "transcendence"—was experienced there.

In his writing on the social construction of reality in everyday life, which stemmed from the work of Hegel, Husserl, and Dilthey, Alfred Schutz suggested an idea about transcendence that moved the discussion away from transcendence in the universe while not ruling out that kind of transcendence either. If we begin with the here-and-now reality in which we live most of the time, Schutz argued, then we can think of transcendence not immediately as something about the cosmos but as a continuum along several dimensions from the small transcendences that happen routinely in everyday life to the large-scale transcendences that may in fact involve conceptions of the universe. Small transcendences occur when we shift our attention away from the here and now by remembering something that happened yesterday, planning what we want to do tomorrow, or imagining what it would be like to live in another place. These small transcendences are supported by language that facilitates memories, plans, and the imagination. Medium-scale transcendences take longer and generally require more reflection than the fleeting transcendences of the moment. Examples might include spending hours engrossed in reading a novel or escaping the familiar spaces of home and work by traveling. Schutz also considered dreams and extended engagement in play and fantasy as medium-scale transcendences. Large-scale transcendences represented the greatest departures from daily reality. They included thoughts and experiences at the farthest edges of personal reality and reality in general, such as anxieties about personal insignificance and death, fear and feelings of astonishment, and ideas about infinity and eternity. Transcendence of this kind, Schutz argued, refers to that which is wholly set apart. It is a language with which to posit a quality of existence apart from human perception and imagination.[14]

Placing the several levels of transcendence, as Schutz did, in relation to the here and now of everyday reality had the important implication of suggesting that transcendence as personally experienced can be thought of as self-transcendence. The smallest transcendences are the moments in which a person imagines being in another time or place. The largest transcendences fully locate the person in the wholeness represented by the cosmos or God. What is being transcended is the self—the person's self-awareness, not in the abstract, but contextualized in the specific here and now reality in which the person lives. Put differently, transcendence is viewed from the perspective of the individual and is concerned with how and to what extent the individual experiences transcendence. The large-scale transcendences of the cosmos that appear in discussions of religion, in this perspective, are of interest as they are experienced by individual persons and are possible to consider in relation to the smaller-scale transcendences that are routinely experienced in everyday life.[15]

Play as Self-Transcendence

Play, which for Schutz was one of the many ways through which self-transcendence was experienced, became the topic that most directly related the quest for transcendence to the practices in which individuals were likely to experience joy. Bellah, Berger and Luckmann, Harvey Cox, and many of their contemporaries referred to the opportunities for transcendence to be experienced joyously through play.[16] They drew ideas about play from Piaget and from the signal theoretical contributions of Johan Huizinga, Jürgen Moltmann, Roger Caillois, and a few others. Huizinga's 1938 book *Homo Ludens: A Study of the Play Element in Culture* was particularly influential. In the same way that Schutz contrasted the multiple realities that differed from everyday reality, Huizinga conceived of play as a noninstrumental, expressive, and even poetic or artistic practice. Play was in these respects like ritual and indeed was most evident in the ritual release from work that occurred on feast days. It was set apart from everyday life, nonserious, ephemeral, fragile, and something that for Huizinga evoked a certain sadness because it was threatened by modern urban life. In play, Huizinga wrote, "something invisible assumes an inexplicit, beautiful, actual, sacred form. The participants are convinced that the ritual brings about a certain salvation and activates a higher order of things than the one in which they usually live." This was not the kind of transcendence that necessarily referred to God or that was organized by religion but was a mystical sense of community among people and harmony in the world. In play, there was an "overarching notion of a community," he wrote, "which recognized its members as 'humanity' with rights and claims to be treated as 'human beings.'"[17]

For Bellah, Berger, Cox, and the others who wrote about it in the 1960s, play was conceived as an actual contemporary social practice engaged in for pleasure, catharsis, and self-realization and through which transcendence could be achieved; play also served as a kind of symbol or metaphor of alterity with which to contrast vibrant engagement with drudgery, freedom with constraint, transcendence with humdrum existence, and joy with misery.[18] The relevance of play for religious communities had a longer history as well. Though largely forgotten, one of the most influential nineteenth-century contributions was the widely reprinted essay on "Work and Play" delivered in 1848 as a lecture to the Phi Beta Kappa Society of Harvard University by Connecticut Congregationalist minister Reverend Dr. Horace Bushnell.[19] Described by a person in the audience as "a strain of lofty music" and by another as filled with the "finest and loftiest speculations," the oration anticipated many of the arguments about play and transcendence that scholars would emphasize again more than a century later.[20]

Bushnell, a devoted parent, had written in his book *Christian Nurture* (1847) about the value for children of play and pastimes and had referred favorably to parents frolicking with their children.[21] In that spirit, he asked his Harvard audience to contemplate children playing on the floor of their home with a kitten: their play was for no other purpose; it was "its own joy." This was the essential contrast between work and play. "Work," he said, "is activity *for* an end; play, activity *as* an end." The one was done to acquire the resources for enjoyment; the other was enjoyment itself. Children at play were "full of animated glee, unable to contain the brimming life that is [in them.]" The second difference was that "work is done by a conscious effort of will," whereas "play is impulsive, having its spring in some inspiration, or some exuberant fund of life at the back of the will." He affirmed that both work and play were necessary. Work created the opportunity for play. But the two were also in tension. Work tended to be done with aversion; it "dried away the playful springs of animal life." Play was done without aversion; it bathed the "inward feeling."[22] In brief, play was an end in itself; it was spontaneous and joyful.

The connection Bushnell perceived between play and something akin to transcendence was two-fold. The first connection was symbolic. As a symbol, play provided a metaphoric conception of what heaven must be like, helping in that way to inspire the imagination. Play was a symbol, he said, of the "noblest exercise and last end of man, the pure ideal in which his being is consummated." He saw in play the same kind of effortless, purposeless, spontaneous joy that would be experienced in heaven. Play especially was symbolic of the soul's freedom in heaven. "Play," he said, "is the symbol and interpreter of liberty." The "ethereal nature of a soul," he argued, demanded that work in this life be understood as a "temporary expedient" through which spiritual discipline was learned. "To imagine a human creature dragged along . . . under the perpetual friction of work, never to ascend above it, a creature in God's image, aching for God's liberty, beating ever vainly and with crippled wings, that he may lift himself into some freer, more congenial element: this, I say, were no better than quite to despair of man." There had to be something better. Play expressed "a state unrealized, where action is its own impulse, where the struggles of birth are over . . . where all that is best and highest is freest, and joyous because it is free, where to be is to be great because the inspiration of the soul is full." The second connection was practical. Religion should in its own way be playful. "Religion must in its very nature and life be a form of play—a worship offered, a devotion paid, not for some ulterior end, but as being its own end and joy." Religion of that kind would conceive of life as the "simple flow of love and thought—no longer colored in the prismatic hues of prejudice and sin." Spiritual play would be "delivered of self-love, fear, contrivance, legal constraints, termagant passions, in a word, of all ulterior ends not found in goodness itself."[23]

Although play was childlike in its impulsiveness and spontaneity, Bushnell understood that effort was required for it to be "spiritual play" of the kind steeped in nothing but "goodness itself." "The play state of the soul" required mental and spiritual work, discipline, not of the kind learned in schools and colleges, but from "the struggles we encounter and the scenes through which we pass in the great school of life." Through these struggles, we grasp our "thoughts, tempers, passions, aspirations, and wants" and "our capacities of taste, fancy, observation, and reason are discovered and limbered for the free activity of spiritual play."[24]

Each of the essential ingredients of play that Bushnell identified continued to be emphasized in subsequent discussions of the topic. Play was activity engaged in for no other purpose—an intrinsic good, an end in itself. Play was spontaneous, impulsive, nondeliberative—arising from some inner need or compulsion. And play was joyous—nonaversive, enjoyable, naturally characterized by laughter, exuberance, mirth, and lightheartedness. Children were naturally playful. "When people are petrified by dignity and propriety," the Brooklyn Unitarian minister Reverend John White Chadwick wrote in the 1870s, "children are God's Messiahs, sent to preach anew the gospel of an innocent amusement and hilarity."[25] Herbert Spencer wrote of children impulsively "jumping for joy."[26] Adults who were playful did not let themselves be consumed by work and worry; they were capable of deflecting anger or undue seriousness in conversation through a lighthearted remark, delicate humor, and a smile.

The relationship of play with religion and the spiritual life was conceived in ways resembling Bushnell's but also with differing emphases. Chadwick, for example, agreed that religion should be less dignified and more playful, and regarded play as a fundamental necessity of life, but placed greater emphasis on play's instrumental value. "We work better for our play," he wrote, "and we play better for our work. Work without play tends to become drudgery and play without work to become nausea. Each enhances the value of the other, sweetens it, and gives it grace and power."[27] Reverend Dr. Joseph A. Benton, the prominent Yale-educated San Francisco minister, argued that play was joyous because it was freeing, but cautioned that too much play was wearying. Even a kitten, he noted, soon tires of chasing its tail.[28] As clergy warned about the temptations of worldly pleasure, they acknowledged that the desire for play was a "basic impulse in human nature"—an impulse that the churches should respect. "It is not enough to denounce the saloon and the dance hall," one pastor advised. "Put something better in their place."[29] Writers associated with the playground and folk festival movements emphasized play's deep spiritual significance even though their interest focused more on play's pedagogical value. There was in their writing at least passing reference to the self-transcending aspect of play. Playground advocate Henry S. Curtis, for example, observed that play facilitated a sense of the joy of life "in which the consciousness of self is sunk in absorbing interest and common things are suffused with unifying feeling."[30] Percival Chubb conceived of play as an expression of the higher power behind human life; Dorothy Gladys Spicer, as a "spiritual outlet." Jane Addams likened the heightened sense of empowerment among the women with whom she worked to children's experience at play. The women were, she wrote, "being made slowly conscious of the subtle and impalpable filaments that secretly bind their experiences and moods into larger relations, and they are filled with a new happiness analogous to that of little children when they are first taught to join hands in ordered play."[31]

Thorstein Veblen understood that play was complicated in ways that had practical implications for religious organizations. The leisure class prided itself on not having to spend time working, but the time not spent working had to be filled with something rather than being left standing idle, he argued. Leisure time therefore was given over to pleasurable activities that were socially respectable. Among the men of the leisure class, Veblen observed an enthusiasm about sporting activities that bordered on something inscrutable. The "sporting temperament" seemed to rest on a "spiritual basis" that "shades off into the character of a religious devotee," he wrote. It was comprised of the same "psychological elements that go to make a believer in creeds and an observer of devout forms." College athletics, he thought, was a case in point. It combined the sporting temperament with religious devotion: "The religious zeal which pervades much of the college sporting element is especially prone to express itself in an unquestioning devoutness and a naïve and complacent submission to an inscrutable Providence." Hence, the trend in religion was to bring such activities "under clerical sanction" through sporting clubs, boys brigades, church bazaars, and raffles. These, he wrote, appealed to "the common run of the members of religious organizations." It was this same kind of devotion that increasingly underlay the "devout consumption of goods."[32]

In *The Varieties of Religious Experience*, William James devoted little attention to play but in writing about joy identified characteristics among persons engaged in walking, sports, reading, and meditation that resembled the ones other writers associated with play. The common feature of these times was that they were set apart from ordinary life, often spatially (as in walking in the woods), clearly differentiated from working, and exceptional in the feelings experienced—great joy, ineffable joy, awe, lightness of heart, and buoyance. Like play, the experiences were spontaneous, happening without intention and with a sense later of the person having been fully absorbed in the experience.[33] These were the same features that Huizinga emphasized in *Homo Ludens*. As a voluntary, nonutilitarian, enjoyable activity, set apart from ordinary life, play was both a practice and a metaphor. Play stood for the higher, spiritual, benevolent ends to which humans aspired.[34]

In this idealized view, play differed from entertainment, which was enjoyable of course but was usually a spectator activity and was becoming increasingly commercialized. During the Social Gospel era when churches with the wherewithal to do so built gymnasiums and swimming pools, one of the chief concerns was to keep young people from dance parties and pool halls by providing wholesome alternatives. In the 1920s, motion pictures became the newest focus of clergy concern. Critics argued that motion pictures were dangerous pleasures that wasted time, debased the mind, weakened viewers' moral fiber, and spread false teachings about goodness and evil. Besides the moral criticisms, some of the arguments dealt with emotions. Motion pictures were said to be too emotionally arousing, playing upon the nerves, generating fear, rage, joy, and laughter—with "too much kick," as one writer put it. Motion pictures' proponents argued that visualization was simply another way of telling stories and that films could be an effective way of spreading the gospel and teaching virtue.[35]

The characteristic of play that became most contested by the post–World War II generation of scholars was its spontaneity. Although these writers continued to regard play as more impulsive than deliberative, they also emphasized the constraints that inhibited it or shaped its meaning. The constraints that set limits on the times and spaces in which play happened were external—features of society that were sometimes oppressive. Symbolically and in fact, play was a natural desire, instinctual, a longing for release and happiness, but was hindered by the expectations under which people labored. These expectations were the norms of an increasingly oppressive social order. "Every [person] has a burning desire for happiness and enjoyment," Jürgen Moltmann wrote in the *Theology of Play*, "but our world gives us little cause for rejoicing. To be happy, to enjoy ourselves, we must above all be free. But such freedom has grown scarce. We enjoy ourselves, we laugh when our burdens are removed, when fetters are falling, pressures yield, and obstructions give way." Playing was thus a way to imagine being free, to be in a suspended state, to be doing something that was not compelled. "Liberation from the bonds of the present system of living takes place by playing games," he argued. "We discover with a laugh that things need not at all be as they are and as we have been told they have to be." The very thought of play brought into sharper relief the world's evils. "How can we laugh and enjoy ourselves when innocent people are being killed in Vietnam? How can we play when children are starving in India? How can we dance when human beings are being tortured in Brazil?"[36]

Besides the external constraints, play was less spontaneous than had often been imagined because it had to be conducted according to its own rules. Bushnell's description of a child playing with a kitten was not quite right because the apparent spontaneity happened only within a set of implicit rules of play, such as not harming the cat, not making a mess on the living room floor, and not playing when it was bedtime. Adult play was similarly constrained, both by social norms and by the rules of the game. These rules—literally, as the rules when play consisted of games—were prespecified and accepted by those who played. The rules of play were increasingly structured, Moltmann argued, by the leisure industry, which tended to turn play into work. Whether that was the case or not, playing was a matter of choosing to set time aside from work and adopt an alternative set of rules. Roger Caillois was the clearest writer on this point. "In play," Caillois observed, the person does not become involved any more "than he has decided in advance." The person "limits the consequences of his acts," "determines the stakes," "carefully demarcates the play area," and adopts "special conventions in which acts have meaning only within that context. Outside this area, before and after play, one is no longer concerned with these arbitrary conventions." Indeed, it was the rules, Caillois believed, that made play enjoyable—the rules imposed a kind of temporary security, an escape from the perils of life.[37]

The fact that play was not actually spontaneous but governed by rules and expectations was the key to understanding its relationship with transcendence. Persons engaged in play were almost by definition likely to experience self-transcendence of the kind Schutz described when writing about "small transcendences." The person at play was set apart from the person at work, becoming a different self from the self that was engaged in everyday life. Play was absorbing, not because it was so enjoyable, and not only because it was an escape from daily life, but because the person at play was totally focused on the rules of the game. Play took place in a different space and within a different temporal framework. It was thus a release, albeit temporary, from the self-doubt, worry, contingency, and striving for achievement in everyday life. The person at play, Caillois wrote, "rests, relaxes, distracts, and causes the dangers, cares, and travails of life to be forgotten."[38] That kind of self-transcendence was, in one sense, an abandonment of self, but in another way, it was conducted by a self who had taken steps to be prepared to enjoy play in a certain way. As self-transcendence, play was an escape that could be sought in any number of ways—certainly through meditation or an ecstatic sense of union with the holy, but also in spectator sports, drama, motion pictures, daydreaming, and fantasy.[39]

Cosmic transcendence was a different kind of self-transcendence. The totally other could be imagined as the harmonious, joyful reality that William James described. It could be the sense of cosmic order that Peter Berger had in mind in describing play as a "signal of transcendence." But cosmic transcendence could also be associated with bafflement, danger, uncertainty, and the precariousness of human life. The sacred, Caillois argued, could not be controlled; its power could not be confined to fixed limits in advance, as in ordinary game-playing. "The domain of the sacred is one in which [we are] paralyzed in turn by fear and by hope—a world in which, as at the edge of an abyss, the least misstep, the least movement can do harm irrevocably."[40]

Happiness in Play

As religious leaders contemplated the benefits of play, they emphasized ways that it could be managed to encourage a certain kind of transcendence that evoked deep emotion and fired the imagination with thoughts about the wonder and mystery of God. The Catholic scholar Mary Charles Bryce, for example, argued that play was not only natural and refreshing but also a metaphor for God's freedom, especially of God freely engaged in creating the universe. Play "echoes the delight experienced by God in creating and sustaining creation," she wrote. Its significance for the Christian, therefore, was enlarged by understanding this metaphoric connection. In practice, Christians at play could emulate God's creativity. "The human creator, exercising the special gift of creativity that he or she has, imitates in a small way the creator's sharing and giving of life. Play in its highest form imitates that free-soaring motion that God as creative principle imparted to the world." Understanding play this way also shaped how the joy a person at play was experienced. "Joy is play's distinctive intention. Eternal joy in God's kingdom is the Christian's anticipated fulfillment." The most tangible way to experience joy, she argued, was to engage in liturgy as if it were a playful activity. "Eternal joy in God's kingdom is the Christian's anticipated fulfillment. In the celebration of Christian liturgy, the participants step from time into eternity. Transcending the day-to-day world, they discover that there is more, always more."[41]

In *The Christian at Play*, Fuller Theological Seminary professor Robert K. Johnston offered an evangelical Protestant perspective on play. Johnston felt that Christians had a responsibility to play and was concerned that play should be done differently by Christians than by other people. To that end, he suggested that Christians structure their play according to the examples given in the Bible. One example was the biblical teaching about observing the Sabbath, which meant regarding play as a time of rest from work, a time to remember that God created the world and then rested, and that the Sabbath was a holy day and was joyful because it pointed to the ultimate redemption of the world and reminded people of God's covenant with the world. Other biblical instructions about play, Johnston observed, could be found in Ecclesiastes, where the Bible distinguished time to work from time to play, the Psalms, which called God's people to sing, and stories about the Israelites celebrating the Day of the Lord by singing and dancing. Johnston also thought it likely that Jesus played, at least since he had attended a wedding feast. None of these examples said explicitly how a Christian should play, but they suggested that when Christians played, they should be mindful of God and guided by the ways in which biblical characters played. As far as transcendence was concerned, Johnston took issue with writers (e.g., Peter Berger) who regarded play as a symbol of transcendence, instead of believing that an objective supernatural transcendent reality existed and communicated to humans.[42]

Theologies of play evoked criticism, even as the concept grew in popularity. Criticism acknowledged that the Christian tradition in the West had long been overly dour, deadening, focusing more on divine punishment than on divine grace, and suspicious of worldly pleasure. It was uncontestable, too, that the Bible included examples of festivity, music, and merriment. But there was something troubling about the argument that God was best understood as a playful deity and that humans were most fully human when they engaged in play. The difficulty was not what had bothered religious leaders in the past about people having fun. There was remarkably little concern about churches hosting festivals and fairs or somehow bending the rules of moral propriety. It was rather that theologies of play reflected the current crises of theology and of the churches' place in society. Play was a feeble response to secularism. It was wimpish, faddish. It accommodated too easily to the obsession for self-realization. It too easily replaced doctrine with emotion. At worst, it turned righteous devotion into a kind of game.[43]

One of the responses to the criticism that theologies of play had gone too far—or not far enough—was religious leaders adopting just enough of popular culture that worshipful activities could be entertaining without ceasing to be worshipful. By the late 1970s, the idea of "fandom"—which sports writers had coined earlier in the century for baseball—had gravitated to boxing, football, movies, television programs, and popular stage and musical performers.[44] Fandom was enough like religion—an emotionally compelling "faith" that evoked an experience of "transcendence," was expressed as intense devotion to a charismatic person or group, generated an enhanced sense of well-being, and served as a source of personal identity—that it could become a substitute for conventional religion or it could be turned to religion's advantage.[45] Bringing popular culture into the times and spaces under their control was a way for religious leaders to produce their own versions of fandom. The strategies included producing pop-rock Christian music, hosting popular musical groups at churches, organizing "movie nights," creating superhero characters for children's lessons, drawing comparisons between sports fans and faith communities, and "retheming" biblical stories with scripts from contemporary television plots.[46]

With a less obvious connection to religion, another line of argument about the theological significance of play was that play was a source of virtue. In this understanding, play was hardly spontaneous or free at all but was an activity to be mastered, much like a skill in the workplace, except that play was ostensibly less serious and done in one's spare time. A person's play might consist of playing chess, soccer, or the piano. The play might be enjoyable, but it would be more enjoyable if the player mastered the game. Mastery required effort, patience, endurance, and even courage. These were characteristics developed within the game for no other purpose than to become better at playing the game. They were, however, virtues that could inform the rest of one's life.[47] Moreover, a virtuous self was more substantial, less shallow, more deeply rooted, more responsible, more reliable, and more morally guided than a self whose play was grounded only in spontaneity and was the source only of temporary pleasure. Play in which mastery was the most important criterion resembled spiritual practice in which achieving a closer relation to God by following clearly defined rules was the desired end. Spiritual practice of this kind was performed not because it was spontaneous, instinctual, or enjoyable but because it was the way to achieve a better sense of the sacred. If joy was to be found, it was contingent on advancing from step to step toward an improved understanding of oneself, better control of one's impulses, and closer conformity to the rules of the practice.

Spiritual Explorations

Ideas about play opened up ways other than religion through which its connection with transcendence could be found. Bellah's essay was written at a time of spiritual exploration in which those involved pursued spiritual insight and growth with utmost intentionality, and yet in ways that resembled play.[48] Meditation, music, sacred dance, chanting, communal living, and sexual experimentation were among the kinds of spiritual exploration through which participants playfully experienced the sacred. "Wisdom is in wit; in fooling, most excellent fooling; in play, and not in heavy puritanical seriousness," Norman O. Brown wrote in *Love's Body*.[49] For some, a theological perspective suggested that transcendence of sorts—"spirit," "wonder," "mystery," "revelatory insight," "grace"—would break through, inspiring the recipient with life-giving ways of being and becoming. All that churches, meditation centers, artists' enclaves, or self-help groups had to do was provide space and encouragement. Spiritual exploration required dedication, yet it was experienced as novel, impulsive, and joyous. Participation "triggered experiences of joy, optimism, and hope—elementary religious responses," sociologist Wade Clark Roof wrote in his book about spiritual seekers, "yet potent enough to raise possibilities of a transcendence forcing [them] to ponder the priorities of life."[50]

The idea that sexual activity could be a kind of spiritual exploration represented the most distinctive break with churchly traditions. Through the nineteenth and early twentieth centuries, faith communities were in near universal agreement that sexual activity was a dangerous temptation, not to be played around with, and even in marriage should be engaged in chiefly for reproduction rather than pleasure.[51] Margaret Sanger's advocacy for better understandings of contraception and the subsequent development in the 1960s of the birth control pill expanded the opportunity for sex to be engaged in for pleasure. *The Joy of Sex: A Gourmet Guide to Love Making* topped the *New York Times* bestseller list for eleven weeks in 1972.[52] The subtler meanings associated with play were attached to arguments about sexual activity as well. Freudian theory taught that sexuality was deeply hidden, often repressed, and thus through being discovered was a source of personal insight. In the phenomenological conceptions of everyday reality that Bellah, Schutz, Berger, and others emphasized, the erotic was a transcendent escape from that reality.

The clearest expression in this tradition of the relationship of sexual activity and transcendence was that of French philosopher Georges Bataille. Bataille argued that there was a kind of sacred energy in humans' emotional and intellectual relationship to reality. These energies transcended daily life and flowed most freely when people were not engaged in useful activity, such as during religious rituals and while engaged in sex. Like play, there was something different about these experiences, a different emotional energy, and a different sense of one's identity. Like play, erotic experience could also be an act of transgression committed as a violation of established social boundaries and relationships. For Bataille, erotic experiences were not understood simply as moments of pleasure but as symbols of the exuberance and fullness of life. They represented the transcendence of individuality and at once the fulfillment of individuality. They were similar in this respect to religious experiences.[53]

Other writers perceived similar relationships between erotic experiences and transcendence. Erotic experiences were the means through which a sense of abandon, limitlessness, and even infinity could be felt. Berger's "signals of transcendence" in which a person was awakened to unseen realities could be experienced through sexual activity. Merleau-Ponty regarded "erotic perception" as the kind of transcendence that connects us as lived bodies to other lived bodies.[54] The erotic, feminist writer Audre Lorde argued, was a resource at a deeply "spiritual plane."[55] Experiencing that spiritual plane was enlivening, baffling, and at the same time empowering. Transpersonal psychologist Ken Wilber argued, "It's not just that sex can be 'mind-blowing'; it's that sex can show you the face of God, the smile of the Goddess, the radiance of Spirit—and more unnerving still, not as a force or presence out there, but as your own deepest self and nature."[56] The erotic as an expression of embodied sensations was spiritual insofar as it differed from the purely organic, biological, material aspects of the body. To be spiritual in this respect referred to something that could not be objectified. It was an aspect of the "felt whole" that went beyond propositional knowledge. Unlike religion, which was organized around codified knowledge, spirituality was subjective and personal. Like religion, though, the spiritual aspect of the erotic could include ecstasy, joy, and a sense of communion with the sacred.

Dancing was a kind of playfulness that faith communities had struggled with for years and with which they had made a series of accommodations. "That dancing itself is an agreeable, graceful, wholesome entertainment, nobody will deny," Walt Whitman wrote in 1846, noting that late nights, thin dresses, and indigestible food were nevertheless problematic.[57] When Progressive Era leaders suggested that dancing might be an innocent pastime, taboos on dancing were still in place in most denominations.[58] The strictures had as much to do with the likelihood that it led to illicit sexual relations and happened where drinking was allowed as they did with the fact that dancing was pleasurable. As a popular advice book observed, "Nineteen out of twenty women who fall confess the beginning of their sad state to the modern dance. Late hours, expensive dressing, violent and protracted exertion, and other reasons might be named as a sufficient array of arguments against the objectionable character of this amusement."[59] But by the 1960s, with the exception of fundamentalists, most churches approved of dancing as long as it was not "vulgar."[60] Dancing's proponents pointed to studies documenting its multiple pleasures, health benefits, and expressive value.[61] The connection with transcendence was through the experience of losing oneself or at least in losing track of time and space. Dancing was set apart from everyday life, often in ways that were transgressive of social norms, and was an immersive experience that could be imaginatively associated with the wholeness of existence.[62]

Liturgical dance represented a cautious, tightly regulated incorporation of the pleasurable attributes of dancing into the formalized activities of worship services. Liturgical dance was playful to the extent that it consisted of nondiscursive, expressive bodily movement. It was symbolic in expressing something about the transcendent mystery of life. As in theology of play arguments, liturgical dance was understood as a more wholistic activity that brought the mind, body, and emotions together in an enacted practice, rather than being concerned only with subjective beliefs. Occurring as it did in liturgical space, its meanings were associated with the faith community's understandings of worship and of God, often with biblical references to David dancing before the Lord and sometimes with the aim of moving past an overly staid "liturgically restrictive" tradition or embracing a more multicultural approach to worship.[63] Liturgical dance was in these ways structured to be acceptable within the time and space set aside for worship.

Other performing arts and the visual arts came to be understood more widely in faith communities as a source of transcendence that resembled the characteristics of play. Faith communities' interest in the arts developed into artist in residence programs, exhibits, museum visits, concerts, and amateur art clubs. Art was not exactly playful in the sense of it being recreational; rather, it resembled play in its nondiscursive, nonrational, symbolically expressive aspects. Art was the human attempt to represent that which was beyond comprehension and indeed beyond strict representation. For some, a painting or song somehow spoke to their inner spirit; for others, there was a sense of hope in the beauty and perfection expressed; for still others, there was joy at being temporarily elevated above the mundane troubles of life into an emotionally fulfilling sense of the sacred.[64]

The earlier connections between religion and sports continued, although as fandom that resembled religion rather than as pleasure that religion controlled. Professional and collegiate athletics' popularity gave faith leaders ample opportunities to use sports metaphors in sermons ("Jesus kept his eye on the ball"), encourage fans to hold up banners at events ("John 3.16"), profile athletes who wore religious insignia ("WWJD" bracelets), applaud those who knelt in prayer after a victory, and in other ways certify that certain athletes shared their values. But to many observers it seemed that sports fandom was a kind of surrogate religion: two-thirds of the American public self-identified as sports fans, sports broadcasts were among the most watched television programs, some $60 billion annually was spent on tickets and memorabilia, and fans' in-person behavior at events resembled sacred rituals in emotional intensity.[65] Marci Cottingham's research on sports fandom demonstrated that its similarities to religion also consisted of fans' emotional attachment with other fans, the embodied aspects of their emotion, their vicarious identification with players and teams, the durability of their devotion, the stock of narratives in which their devotion was embedded, and the release from everyday reality that carried them through the ups and downs of ordinary life. In these respects, sports fandom was rich with symbolically encapsulated emotions that contributed to and elevated fans' sense of meaning and well-being.[66]

If it was possible to think of play as a way of experiencing transcendence, it was less clear what transcendence meant. A person who felt transported by a rock concert or a walk in the woods might be prompted to think about God, the universe, wholeness, metaphysical principles, moral priorities, and the meaning of life. But that person might just as well feel an emotional uplift that made life seem better without putting any of that in religious language. Transcendence in that instance was not about some reality that went beyond the known universe but an experience of self-transcendence. As such, play was intensely personal, unscripted, and unregulated, its meaning variously crafted by persons who felt the need to seek wholeness or simply to escape the worries of everyday life.

That would have been a way to understand play if play could indeed be regarded as a personally improvised means of experiencing self-transcendence. However, that understanding did not take sufficient account of the cultural influences on popular expressions of play. The meanings of play and the opportunities for engaging in play were embedded in a popular culture of self-help, comfort, and entertainment—a happiness market—that distributed goods and services in the name of happiness.[67] Faith leaders were not positioned to dominate the happiness market. But they could carve out a niche within it. They could capture a share of the market by bringing versions of play, entertainment, and emotion under their own sponsorship and by casting it in a distinctive theological language.

A Playful Deity

The possibilities for a niche of this kind emerged in the early twenty-first-century phenomenon known as the "fun with Jesus" movement. The idea of having fun with Jesus appeared in scattered locations in the 2010s and became a full-blown movement in the early 2020s. It was promoted in various forms through books, magazines, classes, sermons, social media, movies, music, and merchandise.[68] The central idea was that Christians should live happy, fun-filled, joy-driven lives. The Christian life was characterized as one that could be exceptionally joyful as a person became intimately associated with Jesus who was in his own way quite a fun-loving person to be with and, besides that, by realizing that God, who was also fun-loving, wants everyone to have a totally enjoyable life. As one writer explained, "God, our creator, created fun. He made humankind with a capacity for fun—for sheer enjoyment of life. It gives him pleasure and delight when we have fun and experience joy with him."[69] Having fun with Jesus meant taking pleasure in life, doing things that were entertaining, feeling happy that Jesus was there too, and believing that Jesus smiles, tells jokes, loves going to parties, and wants his friends to have a good time too. Fun with Jesus took biblical teachings about cheerfulness to a new level, arguing that godly people can be happier than anyone ever imagined, and that Jesus is the key.[70]

If Jesus could be recast as a laugh maker, the church could be rebranded, too. As loyalty to denominational brands weakened, church marketing consultants shifted their advertising campaigns to appeals they hoped would reach wider audiences.[71] A $20 million campaign called "Rethink Church," for example, invited people through video clips on TikTok, Instagram, and websites to "find love, joy, and peace" and to develop a "joy-filled outlook on life."[72] Another campaign, called "He Gets Us," spent millions on billboards, videos, and television commercials portraying Jesus as the kind of person who shared ordinary emotions, experienced pleasure and pain, and loved to relax with his friends. "Let the good times roll," an appeal in *Christianity Today* asserted, offering "practical ways to embrace joy in your church." Churches should "foster a culture of celebration," the essay advised. They should plan "joyful social events," "infuse humor and storytelling" into their activities, and "emphasize the value of rest and leisure."[73]

Few of these ideas were new. They had been featured in faith communities before, only with less intensity as a marketing appeal. Their promoters described them as emphases consistent with scripture and as being beneficial for church vitality. Some of the ideas, such as "creating spaces for fellowship" and "celebrating the joys and accomplishments" of the church community had long been practiced in congregations. But churches as places to have fun were also characterized as novel ways to think about God, Jesus, and the joy-filled life. They were posited as an invitation for people who had grown weary of dour teachings about sin, suffering, and divine judgment—especially the younger generation—to feel that having a good time was what God wanted them to do.

The writers who associated play with transcendence in the 1960s probably would not have been surprised by these developments a half-century later. Play was too essential to human flourishing to neglect, they had argued. There was enough of an affinity between play and envisioning something beyond human comprehension that play was likely to be embraced by some faith communities, even when faith more often dealt with sin and salvation. Moreover, for those who considered it important to have fun with Jesus, their understanding of fun was remarkably similar to the earlier arguments about play. Fun with Jesus was set apart from the workaday world; it was impulsive, innocent, and in its own way transgressive of social norms. Even though it was marketed, it was only minimally commercialized, allowing its practitioners to believe that their kind of play was different from secular entertainment. But the transcendence that Bellah, Moltmann, and others wrote about was oriented toward a nontraditional space in which theistic conceptions of wholeness were expected to diminish. It was ill-defined, nontheistic, up for grabs, impulsive, and thus harder for religious authorities to control. In this respect, the 1960s writers may not have envisioned how robustly some sectors of American religion would work to mold conceptions of play to their advantage.

6
Spiritual Discipline
The Hard Work of Finding Joy

The difficulty with play as a pleasurable way of relating to the sacred is that play, at least in its idealized version, is free form, spontaneous, given to creativity and improvisation, and therefore the kind of thing that is hard for any faith community to manage. A faith community can host a "fun night" at the fellowship hall, but play can just as easily be done on one's own and among friends. An alternative is to argue that true spirituality can only be pursued by working at it. Working at it implies following the rules, gaining skill, and spending time to get better and better at what one is doing to achieve a relationship with the sacred. Working at it requires individual effort and can be tailored to individuals' interests. A large measure of personal agency is involved, implying that individuals are morally responsible for whatever happiness they may attain. Working at it, though, implies that there are indeed rules to be followed, skills to be learned, role models to emulate, and authorities to heed. The rules and skills constitute an emotional practice as well as a spiritual practice. They prescribe ways to deal with emotions, to recover from grief and loss, to seek joy in life, to manage anxiety, and to pursue happiness. Like other emotional practices, these spiritual practices are composed of rules and skills that shape how practitioners connect their faith with their emotional lives.

In 2007, a group of information technology "geeks" began meeting in Silicon Valley to exchange thoughts and ideas about what they were doing at work and in their personal lives. The meetings were like hundreds of other affinity groups that brought people together to share stories about common interests. The difference was that this group's common interest was self-tracking. Each of the group's participants tracked some important aspects of their personal lives, such as how much they exercised, how many hours they worked, and what they ate. Some of them kept old-fashioned daily journals; most used the digital technology on their computers and smartphones. The group, calling itself the Quantified Self (QS), saw self-tracking as a method

Nurturing Happiness. Robert Wuthnow, Oxford University Press. © Oxford University Press 2025.
DOI: 10.1093/9780197807071.003.0007

for doing certain things more effectively that were conducive to happiness, such as eating right, getting enough physical exercise, and spending time outdoors. With self-tracking apps such as Symple, Trakr, and TracknShare, and eventually with built-in iPhone apps, individuals could better monitor everything from how many minutes walking to how many cups of coffee they consumed each day, and thus retrieve control over their decisions and activities. Within a few years, the group expanded into an international organization that held regular meetups, organized conferences and symposia, initiated a blog, exchanged research, and became a hub for the self-tracking movement.[1] It was an odd mixture of quantification, digital technology, and self-obsession—odd, to be sure, but a fitting metaphor for a kind of spiritual quest that has also become common in recent years.

The group's founder, Gary Wolf, was interested in the possibilities of self-tracking not only for keeping tabs on exercise and health but also for monitoring moods—especially despondent moods, on the one hand, and joyful moods, on the other hand. Self-tracking fits neatly with methods being developed in psychology to classify moods along measurable axes from pleasantness to unpleasantness and with respect to varying levels of arousal. Individuals could record their moods, quantify the results, and monitor what was making them happy or unhappy. Self-tracking involved summarizing one's moods at the end of each day, or, as the technology developed, responding to texts received at random intervals throughout the day asking for mood ratings.[2] One QS member using a 1 to 10 happiness scale learned that his happiness averaged "7," which was better than he had anticipated and that getting more sleep had the best effects on his scores. Another QS participant drew a face at the end of each day summarizing her moods—happy, sad, confused, melancholic—and then devised a three-point scale to quantify the results. A third QSer attached electrodes to her temples telling her how much of the day she was smiling or not smiling. Yet another QSer published *Nudge Your Way to Happiness: The 30 Day Workbook for a Happier You* and invented "Moodscope," an online mood tracking service that soon had 100,000 paying customers.[3]

Digitized self-tracking could be used for spiritual monitoring, too, and several innovators developed tools to do just that, providing daily prayers, Bible readings, and ways to keep track of answered or unanswered prayers. The "Spirituality Habit Tracker" was an app that could be downloaded for a minimal fee and customized to "keep track of your ascension to your higher self" through prayer and meditation and by communicating virtually with other self-trackers. "SoulPulse" sent smartphone users messages twice a day asking for spiritual self-assessments.[4] A national poll found that 8 percent of the public claimed to use a prayer app on their smartphones every day.[5] "Spiritual" implications were also said to be present in self-tracking devices less specifically concerned with prayer and Bible reading but through which self-trackers achieved "mindfulness."[6] The Narrative Clip, for example, was a wearable device programmed to capture the most meaningful moments in life by automatically taking pictures during those moments, and Moodmetric was a "smart" ring worn to monitor and thus augment meaningful emotions.[7] The traces individuals left of their activities through self-tracking could also be used by researchers interested in spirituality and religion. Trackers could determine whether people were at church on Sunday mornings by checking GPS data and whether they were watching religious services on YouTube. One innovative study compared the Twitter (later, "X") followers of prominent Christian leaders and prominent Buddhist leaders to see if one group's tweets were happier than the other group's (the two were about the same).[8] Another study examined some two million Twitter messages in which Christian tweets more often included happy words than atheist tweets.[9]

In 2016, technology and society authors Gina Neff and Dawn Nafus estimated in their book, *Self-tracking*, that approximately ninety million wearable sensors were being sold annually to consumers interested in monitoring their health, sleep, medications, and moods. Data collected in 2020 by the National Institutes of Health estimated that 30 percent of US adults had wearable self-tracking devices and that 47 percent of them used their devices every day. The study's authors concluded that self-tracking's potential for health purposes was still greatly underused and would likely grow significantly within the next few years. Neff and Nafus cautioned that self-tracking had been around long before digital technology, but that self-tracking was now ripe for both self-enhancement and surveillance by governments and corporations.[10]

Interesting as it was, digitized self-tracking was more telling as a sign of the times than as an activity to which millions of people were turning for spiritual guidance. Self-tracking was but one instance of the datafication of modern life—the surveillance of our movements, money, and identities by ourselves with the assistance of our computers, and by the banks, retailers, and government agencies with which we routinely interact. Datafication in turn is one of the ways in which contemporary life is ordered. Work life and family life are heavily scheduled, and a good bit of self-monitoring is required to keep ourselves on track. Moreover, much of what it means to be keeping on track reflects an epistemology oriented toward self-examination and concerned with competing claims about facts, values, and truth.

Spiritual practice has taken on many of these same characteristics. For some devotees at least, spiritual practice in the early twenty-first century was a matter of dutiful self-monitoring, dominated by an interest in spiritual "growth," and composed of doing things, keeping track of what one was doing, and carefully discerning whether or not one was making progress. Spiritual practice requires regular self-assessments, discipline, skill, information, and step-by-step efforts to get closer to God. A devoted person who was disciplined enough could be happy as a result. But it was hard work.

For most of American history, spiritual practice in Christian faith communities had meant going to church, praying, observing the sacraments, and reading the Bible. The early Methodists who visited camp meetings took their cues from John Wesley who wrote, "If the remaining evil of our fallen nature be not daily mortified, it will, like an evil tumor in the body, destroy the whole man. But if ye, through the Spirit, do mortify the deeds of the body, only so far as we do this, ye shall live the life of faith, holiness, happiness."[11] Horace Bushnell could argue that Christians should be more playful because he understood Christian nurture to occur through Bible reading and prayer in the home and in congregations. Henry Ward Beecher likened spirituality to the organic development of plants, animals, and children—which implied that spirituality needed to grow.[12] The Epworth League at the end of the nineteenth century held much the same view, adding muscular strength to the repertoire of ideas about spiritual growth. Developing one's spiritual gifts meant being a person of Christian character who sought to "grow in grace" (2 Peter 3:18) and exhibit the virtues of patience, kindness, and faithfulness. The spiritual life, then, involved growing as one aged and as one's faith matured, just as an infant naturally grew into a child and then matured into an adult.

Recasting Spirituality

In the 1970s, about the time Robert Bellah, Jürgen Moltmann, and a few others were encouraging people of faith to be more playful, other writers were advancing a harder-to-achieve, more disciplined, effortful way of thinking about spiritual practice. M. Scott Peck's runaway bestseller, *The Road*

Less Traveled: A New Psychology of Love, Traditional Values and Spiritual Growth, argued that life is difficult and that facing these difficulties requires discipline—to be lazy in the face of life's difficulties was evil, he said, while taking effort to deal with them was the way to become spiritually stronger. James Dobson's *Dare to Discipline*, which sold more than two million copies, challenged parents to nurture their children's moral and spiritual development not by coddling them but by teaching them spiritual discernment. Richard Foster's *Celebration of Discipline: The Path to Spiritual Growth* was widely hailed for its call to daily prayer, meditation, fasting, service, and self-examination.[13] There was a growing sense, too, that spirituality was something that developed in distinctly identifiable ways, went through stages of development, and could be measured. Psychologist Lawrence Kohlberg's idea of moral development stages suggested that "stages of faith" could also be identified. A team of Catholic scholars devised a "Catholic Faith Inventory" with 108 questions to create a self-assessment of one's spiritual growth—a precursor to many other "spiritual growth" and "faith maturity" scales with which self-assessments could be quantified by responding to statements such as "I have a real sense that God is guiding me" and "I feel my life is filled with meaning and purpose."[14]

The recasting of spirituality as a more rigorously disciplined practice was inspired among Catholics by the writing of Thomas Merton and by the Second Vatican Council's emphasis on personal spirituality.[15] The Catholic monastic and mystical traditions were rediscovered through the writings of John Cassian, Saint Teresa of Avila, and others, and in the daily practices prescribed in the Rule of Saint Benedict.[16] Retreat centers, located at monasteries or organized as independent contemplative communities, provided set-apart times and places for retreatants to engage in self-reflection, guided meditation, and discussions of spiritual growth.[17] For some, personal and group therapy encouraged spiritual reflection, guided by a trained therapist, while for others the twelve-step movement specified the slow, arduous spiritual work required to address addictions. The human potential movement contributed ideas about self-actualization, self-realization, and the value of positive psychology.[18]

For writers like Dobson and Foster, spiritual discipline was an antidote to the free-wheeling self-indulgence that concerned them about the 1960s—a return to what they regarded as the time-tested, rigorous, self-controlled, effortful way of developing character. Spiritual discipline was an intentional practice, an act of will that demanded dedication. It was for many of the writers who emphasized it as an exercise in Christian observance, the means through which God's grace was imparted, a way of recovering the authoritative traditions within church history that emphasized slow progress toward spiritual perfection rather than quick "born again" salvation.[19] The 1960s, though, had brought its own recasting of ideas about spiritual practice, evident in the popularity of Zen Buddhism, Transcendental Meditation, macrobiotics, yoga, mindfulness, Reiki, and many other activities—from wilderness hiking and pilgrimages to communal living and performance art—that offered a scripted path toward personal fulfillment and wholeness. These practices were new to the American context, and they required practitioners to dedicate a specified time each day to learning techniques that (for them) involved new ways of thinking and feeling as well as new bodily movements.[20]

By the start of the twenty-first century, spiritual practices in which hard, disciplined work was required had become established among organizations specializing in spiritual direction and in many congregations and seminaries. A share of the population was at least nominally attuned to the idea that spirituality should grow and that growth took effort. A nationally representative survey of US adults in 1999, for example, found that 28 percent of those surveyed considered it "extremely important" to grow in their spiritual life—and a majority (57 percent) considered it at least "very important" to do this. When asked how much effort they had devoted to their spiritual life in the past year, 23 percent claimed to have devoted a "great deal"—and a majority (56 percent) said they had expended at least a "fair amount" of effort. A Gallup Poll the previous year found that 82 percent of those polled said they would like to experience spiritual growth in their lives, up from 58 percent four years earlier.[21] Other studies suggested that casual interest in spirituality was widespread and that a small but significant minority of the population had taken up spiritual growth as a serious pursuit. One poll found that 74 percent of those who responded said they would "like to grow spiritually"; when asked if "achieving spiritual growth" was "very important" to them, another poll found the number shrank to 40 percent; yet another study estimated that between 9 and 19 percent of the US population was composed of "highly active seekers or people for whom spiritual and metaphysical concerns are a driving force."[22] Although "spiritual but not religious" was a popular trope in the literature on religion, the vast majority in these studies who expressed the most serious interest in spiritual growth were active church members.

A distinctive feature of these renewed and newly defined interests in spiritual growth was the number of trained specialists dedicated to the work of spiritual direction. One of the first training centers was the Shalem Institute for Spiritual Formation, founded in Bethesda, Maryland, in 1978, by Episcopal priest Reverend Tilden Edwards, whose book *Spiritual Friend: Reclaiming the Gift of Spiritual Direction* became an authoritative guide for spiritual practitioners that drew from both Christian and Eastern religious traditions. Between 1978 and 2003, Shalem trained more than 900 people in its two-year program on spiritual direction. In 2003, Shalem was one of thirty-five centers offering similar training. Spiritual Directors International, an organization to which persons trained in and practicing spiritual direction belonged, had 4,200 members.[23] Among the other spiritual formation centers were the Christos Center for Spiritual Formation, Contemplative Center of Silicon Valley, Emmaus Formation Centre, PAX Center, Peacock Soul Care Institute, Selah, and Soul Shepherding. As the demand for spiritual direction grew, training programs were also initiated at seminaries, divinity schools, and church-related colleges. Among these were programs at Biola University, Chestnut Hill College, Denver Seminary, Duquesne University, Loyola Marymount University, Portland Seminary, and Princeton Theological Seminary. The training offered varied from weekend retreats and online courses to two- and three-year intensive training programs leading to certification in spiritual direction. The aim of both the short- and long-term courses was to teach the rules and skills needed to guide spiritual growth.

It was no accident that nearly all these programs were affiliated with faith communities. Although spiritual discipline was intensely personal, its roots were in religious traditions. Organized religion was the source of childhood training in which many spiritual directors developed their first interest in faith formation. Churches, church-based colleges, and seminaries provided the physical space and administrative staff for many of the training programs. Faith communities were often where full- and part-time spiritual formation directors were employed and where they connected with persons seeking spiritual direction. A national survey of congregations conducted in 2018–2019, for example, found that 29 percent had a full-time staff person specializing in spiritual growth and 15 percent had a part-time staff person specializing in spiritual growth.[24] Spiritual directors' career paths further suggested the relevance of organized religion. Many were retired pastors, part-time pastors, pastors' spouses, chaplains, retired chaplains, adjunct professors, or Christian school teachers and administrators.

The growth of professional spiritual direction and formation also reflected changes in organized religion. Ministerial training and work, while predominantly modeled on the traditional roles of congregation-based preaching and pastoral care, had become more professionalized and specialized during the twentieth century. Congregational ministry increasingly included trained specialists in children's education, youth programs, and music programs. Larger congregations often included specialists in outreach, home visitation, planning and development, budgeting, and administration. The specialized skills for these roles were acquired through specialized graduate programs at seminaries and from college degrees and previous employment in other fields. Although large congregations employed staff with specialized training, organized religion during the last decades of the twentieth century also experienced a decline in many denominations, which resulted in an oversupply of trained clergy, while in other denominations women were excluded from holding positions as ordained clergy. Paid employment outside of traditional church settings as chaplains, hospice care providers, social workers, Christian counselors, and spiritual formation specialists represented an alternative to employment in congregations. Changes within organized religion that facilitated the growth of spiritual direction programs also included the emphasis on individualized self-development in therapeutic and mental health programs, which encouraged practitioners to supplement psychology with spirituality and to be critical of ordinary spiritual offerings in congregations.[25] There were wider opportunities in spiritual practice programs for women to serve in leadership opportunities, and there were opportunities to develop interdenominational and interfaith practices. Many of the Protestant programs, for example, included training from Catholic patristic and mystical traditions; more of the programs also included training in yoga, bodywork, mindfulness, and the arts.[26]

Spirituality as Work

The guiding metaphor in much of the training that spiritual directors, directees, and spiritual growth specialists received was the idea that spirituality is work. Unlike spiritual play in which an experience of transcendence happened spontaneously, spiritual growth required persons wanting to grow to work at it. Working at it meant physically taking the time to engage in spiritual practices and even more so to work on one's inner life. It meant keeping at it, never stopping from working on oneself, doing the inner "soul work" over an extended period of months and years, and periodically asking if one's spiritual practice was "working." Working at it was the key to a spiritual practice that worked.

The anonymously authored fourteenth-century *Cloud of Unknowing* was an inspiration for some. Constant practice was the only way to achieve true discernment, it advised. Spiritual work should be done without ceasing and without moderation. Evelyn Underhill, the twentieth-century author of works on mysticism and spirituality, was another resource. She likened the spiritual practitioner to the sheepdog that works with no regard for the weather or its own discomfort.[27] In practical terms, spiritual work involved spending time alone or with others seeking to gain a deeper awareness of oneself and of God. Practitioners were assumed to have the potential for deeper awareness but had to overcome confusion, illusions, and false pursuits. The time devoted to spiritual work was spent in silence, reading articles and books about the spiritual life, engaging in "interior listening," assessing one's intentions, praying, keeping a journal, and sometimes was accompanied by icons or music.

Work was necessary because spiritual growth was a matter of struggling with something—some worry, deficit, affliction, unfulfilled desire, or attachment—that was difficult to overcome. The struggles were often deeply troubling, either as abrupt personal crises or as long-term problems—addiction, divorce, bereavement, illness, anxiety, and depression. Recovery from those struggles was hard. The harder one worked, the more likely it was that spiritual insight would prove helpful. "I'm making sure that I'm doing my spiritual reading," one spiritual practitioner explained in an interview. "I'm doing meditation, I'm doing walks in nature, I'm working, eating well." Another remarked that he was doing the work of looking at the darkness in his life.[28] The struggles were about personal identity, looking more deeply within oneself with the goal of achieving an inner transformation. The struggle to become a better person and to live peacefully and in harmony with God had to be worked at. Achieving a relationship with God was difficult. It was like being on a "mental staircase," sociologist Thomas DeGloma found in studying dozens of accounts of such struggles.[29] Often there were doubts that one was not working hard enough or engaging in the right practices to achieve closeness with God. That was because spiritual work was not a matter only of doing things; spiritual work was, above all, mental work. If a person took a walk, it was better not just to walk but to think about God and perhaps recite a passage of scripture one had memorized. A good way to start the day was to ask God what clothes to wear and what to have for breakfast.

Spiritual work was important even for those who might not be struggling with deep personal problems because their sense of satisfaction with life was itself a problem. "We are in denial about the depth and magnitude of our discontent," the bestselling author and megachurch pastor Timothy Keller explained. Contentment was thin, fleeting, a false sense that things were okay when in fact they were not okay. The better way was to want something more in life that involved learning better how to love God. You might have been told that God loves you just the way you are, but you don't experience that love until you learn to love God back—the same way that a child can't experience a parent's love unless the child figures out how to love the parent. Doing things for the parent, obeying the parent, and working to please the parent were the best ways to experience the parent's love, and then once that love was experienced, everything else was experienced in a new way. Or, viewed differently, a person simply needed to change, be transformed, become a "new creature," aspire to a higher calling, and work at being an improvement, rather than being satisfied with themselves.[30]

What made it reasonable to regard spiritual formation as work was the idea that God, too, was a worker. The worker God was the God who had worked so hard to create the world in seven days that the seventh day was spent resting up. God was still busily working in the world, trying to redeem it and help individuals to flourish. Jesus came to do the work of saving lost sinners and showing them how to live their lives. He put his disciples to work, preaching, spreading the gospel, and establishing the church. The Holy Spirit was best understood as that which was doing "inner work" in one's life. The role of the person trying to follow Christ, therefore, was to participate in God's work in the world, to be a coworker or "cocreator" with God, and to daily align one's actions with the life of Jesus.[31]

Like work in any field, it was important to do whatever one did correctly, to develop one's skill, and to improve over time. The correct way of doing spiritual work was often scripted. Some of the scripts were quite simple and thus readily at hand for daily use. One example of a script that could easily be memorized was the handy acronym GROWTH—G for go to God in prayer, R for read God's Word, O for obey God, W for witness, T for trust, and H for the Holy Ghost. A simpler one could be used to keep one's mind from wandering during prayer: ACTS—A for adoration, C for confession, T for thanksgiving, and S for supplication. Other scripts ranged from ones that could be worn, such as WWJD bracelets ("What would Jesus do"), to ones that were written down, such as lists of people and topics to be remembered daily in prayer, to prayers that could be recited daily from memory such as the Jesus prayer and St. Patrick's prayer, to scripts recited in classes or listened to on YouTube. There were also more elaborate techniques, such as the *lectio divina* method of closely interrogating scripture for textual, symbolic, and moral meanings, and centering prayer, through which practitioners learned how to discipline their minds, breathe, and come to a different understanding of God and themselves. Scripts in spiritual direction were like the rules in a game. They had to be learned, and, although they could be broken or improvised, they were crucial for keeping on track with one's practice. Learning the scripts, especially through the more difficult practices of extended meditation and memorization, was an arduous process. As one practitioner of *lectio divina* noted about memorizing scripture as she walked or swam, "Memorizing required intense concentration, more than I realized, and I had to work hard to make progress."[32]

Whether it was tightly scripted or unscripted, spiritual work required discipline. It was through disciplined activity that skills and knowledge developed. A person knew instinctively that to get anywhere in life, it was necessary to spend a lot of time learning the requisite skills; instant gratification was tempting, but being disciplined at whatever one did was how progress was achieved. To do anything right required patience; to be a disciplined person of faith was long and arduous. Spiritual disciplines, observed one of the practitioners who was learning about them from Richard Foster's work, "call the practitioner back to a life of slow formation, where old habits are cast aside and new habits are formed."[33] "I'm seeing how I need to grow," another person acknowledged. "I have not got my act together in a lot of ways. Am I praying to God in the right way?" A participant in another study said she was trying to "understand on the detail level what God wants." She was trying to "know more clearly what the right thing to do is." Disciplined activity, though, was not exactly a means to achieve a goal and then move on to something else. Rather, discipline was part of a never-ending process. "The more you dig into it," another person said, referring to his prayer and Bible study, "the more you realize your limitations." He elaborated, "Learning about God takes a lot of discipline to sit down and dig into it. It's not always fun. There's a lot of lists of stuff that's really boring, but it's important to tie it all together." He'd found that building his relationship with God "takes a lot of work."[34]

The discipline that spiritual practice required included keeping at it even when no spiritual growth seemed to be happening. A person could work hard at it but feel like a failure. In her study of an Integral Yoga studio and a Catholic prayer house, sociologist Erin Johnston found that both the teachers and the regular participants periodically felt frustrated and anxious about their lack of progress. The ones practicing yoga struggled with sitting comfortably, and the ones practicing centering prayer were unable to empty their minds without falling asleep. Blaming themselves, they felt stagnant and undisciplined. Getting over those feelings required coming to grips with failure. This happened, Johnston found, as practitioners came to realize that perceived failures were a "constitutive feature" of the practices themselves, just as setbacks and shortcomings are part of life.[35]

Spiritual discipline in these examples referred to the work devoted specifically to Bible study and prayer or to other practices such as meditation and times set apart for self-reflection. For Foster and for many others who wrote about spiritual discipline, though, the idea was to live a life in which everything one did was—or potentially could be—a discipline through which a closer awareness of God was attained. To be spiritually disciplined, in this larger sense, was to be guided in every moment by thinking about God's presence, reflecting on one's thoughts about oneself and God, interrogating one's intentions, and asking what would be pleasing to God. Spiritual discipline necessitated a large measure of self-control over one's thoughts, emotions, and desires. It required taking oneself to task over giving in to impulses, appetites, and temptations. A spiritually disciplined person could interrogate such activities as how to spend time on Sundays, how and with whom to have sex, and what kind of food to eat, or such mental and emotional processes as discernment, decision-making, forgiving someone, and being kind to one's neighbors. A discerning person could think of cooking, camping, walking, singing, giving birth, or dying as a spiritual discipline.[36]

Although it could be scripted, spiritual work was a matter of self-discovery and therefore differed from one person to the next. This understanding of spiritual practice puts the responsibility for spiritual growth on each individual person. For those who could have one, an individual spiritual director was beneficial, serving less as a literal director but more as someone who listened and was a companion on the journey of self-discovery. It was the inner self—the self that was composed of inward thoughts, feelings, and intentions—that a person took responsibility for working to improve. The spiritual gifts that a person engaged in spiritual work hoped to develop included the traditional virtues of patience, kindness, and faithfulness that applied to everyone, but they also required finding one's unique individual talents, interests, identity, and purpose in life. Discovering one's spiritual gifts was thus a process that could take a lifetime, as one aged and as conditions and opportunities changed, and the gifts one discovered could be as specific as deciding on a new opportunity at work or an invitation to join a community organization. As a journey, spiritual growth had goals toward which one's progress could be measured, even if a person did not actually measure them. Measurable goals were specific enough that one could have a sense of making progress toward them. In short, one's progress could be monitored.

Spiritual practice, understood in these terms, fits well with the prevailing cultural ethos, even though "the culture" was often what spiritual growth was intended to transcend. The cultural ethos was meritocratic in the sense of value being attached to individuals who worked hard and who developed the skills necessary to be socially productive. The ideal path was to demonstrate one's skill through verbal acuity in elementary school, mathematical (or athletic) prowess in high school, and a particular talent after that by attaining degrees, joining the military, getting a good job, and being productive. Hard work involved more than simply putting in the hours; it required figuring out what one could do best and then acquiring the skills needed to do that work. Skill was necessary, whether a person was a construction worker, truck driver, computer technician, or brain surgeon, and the skills required were constantly changing as new technologies were developed. Moreover, the pressure to learn more, adapt, keep on top of things, and acquire new skills was present because there was a widening gap between the remuneration received in high-skill occupations and those received in low-skill occupations.[37] Technical skill was rewarded, but it was not all that mattered, either, particularly because skill was required for promoting oneself as well as for doing the work itself. A self-controlling person had to work on oneself to keep from becoming despondent. There were always others with more skill or who were more adept at putting themselves forward, thus contributing to self-doubt and the necessity of working on one's feelings about who one was.[38] Spiritual practice then was one of the ways in which self-doubts and the quest for better feelings about oneself were addressed, and it made sense that skill and effort were necessary.[39]

The culture was also heavily marketized. Marketization was the means through which goods and services were exchanged and the basis on which costs and benefits were calculated. Market culture was characterized by competition, cost-effective budgeting, management by objectives, advertising, branding, and specialized work. Market culture was said to encourage individuals, in their roles as workers and consumers, to be goal oriented, competitive, skilled, efficient, and self-interested. Market logic influenced how noneconomic relationships as well as economic relationships were described, as in such language as "marriage markets," "academic markets," and "religious markets." Market logic applied to religion has meant that religious organizations compete with one another by branding themselves through the personalities of their leaders, styles of worship, and preferred positions on social issues.[40] The British political theorist Luca Mavelli argues that marketization has influenced contemporary religion in two additional ways. First, the dominance of market claims about what is truly important in life (specified goals and the rational pursuit of goals) has eroded the distinction between secularity and religion by attaching a kind of sacredness to secular organizations (the seriousness with which many American Christians take their commitment to Republican politics would be an example). Second, he argues, a "truth market" has developed through the influence of commercialized and politicized news production and entertainment, such that "fake news" and "post-truth" information further challenge the veracity of religious claims.[41]

As markets expanded geographically and became more complex, datafication was crucial to their growth and efficiency. The availability of more detailed and easily shared data has made it possible for jobs and costs to be broken into smaller units and for evaluations to be based on larger quantities of fine-grained information. Datafication provides the basis for the algorithms corporations use to monitor the activities of customers, clients, and employees. Surveys and poll results have penetrated everyday conversation, enabling individuals to categorize themselves as "average," "above average," or "below average" on earnings and expenditures, on sleep and exercise, and on religiosity and happiness, among other things.[42] These data points become "cruel assessments" when meaning in life is rendered in metrics, sociologist Paul Froese writes. "The possibility of failure looms at work, at home, in bed, at play, in worship, and in self-discovery," he observes. "It looms at every turn, because we have become hyper-aware of all the winners in our midst."[43]

The literature on the datafied marketplace has also emphasized the large extent to which the contemporary marketplace is a service economy. Upward of 80 percent of employment in the United States in 2020, compared with 60 percent in 1980, was in the service sector, composed of professional and business services, healthcare and social assistance, and state and local government.[44] Service sector employment requires specialized knowledge not only of technical information but also for human interaction, including social perceptiveness, active listening, speaking, negotiating, and managing feelings. As it has grown, the service sector also became more diversified, requiring more specialized skills and putting service organizations into a better competitive position if they are able to offer these skills. The greater specialization evident among religious organizations—including more specialized directors of spiritual practice—has been consistent with these larger developments in the service sector.[45]

Although these influences have been broadly present in the culture, it has been the churches through which the connections have often been made with individuals' ideas about spiritual work. Like other institutions, churches identify tasks that need to be done and recruit people willing to do the work. Churches are marketized, competing with one another with branded messages, and large churches have often competed by offering specialized services that make use of specialized skills—operating the media center, running a high-quality children's program, and offering professional-grade musical performances. The quantified congregation keeps track of its progress with membership statistics, numbers of online viewers, numbers of sermons given, attendance figures, and budgets. The church's purpose, sociologist Nancy Ammerman found in talking with clergy and church members, was to equip Christians to do the work that God has prepared for them to do and develop the skills they need to be of faithful service. To that end, pastoral leadership scholar David Bronkema observed, there were clear metrics of competency—biblical knowledge, spiritual disciplines, outreach, and service.[46] For church leaders who were worried that Christianity's influence was declining, it was especially appealing to argue that church members needed to roll up their sleeves and work harder in their personal lives and in the church to be spiritually disciplined. That was the remedy; churches had become lax, accommodating to the idea that God's grace could be found in a quick "decision for Christ," "having fun with God," or by simply being a "good person."

In ethnographic studies, church members and pastors talked as if spiritual growth was best accomplished by doing work through the church, for the church, and in the company of other Christians. In her study of several Protestant churches, for example, sociologist Sally Gallagher found that newcomers learned a distinctive vocabulary for talking about spiritual growth, which they picked up from sermons, church bulletins, newsletters, and small group discussions. They learned that spiritual growth required working to know God better and that serving through the church naturally followed. As a Presbyterian pastor she talked with explained, "The church is a place where we grow our faith [and] where we work on representing Christ's concern for the world in an outward way." It wasn't enough to be a good family member or to show kindness to one's neighbors. A good Christian was also supposed to think about God in the process, "keep working on it," and "do good works" through the church.[47]

There was an implicit ordering, the studies suggested, of those in the church who could be counted on when skill was needed and when work had to be done compared with those who sat back and failed to contribute. Some participants were rewarded with praise and public recognition because they threw themselves wholeheartedly into church work; others were less likely to be recognized for anything. There was value especially in the church as an organization being a growing, thriving part of God's work in the world. "We heard members declare that not only is their church bigger," the authors of a study of megachurches wrote, "it is also *better* because they have more opportunities for service and purpose and there are more individuals with various strengths to fill the gaps and satisfy community needs."[48]

In his study of the Oasis Christian Center in Southern California, sociologist Gerardo Marti found that spiritual discipline was supposed to turn the center's participants into "empowered achievers" who were "working in God's orchard." Their spiritual discipline required working against "obstructive spiritual forces," working on their personal "heart issues," and working for "the kingdom." They put the same achievement-oriented work into the church as they did in their secular jobs. The difference was that the church had a "higher purpose." It was building Christ's kingdom. Its mission was to see that people's lives were being changed, that they were working on their spiritual growth, putting in the effort, applying themselves, and holding each other accountable. The center was a church, Marti wrote, "that celebrates achievement and autonomy in the workforce, one that matches the popular ideal of literate, more educated, capitalistically inspired workers who wish to throw off concerns of structural inequality in the belief that ultimately, with the help of God, their effort and talent will pay off. These workers believe in a God-empowered meritocracy."[49]

Whither Happiness?

Where did happiness come into the picture? The prevailing sense of joy that derived from spiritual work was that happiness was the result of working hard, just as satisfaction could be found from expending effort on other tasks. Success at spiritual growth implies being better able to handle one's anxieties about oneself and thus to be cheerful even in the face of adversity. It felt good knowing that one was working hard to be a better person. Spiritual growth enabled people of faith to better enjoy being in the company of other people of faith, to find joy in doing church work, and to rejoice in the work that God was doing in the world. Being happy was up to the person, a choice one made about what kind of mood to have. Christians should meditate on God's word, be grateful, and be hopeful. They were not being good Christians if they went around being unhappy. It was their responsibility to themselves and to God to be happy.

The joy of spiritual work thus resembles the pleasure that derives from accomplishments in other realms. "We are taught that spirituality involves sacrifice, suffering," the writer Jason Garner, a former Fortune 500 CEO, observed. "Our path to spiritual growth is often difficult, it involves looking in the mirror, accepting what we see, and developing habits to override past programming to create the life we want." He had found that joy was a "hard metric" to associate with spirituality. The lack of clear goals made it difficult to know when he was succeeding. "We don't know how to be good at spirituality," he said. He longed for a deep, lasting joy. Yet, he did find joy in spiritual practice itself. Sitting, breathing, and being aware of the whirling in his mind helped. He prized the "joy of exploration, joy of insight, [and] joy of change."[50] Thus, it wasn't that happiness was lacking or impossible to achieve but that happiness was found in the process of doing spiritual work.

How happiness was found was not left up to the individual to simply sense an inward mood change when completing a task. Intensive spiritual practices included scripts guiding not only what to do but also what to feel. Erin Johnston's research among yoga and centering prayer practitioners was instructive in this regard. Both groups of practitioners were told that as they practiced, their emotions would change; specifically, they would come more often to feel calm and at peace with themselves. They were taught that these were emotional goals that they should set for themselves and aspire to achieve. Making progress toward these goals was a measure of the success of their spiritual practices. Because practitioners often felt despondent about their lack of progress, the teachers also encouraged them retrospectively to reinterpret their feelings. In other words, a practitioner who had not felt happiness at the moment could look back and decide that happiness had been present after all. A kind of reflective self-tracking was required to craft these retrospective reinterpretations.[51]

There was, however, a nonstriving kind of joy that some persons who worked hard at spiritual practices came to experience. This kind of joy resulted from determining that they had done all the spiritual work they could do, or, in other cases, feeling that spirituality was not something to be worked for in the first place. Nonstriving spiritual joy was different from working to become a better follower of Christ or working to achieve a more disciplined relationship with God or doing church work. It was not the routine expected satisfaction that came from making progress in one's spiritual journey. It was the joy of not doing any of those things and yet being content with the way things were and the way God was already present in the world and in one's life. It was experienced less in working than in listening, less in talking than in silence, and less in becoming than in being. It was an awareness that the moment was sacred. "Earth's crammed with heaven," Elizabeth Barrett Browning had written, "and every common bush afire with God."[52]

How nonstriving joy came about was different for different people. For some, it happened from working hard at a spiritual practice until eventually realizing that God was in charge. The practice shifted from being drudgery to being enjoyable. As one person remarked, "The pressure is off; it's a joy to pray." For some, it came from being advised that God wanted people to have fun. For others, an experience from time to time of being in nature or at worship or at a festive event produced a momentary sense of well-being that somehow became larger and more enduring. The philosopher Quentin Smith called these experiences "felt meanings of the world." A person could simply be sitting on the veranda on a summer afternoon, watching the trees sway in the sunlight, he argued, when the person's awareness gradually broadens and deepens, and a sense of joy begins to arise. "My perceptual surroundings seem to be infused with an upwardly radiated feeling-flow of joy, a joyous feeling-tonality that has its source, not in the garden, trees, and sky, but in the fulfilled global interior that appears to be 'far behind' and 'far within' these perceptible phenomena."[53]

Felt meanings like this depended on a person having decided in the first place to sit on the veranda and watch the trees swaying in the sunshine. A decision of that kind reflected an agentic view of happiness—a view that placed responsibility for a person's happiness on the individual. The feelings of wholeness also may have arisen from a disposition for such experiences that had been cultivated through reading, meditation, and prayer. Spiritual work may have contributed in these ways. The discipline, skill, and spiritual direction involved served as a guidance mechanism through which a person learned to take greater responsibility for self-care. Yet, working too hard at anything was a way of missing the given fullness of life. Spiritual growth that depended on people pushing themselves to learn more, pray more, and do more was by this standard not the best way to experience the spiritual life's deepest joy. Coming to an understanding of the divine being present without that presence depending on hard work was an attractive alternative.

7
Illicit Happiness
The Fallout from Betrayals of Trust

The preceding chapters have dealt with changing social conditions to which religious leaders devised adaptations that generally preserved their authority as far as informing people about how to experience happiness was concerned. There may have been disputes, but accommodations were made that became widely enough accepted that large numbers of people agreed that these were good ways to be faithful and to be happy at the same time. There are other instances, though, in which religious leaders have pursued illicit means of happiness—lying, cheating, embezzling, and especially engaging in illicit sexual relations. These illicit pursuits of happiness create problems of a different order. They require corrective practices, sometimes involving exceptional displays of shame and remorse, and they pose questions about religious institutions' capacity to maintain the public's trust.

At the start of the twenty-first century, few American churches were as powerful or as well respected as Willow Creek Community Church in suburban Chicago. Its twenty-five thousand members, who worshipped at eight sprawling locations, were part of a televised global association that linked congregations across the nation and internationally.[1] Thousands of pastors visited the church in person and online each year to learn the secrets of dynamic congregational growth from Willow Creek's founder and senior pastor, Reverend Bill Hybels. The ministry was known for its emphasis on happiness. Hybels's sermons and books were filled with advice about living joyfully, following your dreams, and being happy. But on August 8, 2018, Willow Creek's entire board of elders resigned, saying they did so because they had failed to heed accusations of sexual harassment against Hybels that they now believed were credible. "We viewed the allegations through a lens of trust [in Hybels]," one of the leaders explained, "and this clouded our judgment." Said another, "Trust has been broken by leadership and it doesn't return quickly."[2]

Nurturing Happiness. Robert Wuthnow, Oxford University Press. © Oxford University Press 2025.
DOI: 10.1093/9780197807071.003.0008

The breach of trust at Willow Creek was one of many such scandals among religious leaders during the last years of the twentieth century and first years of the twenty-first. In 1987, Pat Robertson protégé Reverend Jim Bakker, whose leadership, with his wife Tammy Faye, of the conservative Christian television program *The PTL Club* had earned a national audience, resigned following the disclosure of his involvement in illicit sexual encounters.[3] One year later, TV evangelist Jimmy Swaggart confessed to hiring and having relations with a sex worker, gave up his ministry temporarily, and then resumed preaching only to be accused of picking up a sex worker again in 1991.[4] In 1999, Ellen F. Cooke, treasurer of the national Episcopal Church, was sentenced to five years in prison for embezzling $1.5 million from the church and evading $300,000 in income taxes.[5] In 2002, *The Boston Globe* published the first of a series of articles detailing widespread sexual abuse by Boston-area Roman Catholic clergy, whose abuses were enabled for decades by Catholic bishops who repeatedly reassigned these priests to new parishes.[6]

During the Willow Creek investigation, in 2018, a grand jury found that Roman Catholic leaders in Pennsylvania had covered up the sexual abuse of more than one thousand children over seven decades.[7] A few months later, an investigation of sexual abuse within the Southern Baptist Convention found that nearly four hundred clergy and lay leaders were alleged to have engaged in sexual misconduct.[8] The following year, Jerry Falwell Jr., whose father led the Moral Majority in the 1980s, resigned as president of Liberty University after photos and stories surfaced about his (and his wife's) extramarital sexual relations and financial dealings.[9]

Whatever one thinks about religion, there is a palpable sense of betrayal when religious leaders participate in moral malfeasance: when they engage in illicit sexual affairs, commit or condone child abuse, or deal in fraudulent financial transactions. Betrayals like these violate the norms separating an appropriate pursuit of happiness from its prurient alternatives, and they are in ways large and small perversions of institutional authority. They prompt doubts that religious leaders can be trusted and pose questions about the organizations they represent. They make it harder for otherwise devout men and women of faith to believe what their leaders tell them. Why should they trust a preacher who is sexually harassing women in the congregation behind closed doors? Why should they send their sons and daughters to confirmation class? What's the point of tithing if a substantial share of the church's income is being used to pay legal bills?[10]

What can be learned from these episodes? Betrayals of trust that happen among leaders in particular places become symbolic representations of larger societal problems that are deemed to necessitate reform. As such, the illicit joy that comes from sexual liaisons, inappropriate sexual contact, and ill-gotten financial gain provides the basis for cautionary tales that should, if properly understood, reinforce the distinction between morally acceptable and morally unacceptable pursuits of happiness. In the process of dealing with betrayals that threaten to subvert the authority of entire institutions, the leaders of these institutions in the best cases initiate corrective behavior that they hope will restore trust. How the betrayals are interpreted becomes the basis for mechanisms through which attempts are made to restore trust: in the case of religious organizations, these mechanisms usually include confessions and investigations, and sometimes require litigation. Although these responses often fall short, they cast light on the broader challenges a nation faces as it seeks to restore trust in basic institutions and democracy.

Church Scandals

Scandals involving religious leaders, and their organizations, are troubling beyond their immediate contexts and the persons most directly affected by them. Religious leaders are the experts who hold formal authority in their organizations, the trained specialists in biblical understanding and public speaking, and the role models within their respected institutions and communities who admittedly fall short of moral perfection, but are supposed to be fundamentally honest, happy, trustworthy, and given to common decency. Scandals raise doubts not only about particular leaders' adherence to moral norms but also about other religious leaders' trustworthiness, and scandals evoke broader questions about the ethical standards religious organizations purport to uphold. Especially when religious leaders make a point in their preaching, as many of them do, about the importance of family values and marital fidelity, scandals involving sex and dishonesty threaten to subvert the very basis of their ministries.

Trust broken is not quickly restored. There is always the suspicion that a person who has broken the rules once will break them again. Nor is mistrust easily contained. Suspicion spreads. If someone as well respected as the leader of a large megachurch or a popular television ministry cannot be trusted, what about other leaders? What about the institutions they represent? What about religion? Confidence in religious institutions suffers when scandals occur too often, too publicly. As sociologist Jeffrey Guhin noted about Falwell, "Falwell makes people wonder if religion is actually just jerks reciting pieties and making money."[11] Evidence suggests that confidence in religious institutions was indeed falling dramatically. Gallup polling, for instance, recorded a decline in those who had a great deal or quite a lot of confidence in the church or organized religion from 68 percent among those polled in 1975 to only 31 percent in 2022.[12]

Not only did confidence in religion decline, but affiliation also plummeted: polls suggest that nearly 30 percent of Americans no longer identify with any religious tradition.[13] A shift of this kind poses serious questions not only about religion but also about the role it plays in society. Among these are whether the United States, which has long been the outlier among advanced industrial democracies in its residents' religious commitment and practices, is drifting toward a fuller embrace of secularity and, if so, whether that has implications for how we lead our lives and how we think about religion's role in supporting American democracy.

Indeed, there is widespread concern that religion's decline—and the decline of trust in religion—does not bode well for American democracy.[14] Many of our deepest values—especially the importance we attach to human dignity and freedom—are grounded in religion. Thus, we need to understand why trust in religion is declining, what religious leaders are doing to restore trust, what can be learned from the outcomes of these methods, and whether the strength of America's historic religious diversity is being weakened by secularity and polarization.

Trust is commonly conceived of as an attitude, a generalized belief, an implicit agreement, or an unspoken norm that bonds people together and facilitates the civic cooperation so sorely needed in a democratic society. Research demonstrates that trust and happiness go hand in hand.[15] But to understand trust, we must also consider the events that sometimes weaken it—betrayals, for example—and how these events take on meaning as symbols of social disorder. In this symbolic role, betrayals of trust are events that evoke public deliberations about how they should be interpreted and what should be done to prevent them from happening again. The deliberations in turn influence the measures that are taken to restore the trust that has been broken. Many betrayals are private, affecting only a small circle of confidants, victims, and acquaintances; others have far-reaching effects. The Watergate scandal, for example, led to a significant decline in confidence not only in the Nixon administration but also in the US Congress, the Supreme Court, the military, higher education, the press, major companies, and organized religion.[16]

Betrayals of trust in religious organizations are probably no more frequent than in other settings, but these betrayals are particularly problematic because of the norms religious organizations seek to reinforce. These norms vary among religious traditions but generally include an ethic of mutual concern, such as is expressed in the Golden Rule or the injunction to show love toward one's neighbor; prescriptions favoring such virtues as truthfulness and sincerity; proscriptions against such ethical violations as theft and adultery; and conceptions of these ethical standards as being divinely ordained and universally applicable. Additionally, religious organizations provide both resources through which these ethical conceptions are taught and rituals that serve as occasions for bonding and commemoration. Moreover, the constitutional protection of religious liberty sometimes reduces the legal scrutiny and regulatory supervision of religious institutions and thus puts the onus on these institutions' leaders to earn the public's trust to police themselves. Exposure to ethical instruction and ritual observance of course does not guarantee conformity, nor does it imply that trust cannot be cultivated by individuals and organizations in the absence of religious convictions. However, the prominence of norms that are meant to facilitate trust within religious communities does imply that betrayals of trust are likely to necessitate repair work for religious organizations. In short, it is not only the frequency or severity of betrayals that matters but also how and how effectively religious organizations attempt to recover from these events.[17]

Discussions of church scandals often interpret the betrayals of trust in terms of some failing of the person committing the betrayal. The failing is described as a misguided sense of morality or a frustrated pursuit of personal happiness. For example, Hybels's betrayal was described as that of a person who appeared by all external standards to have achieved great success but was inwardly unhappy.[18] Jerry Falwell Jr.'s problem was attributed to his unhappiness at having to follow in his father's footsteps; illicit sex and shady financial dealings were Falwell's misguided effort to achieve happiness.[19] In addition, unhappiness figures into the standard accounts of such betrayals as their expected outcome. The betrayal deepens the betrayer's unhappiness. There is a theological aspect to the standard account as well when the betrayal happens at a church. The betrayer is said to have pursued happiness in worldly ways rather than by trusting in God.

The notable feature of these ways of thinking about church scandals is that they focus on the individual—the person who has sought happiness wrongly and suffers unhappiness as a result. It is not surprising that faith communities would focus in these ways on the individual, given the typical emphases on personal spirituality, sin, and salvation. But, of course, betrayals of trust have wider implications too. They evoke mistrust that spreads through the community in the form of hurt, suspicion, and questioning. The questioning focuses not only on the individual who commits the betrayal but also on the institution in which the betrayal has occurred.

Cautionary Tales

In his examination of 1990s responses to sex scandals in politics and the entertainment industry, sociologist Joshua Gamson found that the responses typically featured "institutional morality tales"—narratives that deflect attention from individuals' indiscretions and focus instead on institutional pathologies. "These institutional frames," Gamson writes, suggest that "*personal* behavior at first presented as 'shocking' . . . may be quite typical of those in the institutional *role*, that the individual *nonconformity* to sexual norms may reveal a sort of *conformity* to institutional norms."[20] In other words, there may be something toxic about the institution's subculture—its implicit workplace norms about what is possible to get away with. Especially when multiple scandals occur, the impetus among those concerned about the scandals is to generalize, positing reasons to worry that the institution affected and perhaps similar institutions are not as good as they used to be—not doing things right anymore in recruiting the right kind of leaders, training them, upholding norms of integrity, monitoring leaders' actions, and punishing misdeeds: in short, feeding the erosion of trust in the institutions themselves. This impetus, Gamson found, was driven partly by journalists' interest in making the story about something larger than any one incident, such as about the public's gullibility, the corrupting influence of capitalism, the superficiality of contemporary culture, insufficient attention to the problems of male dominance, and hypocrisy among proponents of traditional values. But the fault was not entirely the journalists' penchant for enlarging the story. The persons at the helm of institutions also worried that the barrel might be rotten rather than only the apples in the barrel.

Perhaps the tendency Gamson observes is present in religion as well. A scandal in religion occasions a cautionary tale not only about an individual but also about religious institutions. A breach of trust by a trusted leader poses questions about the health of the institution the person represents. The questions become calls to action. Willow Creek's response to the accusations against Hybels—after the board of elders resigned for failing to investigate the charges and oversee Hybels—was to determine what the church could do better to prevent similar incidents from happening again. Evangelical publications and websites in turn questioned whether evangelicalism as a national phenomenon had become complacent or insufficiently attentive to fleshly temptations.[21]

But the cautionary tale that church scandals produce tends not only to be about a specific congregation or even about a particular brand of religion. Church scandals evoke cautionary tales about cultural malaise. The church at large is beleaguered and less influential, the narrative suggests, because of the broader culture's increasing secularity—its hedonism, its pursuit of pleasure in the wrong places, and its permissive materialism. The year following the investigation of alleged widespread sexual misconduct by Southern Baptists, in an essay titled "Why I am a Baptist," R. Albert Mohler Jr., president of Southern Baptist Theological Seminary, traced the history of Baptists' preaching, doctrines, evangelism, growth, notions of citizenship, emphasis on separation of church and state, past instances of persecution for their beliefs, and decades-long confrontations with the corrosive effects of modernity. "An increasingly aggressive secularism, joined by forces aligned with moral progressivism," he warned, "renders all traditional theistic beliefs subversive and retrograde. The entire inheritance of Christianity and Christendom is dismissed as inimical to the project of secular liberation."[22]

The story of a church beset by "aggressive secularism" can be an appealing narrative with which to explain the dramatic drop in public confidence in religion. In this account, declining trust is the evidence that secularity is winning. The facts that nearly one in three adults is religiously unaffiliated and nearly half rarely or ever attend religious services—captured in polling report headlines such as "In U.S., Decline of Christianity Continues at Rapid Pace"—offer further evidence for this view of secularity's ascendancy.[23] But secularity is not the only possible explanation. The recent decrease in religious participation is concentrated among young adults and has been attributed to the economic difficulties young adults experience: student loans, uncertainties about careers, the necessity of changing jobs and retraining for different occupations, corporations' increasing reliance on temporary labor, and uncertainties about health insurance, often coupled with credit card debt and geographic mobility—all of which are associated with delayed marriage and childrearing. The life courses of young adults thus deviate markedly from the settled family and neighborhood lifestyles around which many congregations have been built.[24] Were these factors not enough to explain young adults' disaffiliation from religion, researchers have also documented alienation induced by religious leaders who align themselves with political candidates and policies, especially on the right.[25] This evidence on the face of it therefore suggests that religious leaders seeking to curb what they regard as secularity by engaging in partisan politics may be harming rather than strengthening their own institutions.

The alignment of religious leaders with partisan politics is reason to be interested in another aspect of the relationship of religion and trust: the politicization of trust, or as columnist E. J. Dionne Jr. has termed it, "the weaponization of mistrust."[26] The question of trust with respect to religion is not confined to whether the public does or does not have confidence in religious leaders and their institutions. The more pressing question is whether religion, especially when it is politically weaponized, encourages or discourages trust in other institutions: science, medicine, higher education, government, and the media? For example, do religious leaders espouse beliefs that credit the leaders of these other institutions with contributing to the general good and pursuing happiness in legitimate ways, or do religious leaders issue statements that cast doubt on the motives and values of everyone with whom they disagree? The history of religion in this regard is quite mixed, as debates about the teaching of evolution, faith healing and scientific medicine, and antivaccination crusades have shown. Much depends on which kind of religious organization, which issues, and which context. In the current "post-truth" context, in which any statement can be called "fake news"—or denied having been uttered at all—distrust has become a political weapon wielded for partisan purposes, including by religious leaders.[27]

The idea that religion is beleaguered by aggressive secularism poses two important questions: Who perceives religion to be besieged this way? And who do they perceive the purveyors of secularism to be? Both questions are about trust, asking, in other words: Who among religious leaders are the most mistrustful of the secular society? And which institutions, leaders, and organizations do they distrust the most?

In a study published in 1998, sociologist of religion Christian Smith suggested an answer to the first question, writing that White evangelical Protestants cultivated an image of themselves as an embattled subculture.[28] More recently, sociologists Andrew L. Whitehead and Samuel L. Perry have identified what they describe as Christian nationalism among a similar population of White evangelical Protestants.[29] Although neither study is specifically concerned with trust, both imply that White evangelical Protestants are at least one prominent group within American religion that is distrustful of the wider society—an implication, incidentally, that corresponds with studies showing that social capital among White evangelical Protestants tends toward in-group bonding rather than bridging with outsiders. Other groups, including Jews, Roman Catholics, Christian Scientists, Jehovah's Witnesses, and Muslims, have been literally and figuratively embattled within the larger society as well, but White evangelical Protestants have been of particular interest in recent decades because of their apparent influence in electoral politics. Their sense of embattlement has perhaps increased as well, at least if diminishing membership matters. According to one estimate, the White evangelical Protestant population declined from 21 percent of the American population as recently as 2008 to only 15 percent in 2019.[30]

The second question, of whom they distrust, is best answered with reference to the traditions of White evangelical Protestantism. These include an emphasis on the spiritual lives of individual persons and an ambivalent stance toward secular authority. The emphasis on individual spirituality is traceable to the Protestant Reformation in teachings about personal salvation and in practices oriented toward moral discipline such as temperance, sobriety, and marital fidelity. Ambivalence toward secular authority is expressed in the New Testament injunction of obedience to government, on the one hand, and, on the other hand, to qualified obedience when the government is perceived as acting in violation of a higher divine authority. Taken together, moral discipline and qualified obedience to governmental authority provide a basis for White evangelical Protestants to be distrustful of institutions such as the media and entertainment industry insofar as they are perceived to promote moral relativism and to be distrustful of government when government is perceived to act in ways contrary to evangelicals' understanding of God. Distrust of government, though, is subject to partisan interpretation such that in recent decades White evangelical Protestants have been profoundly less trusting of Democrats than of Republicans, whom they perceive as allies on issues of religious freedom, opposition to abortion and homosexuality, and, as far as White Christian nationalism is concerned, opposition to racial and ethnic diversity and immigration. When an illicit activity by a White evangelical Protestant leader causes a scandal, therefore, the mistrust that results may be projected onto almost any of these "others"—gays, Blacks, immigrants, and Democrats—rather than focusing on problems among White evangelical Protestants themselves.

Responses to the 2020 and 2021 COVID-19 pandemic amply illustrated religious leaders' beliefs about whom and whom not to trust. As the Trump administration questioned scientists and health experts' advice and issued misleading statements about the scope and risks of the pandemic, White evangelical Protestants aligned themselves with the president, with only 31 percent disapproving of Trump's handling of the pandemic, compared with 65 percent of the general public who disapproved.[31] One of the first US religious leaders to die from COVID-19, an evangelical pastor in Virginia, reportedly distrusted the media's warnings about the seriousness of the virus and the importance of social distancing, believing instead Trump's portrayal of a liberal media hyping the story. The man's daughter recalled, "I was frustrated with the way that the media was very agenda driven—and it's on both sides. I feel like the coronavirus issue turned into something that was 'party against party' instead of one nation under God."[32] Most religious leaders, especially mainline Protestant and Roman Catholic clergy who were subject to denominational authorities, and thus did not typically have individual control of their messaging to their congregation, heeded health officials' warnings. However, defiance of social distancing and mask wearing increased as the pandemic continued, with religious leaders especially of large predominantly White nondenominational evangelical congregations challenging the authority of governors to impose regulations and, in some cases, questioning health officials' credibility.

White evangelical Protestants' sense of themselves as an embattled minority illustrates another important dynamic in understanding the relationship between religion and trust: "Organized religion" is not one thing, as survey questions sometimes imply. Rather, organized religion in the United States is highly diverse, varying in tradition, theology, national origin, region, ethnicity, and race, which means that religious groups hold varying levels of trust or distrust toward institutions and one another. These variations may not be expressed specifically in the language of trust, but are evident in the frequent conflicts that have characterized religious groups throughout the nation's history, including tensions between Christians and Jews, Protestants and Catholics, and among Protestant denominations and sects. The recent decline in confidence toward organized religion, therefore, is likely in part to reflect distrust of religious groups toward one another, such as White evangelical Protestants who distrust liberal Protestants, and vice versa.

Restoring Trust

Narratives about what has gone wrong when trust is betrayed tend to expand in multiple directions that reflect religious communities' varied concerns. These stories also suggest what should be done to restore the trust that has been transgressed and return the community to its previous enjoyment of faith and fellowship. If we take as three examples the Swaggart scandal, the Willow Creek sexual harassment allegations, and the Catholic sex abuse cases, we see three of the most common means by which attempts are made to restore trust. Swaggart tearfully confessed to his congregation and television audience that he had sinned and asked God's forgiveness. Willow Creek launched an independent advisory committee investigation that emphasized greater personal discipline, accountability, and administrative oversight.[33] The Catholic sex abuse scandals extended over such long periods, included so many victims, and involved such a lack of transparency on the part of church officials that many of the cases resulted not only in laicization of clergy and the resignations of bishops but in litigation and criminal prosecution.[34] In short, repair work in these cases consisted of confession, investigation, and litigation.

In none of these three cases was the means employed entirely effective. Following his confession and a subsequent incident of sexual misconduct, Swaggart's ministerial license was revoked by the Assemblies of God denomination he was affiliated with, after which he continued to preach independently to a large audience of radio listeners and television viewers. They were apparently eager to believe that Swaggart was repentant and that God was working to bring other sinners to repentance through him. Willow Creek's investigative committee, which commenced its work after Hybels took early retirement, concluded that the church's leadership needed to be more careful in handling sexual harassment cases, including instituting written guidelines and a third-party off-site hotline for reporting misconduct, but the flaws of these recommendations were exposed by another such case only a few months later. The report left it to the church's leadership to devise its own plan of action. The Catholic sex scandals resulted in monetary settlements with some of the victims, but the fact that abuse had been concealed so often without penalty or transparency left doubts as to how thoroughly the problem was being addressed; in surveys, many Catholic parishioners have said they remain distrustful of clergy and have reduced their attendance at services and financial support of the church.[35] Unsurprisingly, confession, investigation, and litigation in these cases were limited by the extent to which they carried enforceable rules and obligations. They were also limited by the declining credibility of these very mechanisms resulting from cynical abuses of how they were meant to function: by insincere confessions staged for media consumption, from investigative committees producing toothless reports that languish in bureaucratic darkness, and by litigation that drags on for years before inconsequential penalties are levied. The efforts to address these scandals were subject to all these limitations.

Their relative ineffectiveness, however, did not imply these efforts were without meaningful consequences. The scandals became institutional morality tales that publicized the incidents, defined them as transgressive of institutional norms, and demonstrated that the institutions' leaders felt an obligation to do something about them. The Swaggart case was a cautionary lesson about accepting public confessions at face value and about the importance of truthfulness and accountability.[36] Willow Creek's investigation similarly cautioned against putting too much trust in and giving too much unchecked power to charismatic leaders, while also serving as a lesson to other evangelical churches about the need to adopt clearer policies about gender equality and sexual harassment.[37] The Catholic abuse cases, among other things, prompted wide-ranging discussions of pedophilia and new demands for clergy reform.

Collectively, the responses resembled what anthropologist Mary Douglas described in the 1960s as rituals of rejuvenation: they contributed to the renewal of the moral order by dramatizing concerns about purity and danger.[38] Moreover, rejuvenation involves concrete steps that extend beyond the immediate discussion prompted by a particular scandal. Institutions are, among other things, arrangements of formal and informal norms that govern how people act and expect others to act in given situations. Restoring trust in an institution therefore requires clarifying and reinforcing these norms. Swaggart may have continued preaching, but not under Assemblies of God auspices, which demonstrates the Assemblies' rejection of his behavior. Willow Creek learned that it, like any large organization claiming to be trustworthy, needed to have formalized rules about handling allegations of sexual harassment. Catholic leaders, with varying amounts of credibility, sought to demonstrate that they were capable of exposing sex offenders and cooperating with the law in punishing them.

What religious leaders have done to restore trust, then, is not so different from how other institutions, including our political system, attempt to restore trust. Evoking confessions of wrongdoing can appear impossible in the political arena, but public pressure to depose untrustworthy leaders is an elemental part of the electoral process. So are investigations and litigation, as those surrounding the January 6, 2021, insurrection illustrated. Although these processes are often lengthy and bitterly contested, they are the means through which we attempt to call attention to mistrust. And as the examples in religion illustrate, these mechanisms facilitate valuable discussions of crucial social norms, even when trust itself is difficult to restore.

The potential gains through confessions, investigations, and litigation notwithstanding, the decline of trust in religious institutions, coupled with dissension about whom and whom not to trust, is detrimental to the collective good. Democracy benefits when citizens trust one another and the institutions that make up civil society, when trust is sufficient to facilitate reaching out to strangers as well as acquaintances, joining voluntary associations, taking part in political activities, and working together for the common pursuit of life, liberty, and happiness. Trust that is grounded in religious convictions has long been a source of common values and a basis on which to build consensus. Even as religion sometimes inflames passions and promotes incommensurate ideas, Americans have historically conceived of it as a kind of civil institution that promotes agreement more than disagreement. It is understandable therefore to wish that more Americans held something like a common faith—even if faith were only belief in faith itself—and consider it deplorable when religious communities target each other rather than working together to promote peace and harmony.

Dissension and Democracy

However, the dissension so obviously present among religious leaders points to a feature of American religion that in the past—under the right conditions—has served democracy well. Dissension among religious groups provides checks and balances in the same way that divergent views between political parties and special interest groups do. America's "variety of sects," as James Madison termed them, motivated the separation of church and state. And the contending factions that have vied with one another have also limited the tendencies of any group to become a religious establishment.[39] Along these lines, legal scholar Kent Greenawalt, writing about religion and the politics of liberal democracy, suggests that trust is possible not despite religious diversity but because of it. "If one believes that comprehensive views themselves are so diverse that one has little fear if decisions are reached by individual citizens and legislators in accord with comprehensive views," he writes, "one might not worry much about their employment." The reason, among others, is that despite impassioned and uncompromising religious advocacy, the reality of diversity can alter the standards of judgment on which political decisions are made and promote healthy skepticism toward political claims.[40]

Greenawalt is mindful of the fact that American religion—like American democracy—is pluralistic. In religion as in politics, we are a diverse society. We agree on basic principles, such as the rule of law and the peaceful transition of power, but we disagree deeply about many other things. Political parties, special interest groups, racial and ethnic groups, and religious groups all contend with one another for power, rarely engaging in direct deliberations or coming to a consensus that resolves their disagreements, but bringing diverse ideas, arguments, and proposals to bear on policy decisions. Unlike in relatively homogeneous societies where common cultural traditions provide a basis for deliberative democracy to be practiced, the diversity of a society like the United States demands greater respect for differences and heightened expectations about the persistence of fundamental disagreements. The contention is messy and indeterminate yet is the means through which a pluralistic democracy adapts to challenging circumstances.[41]

From this perspective, democracy can withstand, perhaps even be strengthened by, the kinds of contention evident among religious groups today. Faith communities are organized along racial and ethnic as well as theological lines, often serving as the local centers in which constituents support one another, learn about issues of common importance, and facilitate their coreligionists' access to information about leisure activities, schools, health care, social services, and opportunities for volunteering. The fact that faith communities disagree with one another adds incentive for them to advocate for their distinctive beliefs and, in many instances, results in mutual criticism and calling foul on adversaries' tactics.[42] Of course, the winner-take-all approach that seems to have characterized White evangelical Protestants' alignment with Republicans in recent decades is regarded by many as a threat to the civil liberties democracy is meant to preserve. Yet the 15 percent of the electorate composed of White evangelical Protestants is countered by numerous religious and secular groups who hold differing views. The extent of this diversity suggests, as a long-time observer of American religion, Kenneth L. Woodward has argued, that White evangelical Protestants can hardly be credited with—or blamed for—electoral outcomes that in reality are the result of complex aggregations of constituencies and political strategies.[43] The diversity of American religion is also a significant factor in the debates—divisive as they have been—about the standards by which citizenship should be determined, elections should be held, and presidents should be judged. Long-standing advocacy groups such as the ACLU and NAACP have been joined in recent years by groups such as the Clergy Emergency League, (revived) Poor People's Campaign, Interfaith Center for Public Policy, Clergy and Laity United for Economic Justice, Vote Common Ground, and Black Lives Matter, as well as by local and regional clergy councils and lay organizations that advocate for immigrant rights, affordable housing, and universal health insurance.

Pluralism means that advocacy groups in religion, just as in politics, will take different sides on issues and will directly challenge their adversaries' arguments. Pluralism is also operative when advocacy groups mobilize constituencies with divergent interests, as illustrated by some faith-based groups orienting their efforts toward immigrant rights while others focus on homelessness, racial reconciliation, or police reform. Apart from advocacy, pluralism is the condition that encourages institutions to work to restore trust. Leaders of religious organizations are motivated to restore trust because, in the absence of it, constituents will vote with their feet, taking advantage of a vastly diverse American religious landscape and choosing to worship elsewhere, or not worship at all. Attendees at Willow Creek could decamp to a different church if they no longer trusted Willow Creek's leadership, and college students could opt to study somewhere other than Liberty University if its board of trustees did not restore the institution's trustworthiness. An amendment to the concept of pluralism, then, is that religious organizations do not have to attack one another if pluralism provides opportunities for constituents to register their dissent by moving their loyalties to other organizations.

But without a basic level of trust among the parties involved, pluralism falters. Profound disagreements must include at least minimal agreement about the norms of involvement. Disputants must treat one another not as enemies but only as adversaries, and disagreements must be negotiated within the law through deliberation, legislation, the courts, and peaceful confrontations. There must be a basic threshold of trust that those with whom one disagrees will play by the ground rules of civility, adhering to norms of honesty and respect for well-established norms of human rights and freedoms. Despite serious disagreements, America's various faith communities have in the past generally exhibited adherence to these norms, even to the point of arguing less exclusively about divinely revealed truth than about procedures and practicalities. In surveys, White evangelical, White mainline Protestant, Black Protestant, Catholic, and Jewish respondents rate each of the other groups warmly, if not quite as positively as they do their own, the exceptions being colder feelings toward Muslims and atheists.[44] More to the point, religious groups with widely divergent views about religious freedom, abortion, homosexuality, conscientious objection, welfare, immigration, and capital punishment—including advocacy groups that have formed to press for particular issues—have, with only a few exceptions, worked to achieve their goals through lobbying, voting, and the courts.

The pursuit of happiness through such illicit pleasures as adulterous sexual liaisons and fraudulent financial schemes, then, is a betrayal of trust with potential consequences far beyond those immediately involved. The decline of trust in religious institutions should be considered in terms of its cultural fallout and the remediation needed to restore trust in our basic institutions. Declining trust is an opportunity for religious and secular groups alike to fight for their convictions and, in so doing, clarify through instances of confession, investigations, and even litigation the operative social norms as well as the beliefs for which they stand. The fighting itself can be a good thing, bringing to the table alternative values and elevating the importance of clarifying those values. But it is the terms under which the fighting takes place that matters. The disputes must be conducted in good faith, expressing what people sincerely believe to be true and understanding that to disagree requires respect for those with whom one disagrees. The danger to religion, as well as to democracy, lies in cynical distortions of sincere convictions. Democracy is truly endangered when leaders refuse to believe that those with whom they disagree are worthy of the elemental trust that all deserve.

The task of restoring trust in basic institutions—of recovering the foundational trust in human goodness that seems so often to be the victim of abject betrayals—and of rejuvenating faith in American democracy is, at this moment in our nation's history, a high priority. Any hope that the United States can find common ground in the beliefs and practices that once inspired religion as a source of consensus is ill founded. The more likely scenario is that religious groups in alliance with or in opposition to one another, as well as in conjunction with secular groups, will either keep fighting for what they think is uniquely true or retreat into a privatized faith that encourages individuals to seek spiritual gratification in purely personal ways. Neither of these possibilities is very encouraging for the health of democracy. Especially when religious groups willingly dispute the basic facts of scientific medicine, endorse the false claims of political operatives, and deride people whose religious convictions differ from theirs—when religious groups fail to treat one another according to basic principles of trust and toleration—then religion functions more to facilitate authoritarianism than to support democracy.

For religious leaders to restore the public's—and, indeed, their own members'—trust in the religious institutions that have served America so well in the past, they certainly do not have to all agree on the important moral and social issues of the day. But they must be attentive to the basic principles within their own traditions of how to live amicably and respectfully among those with whom they disagree. Perhaps religious leaders can once again appreciate that their own traditions are strengthened by America's pluralism. And perhaps that realization can be a source of inspiration for upholding the underlying principles of law, trust, and common respect on which democracy is based.

Regarding the question of how faith communities shape emotional practice, these considerations show that the pursuit of happiness through illicit behavior such as sexual misconduct, stealing, and lying has prompted not only warnings and punishments for such behavior but also remedial practices, including investigations, acts of contrition, and testimonials of forgiveness and redemption. Many of these remedial practices are deeply emotional and are deemed more sincere when intense emotion is displayed. A kind of emotional equilibrium may be achieved when the happiness that was ostensibly experienced from the illicit behavior is balanced by sufficient remorse. Emotional repair work, therefore, is part of the process through which religious institutions retain or lose public support.

8
Conclusion
Nurturing Happiness

There is an inherent tension in Christianity between teachings that emphasize God's unconditional love and teachings that stress individuals' need to believe something, do something, and work harder to be better at what they believe and do. The tension is not easily resolved. God's unconditional love and doing better to serve God can both be sources of happiness. The difficulty stems less from theology, which can be subtle and complex in how it addresses happiness, but from religion as a social institution. Churches have an incentive to offer happiness to their adherents but to do so at a price. The message they embrace says, in effect, that God loves you unconditionally, just the way you are, but we, the church, are here to interpret that message, loudly, clearly, even uniquely, and thus to guide how you think about happiness and experience it. Churches have a vested interest in helping people to experience happiness but also to guide their happiness in ways that further the churches' mission in the world.

Whether we appreciate what they do or whether we think the world would be better without them, faith communities are assemblages of power. They hold out what they regard as authoritative interpretations of scripture, authorize certain persons to make decisions and to lead worship services, and expect participants to give voluntarily of their time and money. Faith communities also instantiate formal and informal norms about when services should be held, what should happen, what to expect, and how to behave when present at a particular time and place. These norms include expectations about how to be happy. Happiness of a certain kind is facilitated by warm greetings, music, and uplifting messages. The norms about the kinds of pleasure that are appropriate and those that are not extend into everyday life. None of this depends on heavy-handed enforcement. Compliance is voluntary, and a great deal of noncompliance is tolerated.

These observations add to the literature that has focused on feeling rules. Feeling rules are norms that persons in power put into place to guide how

Nurturing Happiness. Robert Wuthnow, Oxford University Press. © Oxford University Press 2025.
DOI: 10.1093/9780197807071.003.0009

people under their supervision should express their feelings. Just as store clerks and flight attendants are expected to express cheerfulness, even though they may not feel cheerful inside, so participants at worship services are usually expected to be happy about being there and to express that happiness when greeting their fellow congregants. These expectations are often reinforced by uplifting music and smiling worship leaders. The shaping of emotional practice, though, is more complicated and interesting than that. As we have seen, happiness is shaped by compare-and-contrast metaphors, such as the ones describing heavenly and earthly joy in colonial America, that prioritized kinds of happiness, sharpened the distinctions among them, and provided language with which to describe happiness. A second kind of emotional shaping occurs when multiple emotions are present, such as the ecstatic joy and convivial happiness that worshippers experienced at camp meetings in the early nineteenth century and are spatially separated to manage what is appropriate in each situation. Exuberant expressions of emotion are especially subject to such management techniques. A third kind of emotional shaping involves bringing familiar emotions, such as happiness associated with friendly socializing, into a new location, such as a church parlor or at a "ladies' fair," and providing guidance for what to do and say in this novel situation. A fourth kind consists of demonstrating the connection of happiness to other activities, such as at a Progressive-era social service project, or of associating "transcendent" meaning with playful activities. Shaping of these kinds depends on religious leaders having the authority to orchestrate messages about happiness and to control the times and spaces in which happiness occurs. Their power in turn is subject to conditions beyond their control and thus requires improvisation.

The episodes we have considered demonstrate how much the relationship between faith communities and happiness depends on specific times and places. Happiness, like anger, fear, and sadness, is an emotional practice that is influenced by the situations in which it occurs, by who else is present, the kinds of authority they represent, the cues they provide about what feelings are appropriate to experience and to express, and by what has happened in similar situations in the past. Is the situation composed of people smiling and laughing or are they tight-lipped, worried, and grouchy? The cues given by religious teachings can go either way. There is a baseline message that people of faith should be joyful—but not in all times and places. This was the reason that faith leaders took pains to establish the rules about when and where the gathered community could be joyful. Happiness as they understood it was not a generalized sense of well-being that could be aggregated and scored. Happiness was conditioned by the ups and downs of daily life. Deathbed scenes were sad, but sadness was circumscribed by testimonies of joyful expectations. Exuberant emotion that would never have been expressed openly among one's neighbors could be expressed freely at a camp meeting revival. Festivity that would profane the sanctity of a worship space was fine in the church parlor or even in the sanctuary at some other time than Sunday morning. There were also times to orchestrate emotional repair work. The mourning bench and the confessional served this purpose. It was an important part of the community of faith to impart ideas about God's prevailing love for the world, but it was equally important to guide the community in how to express itself emotionally.

Faith communities over the years played an important role in training the self-dispositions that people brought to their situations. Whatever might be going on in their lives, people of faith learned that God wanted them to be cheerful. There were biblical stories to be learned and songs to be sung. Importantly, faith communities provided a nuanced repertoire for talking about happiness. Happiness could be composed of true joy or superficial joy, enduring joy or fleeting joy, mirth or mere contentment, extravagant joy, or even, as some called it, somber joy. When more than one kind of happiness was present, faith communities worked out ways of distinguishing them. The camp meeting participants who fell to the ground in ecstasy were separated from the worshippers whose joy was merely worshipful and the spectators who were happy merely to be present. Moreover, the rules governing the expression of joy were always gendered. The joyful bachelor flirting with young women at a ladies' fair got away with more than the young women did in return. The women who worked all day cooking and baking for a church fair experienced more happiness when it was over than in the moment. The rules were age-graded as well. Children's play could be taken as a symbol of the spontaneity that adults might want to experience but could not in their workaday lives. The selves for whom happiness was possible were further distinguished by the relationships that faith communities conceived between joy and transcendence. The happiness that individuals derived from ordinary life was sharply distinguished from the self-transcendence that occurred from holistic unity with the divine.

As much effort as was put into the rules about when, where, and how happiness was to be experienced, faith communities rarely held that happiness itself should be the primary goal of a person's life. The happiness that faith communities encouraged was nearly always a byproduct of some other activity engaged in for a different purpose. The day-to-day cheerfulness that Christians were taught in early American preaching was a byproduct of working to glorify God and thinking in joyous expectation about being with God in heaven. Camp meeting revivals were organized to save souls, and the joy experienced at the meetings was happiness not only in witnessing others being saved but the convivial joy that happened simply from mingling with friends and neighbors. Ladies' fairs had to be pleasurable to attract visitors but that was a means to the fairs' higher end of raising money for worthy purposes. The happiness that came with doing church work was a byproduct of playing a part in doing God's work in the world. Illicit joy was most notably wrong-headed when it subverted the ministries of those involved.

If happiness was a byproduct of activities done for a different religious purpose, happiness nevertheless was empowering for the individuals experiencing it. The spontaneous happiness that children experienced at play or the sudden, unexpected revelry that came during a moment of mystical self-abandon was less often the way in which faith communities described happiness than the kind that involved an empowering sense of agency. Happiness is derived from making good choices, deciding to be a person of faith, and doing good works as a person of faith. It came from achieving personal goals in life but also from feeling that there was joy in pursuing those goals. Happiness in this respect was indeed a pursuit more than it was an accomplishment. It was a pursuit to a considerable extent because it involved figuring out what one wanted in life. Being unsure of one's intentions was a reason to expend effort on oneself, examining, clarifying, and assessing one's intentions. The idea that one's happiness depended on the happiness of all was hard to contemplate except in the context of one's immediate friends and family. The early preachers who argued that cheerfulness was beneficial to family life and personal relationships would have shaken their heads at the idea that happiness could be quantified, but they had something like self-tracking in mind when they urged believers to include self-assessments in their daily prayers.

The relationship between religious faith and happiness in the episodes we have considered demonstrates the value of regarding religion as a social practice embedded in institutions. Institutions are power arrangements composed of formal rules and informal norms, including rules about experiencing and expressing feelings. Through the decades, faith communities repeatedly confronted the task of determining what kinds of happiness were appropriate to encourage or condone and what kinds were not. Should the faithful be happy simply as a matter of course or should their happiness be contingent on thinking about heaven? Should casual socializing be allowed at camp meetings or discouraged? Was dancing less deplorable if it was sponsored by a church or even more deplorable? Was it a good idea to encourage a bit of flirtation to make a ladies' fair profitable or was that a bad idea? Should the church organize a money-making event at all? What if that event included a lottery? How should happiness be separated from work? How should it be included within—or set apart from—business, games, and entertainment?

Faith leaders' answers to these questions reflected the challenges and opportunities brought to them by the changing times in which they lived. As Americans settled down, farmed, opened factories, and founded towns, the asceticism that governed life in an earlier era gave way to doctrines that made room for more merriment to be incorporated into daily life. The exuberance of the Great Awakening in the 1740s opened the way for revival preaching and camp meetings in the nineteenth century to show that exuberance could be handled even when it burned with fiery zeal. It took a while for faith communities in the larger towns and cities to figure out how to organize church fairs without straying too far into the business of entertainment. The relationships among play, work, and transcendence were debated in new ways as the society became more marketized. Illicit pursuits of happiness were always troublesome. Many of the festive activities that seemed problematic at first set the pattern for such routine events as church suppers, rummage sales, picnics, holiday celebrations, and summer camps.

Faith communities' decisions in dealing with these questions implied moral judgments. Whether a person should experience godly happiness or be content with worldly pleasure was a moral judgment. The value of experiencing exuberant joy at a camp meeting was a moral judgment. There were moral distinctions between the ways that good Christians were supposed to be cheerful and the ways that the unregenerate pursued happiness. There were moral distinctions in discussions about church fairs and festivals. Although the language changed, many of the moral distinctions remained. There were always dedicated leaders who believed that their views about God, the church, sex, and politics were the keys to true happiness.

For those who study religion's current role in shaping emotional practice, there are many implications from the examples we have considered. Religion's discursive power is likely to be present in how dialogic distinctions are drawn between kinds of happiness, elevating the status of some (calling them "sacred," "godly," "lasting," or "pure") and contrasting them with other kinds ("superficial," "worldly," "temporary," or "illicit"). The spatial arrangements that figured importantly in camp meetings have twenty-first-century parallels in how different kinds of happiness are expected in different places. The emotional division of labor that still defines differences in expected emotional practices according to race and gender bears similarities to the differences that distinguished the camp meeting practices for enslaved persons and enslavers and that differentiated men and women. The gendered patterns evident in ladies' fairs have parallels today in how women and men are expected to participate in pleasurable activities. Religious rituals may facilitate the pursuit of happiness, but there is a division of labor in these rituals that corresponds with different expectations about who will be "moved" the most. Emotional practices in many religious venues carry expectations about how structured, how improvisational, how disciplined, and how effortful the practices should be. Studies of religion's shaping of emotional practice must also take account of whether religious leaders can make compelling arguments about happiness at work, in the home, and among friends or whether those arguments are being made by the media and the entertainment industry. In short, careful investigations of religion and emotional practice must pay close attention to the structuring effects of discourse, places, norms, and power arrangements.

The study of religion has rightly become more cautious about ideas of secularization. But observers who suggested that faith communities were gradually accommodating to the pleasures of the secular world had a point. Churches that considered May Day festivals and even Christmas celebrations as being fraught with moral danger, let alone skating parties and dancing, gradually accommodated to these temptations. And churches that at one time challenged people of faith to control how they expressed happiness in public have largely adopted the culturally convenient view that happiness is a subjective mood that a person can choose to experience privately in any situation. The trajectory in these long-term developments was from the church as an authoritative institution in which clergy could set the terms for enjoying life toward the circumstances that we know today in which individuals make up their minds about what to believe and often do so in terms of how they feel about particular beliefs and practices. It would be mistaken, though, to emphasize the long-term trends without considering the situations in which impactful decisions were made. While these decisions took account of what was happening in the wider culture, they were especially concerned with how happiness was to be encouraged and experienced within faith communities themselves. It was understood that happiness was a virtue, a pleasure that was inspirational and rewarding. Always, the question was how properly to understand it and how appropriately to experience it.

Notes

Introduction

1. E.g., John Corrigan, *Business of the Heart: Religion and Emotion in the Nineteenth Century* (Berkeley and Los Angeles: University of California, 2021); Caroline Wigginton and Avram Van Engen, eds., *Feeling Godly: Religious Affections and Christian Contact in Early North America* (Amherst: University of Massachusetts Press, 2021); Owen Flanagan, Jr., ed., *Against Happiness* (New York: Columbia University Press, 2023); Ann Taves, *Fits, Trances, and Visions: Experiencing Religion and Explaining Experience from Wesley to James* (Princeton, NJ: Princeton University Press, 1999); Ann Taves, *Religious Experience Reconsidered: A Building Block Approach to the Study of Religion and Other Special Things* (Princeton, NJ: Princeton University Press, 2009); Courtney J. Bender, "Touching the Transcendent: Rethinking Religious Experience in the Sociological Study of Religion," in *Everyday Religion: Observing Modern Religious Lives* (New York: Oxford University Press, 2007), 202–27.
2. Wayne Proudfoot, *Religious Experience* (Berkeley and Los Angeles: University of California Press, 1985), 76.
3. Robert N. Bellah et al., *Habits of the Heart: Individualism and Commitment in American Life* (Berkeley and Los Angeles: University of California Press, 1984).
4. Philip Rieff, *The Triumph of the Therapeutic: Uses of Faith After Freud* (New York: Harper & Row, 1966).
5. Eva Illouz, *Saving the Modern Soul: Therapy, Emotions, and the Culture of Self-Help* (Berkeley and Los Angeles: University of California Press, 2008); Katja Rakow, "Therapeutic Culture and Religion in America," *Religion Compass* 7, 11 (2013), 485–97; Shane Sharp, "How Does Prayer Help Manage Emotions?" *Social Psychology Quarterly* 73, 4 (2010), 417–37.
6. See especially Tim Lomas, *Happiness* (Cambridge, MA: MIT Press, 2023); Darrin M. McMahon, *Happiness: A History* (New York: Atlantic Monthly Press, 2004); and the abbreviated history in Darrin M. McMahon, "From the Happiness of Virtue to the Virtue of Happiness: 400 BC–AD 1780," *Daedalus* 133, 2 (Spring 2004), 5–17; and on happiness in philosophical and literary work, Jeffrey R. Di Leo, *Happiness* (New York: Routledge, 2022).
7. P. Radhika, B. Roopasree, and J. K. Mukkadan, "'Happiness'—The Role of Neurochemicals," *International Journal of Science and Research* 9, 9 (September 2020), 174–8; Morten L. Kringelbach and Kent C. Berridge, "The Neuroscience of Happiness and Pleasure," *Social Research* 77, 2 (2010), 659–78; Rebecca Alexander, "The Neuroscience of Positive Emotions and Affect: Implications for Cultivating Happiness and Wellbeing," *Neuroscience & Biobehavioral Reviews* 121 (February 2021), 220–49.
8. Ed Diener and Robert Biswas-Diener, *Happiness: Unlocking the Mysteries of Psychological Wealth* (Oxford, UK: Blackwell, 2008); Robert Biswas-Diener, Ed Diener, and Maya Tamir, "The Psychology of Subjective Well-Being," *Daedalus* 133, 2 (Spring 2004), 18–25; on the role of meaning in contrasting emotions from pleasurable feelings, see James A. Russell, "Emotion, Core Affect, and Psychological Construction," *Cognition and Emotion* 23, 7 (2009), 1259–83.
9. Charles Darwin, *The Expression of Emotion in Man and Animals* (New York: D. Appleton and Company, 1899 [1872]), 811; Fraser W. Smith and Philippe G. Schyns, "Smile through Your Fear and Sadness: Transmitting and Identifying Facial Expression Signals over a Range of Viewing Distances," *Psychological Science* 20, 10 (2009), 1202–8; Charlotte Vkrijen et al., "Spread the Joy: How High and Low Bias for Happy Facial Emotions Translate into Different Daily Life Affect Dynamics," *Complexity* 18 (2018), 1–15.
10. Bent Greve, *Happiness* (New York: Routledge, 2023); Daniel M. Haybron, *The Pursuit of Unhappiness: The Elusive Psychology of Well-Being* (New York: Oxford University Press, 2008), 139; Daniel Nettle, *Happiness: The Science Behind Your Smile* (New York: Oxford University Press, 2005), offers an extended discussion of the arguments about extroversion and introversion.

11. Fred Feldman, *What Is This Thing Called Happiness?* (New York: Oxford University Press, 2010), 127–36; on hedonic adaptation, see especially Philip Brickman and Donald T. Campbell, "Hedonic Relativism and Planning the Good Society," in *Adaptation Level Theory: A Symposium*, ed. M. H. Apley (New York: Academic Press, 1971), 287–302; and Shane Frederick and George Loewenstein, "Hedonic Adaptation," in *Well-Being: Foundations of Hedonic Psychology*, eds. Daniel Kahneman, Edward Diener, and Norbert Schwarz (New York: Russell Sage Foundation, 1999), 302–9; for an argument distinguishing fluctuating and durable happiness, see Michael Dambrun et al., "Measuring Happiness: From Fluctuating Happiness to Authentic-Durable Happiness," *Frontiers in Psychology* 3 (2012), 1–16; Brent Dean Robbins, "Joy," in *The Encyclopedia of Positive Psychology*, ed. Shane J. Lopez (Malden, MA: Wiley-Blackwell, 2009), 540–4.
12. See especially Claude S. Fischer, *Lurching toward Happiness in America* (Cambridge, MA: MIT Press, 2014); Alan B. Kreuger, ed., *Measuring the Subjective Well-Being of Nations: National Accounts of Time Use and Well-Being* (Chicago: University of Chicago Press, 2009); Angus Deaton and Arthur A. Stone, "Economic Analysis of Subjective Well-Being: Two Happiness Puzzles," *American Economic Review* 103, 3 (2013), 591–97; Panel on Measuring Subjective Well-Being in a Policy-Relevant Framework, *Subjective Well-Being: Measuring Happiness, Suffering, and Other Dimensions of Experience* (Washington, DC: National Academies Press, 2013); and Luigino Bruni and Pier Luigi Porta, eds., *Handbook of Research Methods and Applications in Happiness and Quality of Life* (Northampton, MA: Edward Elgar, 2016).
13. Haya Stier and Amit Kaplan, "Are Children a Joy or a Burden? Individual and Macro-level Characteristics and the Perception of Children," *European Journal of Population* 36, 2 (2020), 387–413.
14. Sonja Lyubomirsky and Kristin Layous, "How Do Simple Positive Activities Increase Well-Being?" *Current Directions in Psychological Science* 22, 1 (2013), 57–62; John P. Robinson and Steven Martin, "What Do Happy People Do?" *Social Indicators Research* 89, 3 (December 2008), 565–71; Zhanjia Zhang and Weiyun Chen, "A Systematic Review of the Relationship between Physical Activity and Happiness," *Journal of Happiness Studies* 20 (2019), 1305–22; on joy as power, see Gilles Deleuze, *Spinoza: Practical Philosophy*, trans. Robert Hurley (San Francisco, CA: City Light Books, 1988 [1970]), 100.
15. See especially Sara Ahmed, "The Happiness Turn," *New Formations* 63 (2007), 7–14; Sara Ahmed, "Killing Joy: Feminism and the History of Happiness," *Signs: Journal of Women in Culture and Society* 35, 3 (2010), 571–94; and Sara Ahmed, *The Promise of Happiness* (Durham: Duke University Press, 2010).
16. Fernando Marmolejo-Ramos et al., "Placing Joy, Surprise and Sadness in Space: A Cross-Linguistic Study," *Psychological Research* 81, 4 (July 2017), 750–63; Kyoshiro Saski, Yuki Yamada, and Kayo Miura, "Post-Determined Emotion: Motor Action Retrospectively Modulates Emotional Valence of Visual Images," *Proceedings of the Royal Society of London, Series B: Biological Sciences* 282, 1805 (2015), 1–20.
17. Peggy A. Thoits, "The Sociology of Emotions," *Annual Review of Sociology* 15 (1989), 317–42; Sara Ahmed, *The Cultural Politics of Emotion*, 2nd ed. (Edinburgh, UK: Edinburgh University Press, 2014); Catherine Lutz and Lila Abu-Lughod, *Language and the Politics of Emotion* (New York: Cambridge University Press, 1990); Ann Swidler, *Talk of Love: How Culture Matters* (Chicago: University of Chicago Press, 2001), 6; Mark Cieslik, "'Not Smiling but Frowning': Sociology and the 'Problem of Happiness,'" *Sociology* 49, 3 (2015), 422–37.
18. Arlie R. Hochschild, "Emotion Work, Feeling Rules, and Social Structure," *American Journal of Sociology* 85, 3 (1979), 551–75; Arlie R. Hochschild, *The Managed Heart: Commercialization of Human Feeling* (Berkeley and Los Angeles: University of California Press, 1983); Adia Harvey Wingfield, "The (Un) Managed Heart: Racial Contours of Emotion Work in Gendered Occupations," *Annual Review of Sociology* 47 (2021), 197–212.
19. How this emphasis on individual happiness differed from, and represented a decisive shift away from, the ideal "pursuit of happiness" mentioned in the Declaration of Independence, which held that the happiness of any must variously include the "happiness of all," "happiness of the community," and "happiness in the welfare of the whole" is described insightfully in Barry Alan Shain, *The Myth of American Individualism: The Protestant Origins of American Political Thought* (Princeton, NJ: Princeton University Press, 1994).
20. Theodore R. Schatzki, Karin Knorr Cetina, and Eike von Savigny, eds., *The Practice Turn in Contemporary Theory* (New York: Routledge, 2001); Theodore R. Schatzki, *Social Practices: A Wittgensteinian Approach to Human Activity and the Social* (New York: Cambridge University

Press, 1996); Joseph Rouse, "Practice Theory," in *Philosophy of Anthropology and Sociology*, eds. Stephen P. Turner and Mark W. Risjord (New York: Elsevier, 2007), 499–540; and Davide Nicolini, *Practice Theory, Work, and Organization: An Introduction* (New York: Oxford University Press, 2012).

21. Andreas Reckwitz, "Toward a Theory of Social Practices: A Development in Culturalist Theorizing," *European Journal of Social Theory* 5, 2 (2002), 243–63, quote on page 254.
22. Ian Buchanan, *Michel de Certeau: Cultural Theorist* (London: Sage, 2000); Veronica Ng, "The Problem of *Place*: A Foucauldian and Discursive Analysis on *Place*," in *Space and Place, vol 3: Exploring Critical Issues*, eds. Didem Kilickiran, Christina Alegria, and Carl Haddrell (Oxford: Inter-Disciplinary Press, 2013), 185–204; see also Schatzki, *Social Practices*, 89, on "teleoaffective" structures.
23. See, e.g., the treatment of emotional attachment in Walter E. A. Van Beek, *The Forge and the Funeral: The Smith in Kapsiki/Higi Culture* (East Lansing: Michigan State University Press, 2015).
24. Monique Scheer, "Are Emotions a Kind of Practice (And Is That What Makes Them Have a History)? A Bourdieuian Approach to Understanding Emotion," *History and Theory* 51, 2 (May 2012), 193–220; Hochschild, "Emotion Work, Feeling Rules, and Social Structure."
25. Hochschild, *Managed Heart*, 56–75.
26. Marci D. Cottingham, *Practical Feelings: Emotions as Resources in a Dynamic Social World* (New York: Oxford University Press, 2022), 19–20; on happiness as embodied practice, see also Richard Gibbons, "Considering the Body in Happiness Research," in *Researching Happiness: Qualitative, Biographical and Critical Perspectives*, ed. Mark Cieslik (Bristol, UK: Bristol University Press, 2021), 113–32.
27. William Sander, "Religion, Religiosity, and Happiness," *Review of Religious Research* 59, 2 (June 2017), 251–62; Morgan Green and Marta Elliott, "Religion, Health, and Psychological Well-Being," *Journal of Religion and Health* 49, 2 (June 2010), 149–63; Rodney Stark and Jared Maier, "Faith and Happiness," *Review of Religious Research* 50, 1 (September 2008), 120–5; Andrew Greeley and Michael Hout, *The Truth about Conservative Christians* (Chicago: University of Chicago Press, 2006), 150–61.
28. Chaeyoon Lim and Robert D. Putnam, "Religion, Social Networks, and Life Satisfaction," *American Sociological Review* 75, 6 (2010), 914–33; Stark and Maier, "Faith and Happiness"; Eduardo Perez-Asenjo, "If Happiness Is Relative, Against Whom Do We Compare Ourselves? Implications for Labor Supply," *Journal of Population Economics* 24, 4 (2011), 1411–42.
29. On the practice approach to the study of religion, see especially Nancy T. Ammerman, "Rethinking Religion: Toward a Practice Approach," American *Journal of Sociology* 126, 1 (July 2020), 6–51; and Nancy Tatom Ammerman, *Studying Lived Religion: Contexts and Practices* (New York: New York University Press, 2021). My work on practice, most recently in *What Happens When We Practice Religion? Textures of Devotion in Everyday Life* (Princeton, NJ: Princeton University Press, 2020), emphasizes the interplay of habits and improvisation, situational cues and material affordances, intentions in action, feeling rules, embodied routines and representations, and the evolution in social studies of religion from classificatory concepts to a focus on structuring processes.
30. Charles Mathewes, "Toward a Theology of Joy," in *Joy and Human Flourishing: Essays on Theology, Culture, and the Good Life*, eds. Miroslav Volf and Justin E. Crisp (Minneapolis, MN: Fortress Press, 2015), 63–95, quote on page 68.
31. General conceptions of symbolic and social boundaries are found in Michèle Lamont and Virag Molnár, "The Study of Boundaries in the Social Sciences," *Annual Review of Sociology* 28 (2002), 167–95; and Andreas Wimmer, "The Making and Unmaking of Ethnic Boundaries: A Multi-Level Process Theory," *American Journal of Sociology* 113 (2008), 970–1022; on boundary work in faith communities, see especially Grace Yukich, "Boundary Work in Inclusive Religious Groups: Constructing Identity at the New York Catholic Worker," *Sociology of Religion* 71 (2010), 172–96; on religion and science, see especially Thomas F. Gieryn, "Boundary-Work and the Demarcation of Science from Non-Science: Strains and Interests in Professional Ideologies of Scientists," *American Sociological Review* 48, 6 (December 1983), 781–95; on moral justifications, see especially Stephen Vaisey, "Motivation and Justification: A Dual-Process Model of Culture in Action," *American Journal of Sociology* 114, 6 (May 2009), 1675–715.
32. Amy C. Wilkins, "'Happier than Non-Christians': Collective Emotions and Symbolic Boundaries among Evangelical Christians," *Social Psychology Quarterly* 71, 3 (September 2008), 281–301; social scientists have also contributed to this kind of "we-are-happier-than-they-are"

thinking; see, e.g., Chih-Yu Chen and Tsung-Ren Huang, "Christians and Buddhists Are Comparably Happy on Twitter: A Large-Scale Linguistic Analysis of Religious Differences in Social, Cognitive, and Emotional Tendencies," *Frontiers in Psychology* 10 (February 2019), 1–8; and Ryan S. Ritter, Jesse Lee Preston, and Ivan Hernandez, "Happy Tweets: Christians Are Happier, More Socially Connected, and Less Analytical Than Atheists on Twitter," *Social Psychological and Personality Science* 5, 2 (2014), 243–49.

33. C. S. Lewis, *Surprised by Joy: The Shape of My Early* Life (New York: Harcourt Brace, 1955), 74.
34. Émile Durkheim, *The Elementary Forms of Religious Life*, trans. Karen E. Fields (New York: Free Press, 1995 [1912]), 225, 320; Karen Barad, *Meeting the Universe Halfway: Quantum Physics and the Entanglement of Matter and Meaning* (Durham, NC: Duke University Press, 2007), 93, uses the metaphor of symbolic boundaries to describe the shifts in personal narratives from defeat and despair to contentment and joy as "boundary-drawing practices."
35. Sara Ahmed, *The Promise of Happiness.*
36. Robert Wuthnow, *Religion's Power: What Makes It Work* (New York: Oxford University Press, 2023).
37. Readers interested in other times and places in which faith communities have shaped expressions of happiness and other pleasant or unpleasant emotions, including sorrow and guilt, would benefit from such works as Lindsey Stewart, *The Politics of Black Joy: Zora Neale Hurston and Neo-Abolitionism* (Evanston, IL: Northwestern University Press, 2021), which describes the portrayal in abolitionist literature, Negro spirituals, and twentieth-century writing of enslaved persons as joyful and sorrowful; Nancy Tatom Ammerman, *Studying Lived Religion*, especially Chapter 6, which describes emotions in a wide variety of religious practices; Peter J. Thuesen, *Tornado God: American Religion and Violent Weather* (New York: Oxford University Press, 2020), which traces Midwestern faith communities' efforts to deal theologically and practically with the physical and emotional devastation wrought by natural disasters; Alyssa Maldonado-Estrada, *Lifeblood of the Parish: Men and Catholic Devotion in Williamsburg, Brooklyn* (New York: NYU Press, 2020), which is one of the best ethnographic studies of Catholic men's emotional investment in parish religious practices; Lila Abu-Lughod, *Veiled Sentiments: Honor and Poetry in a Bedouin Society* (Berkeley and Los Angeles: University of California Press, 2016 [1986]), which provides an excellent anthropological approach to the cultural construction of emotion among Muslim women; and David Morgan, *The Embodied Eye: Religious Visual Culture and the Social Life of Feeling* (Berkeley and Los Angeles: University of California Press, 2012), which provides an insightful overview of the relationship of religious art and emotion.

Chapter 1

1. On the emotional practices of early American Protestantism and its antecedents, see especially Perry Miller, *Errand into the Wilderness* (Cambridge, MA: Harvard University Press, 1952); Philip Greven, *The Protestant Temperament: Patterns of Child-Rearing, Religious Experience, and the Self in Early America* (New York: Knopf, 1977); Michael P. Winship, *Hot Protestants: A History of Puritanism in England and America* (New Haven, CT: Yale University Press, 2018); Charles E. Hambrick-Stowe, *The Practice of Piety: Puritan Devotional Disciplines in Seventeenth-Century New England* (Chapel Hill: University of North Carolina Press, 1982); Charles Lloyd Cohen, *God's Caress: The Psychology of Puritan Religious Experience* (New York: Oxford University Press, 1986); and Janice Knight, *Orthodoxies in Massachusetts: Rereading American Puritanism* (Cambridge, MA: Harvard University Press, 1994). Among surveys of how heaven has been conceived over the centuries in Western religious traditions, see especially Colleen McDannell and Bernhard Lang, *Heaven: A History* (New Haven, CT: Yale University Press, 1988). My discussion of happiness here is limited to the work of colonial-era Protestant religious authorities; for a helpful survey of other traditions during this period, see Jon Butler, *New World Faiths: Religion in Colonial America* (New York: Oxford University Press, 2008).
2. On rhetorical skill, see especially Harry S. Stout, *The New England Soul: Preaching and Religious Culture in Colonial New England* (New York: Oxford University Press, 2012), who describes New England preaching in terms of the five components of classical rhetoric: invention, arrangement, style, delivery, and memory.
3. The centrality of "moral judgment" in eighteenth-century discussions of the "affections" is described in Mark Valeri, "Conversion, Free Will, and the Affections in Eighteenth-Century New England," in *Feeling Godly: Religious Affections and Christian Contact in Early North America*, eds. Caroline Wigginton and Abram Van Engen (Amherst: University of Massachusetts Press, 2021), 29–48.

4. On discursive power, see especially the theoretical background provided in Isaac Ariail Reed, "Power: Relational, Discursive, and Performative Dimensions," *Sociological Theory* 31, 3 (2013), 193–218; and the approaches to discourse developed in M. M. Bakhtin, "Discourse in the Novel," in *The Dialogic Imagination: Four Essays*, eds. Caryl Emerson and Michael Holquist (Austin: University of Texas Press, 1981), 259–42; and Michel Foucault, *The Archeology of Knowledge and the Discourse on Language*, trans. A. M. Sheridan Smith (New York: Pantheon, 1972). See also my discussion in *Religion's Power: What Makes It Work* (New York: Oxford University Press, 2023), 48–103.
5. On the religious authorization of discursive practices, especially with reference to doctrines and beliefs, see Talal Asad, *Genealogies of Religion: Discipline and Reasons of Power in Christianity and Islam* (Baltimore, MD: Johns Hopkins University Press, 1993); although Asad's concern in this work was primarily about the relationship of power to conceptions of truth, his critique of Geertz included Geertz's discussion of religious "moods."
6. This approach follows the work on discursive vocabularies of emotion that has been emphasized by Barbara H. Rosenwein in *Emotional Communities in the Early Middle Ages* (Ithaca, NY: Cornell University Press, 2006) and *Generations of Feeling: A History of Emotions, 400–1700* (Cambridge, UK: Cambridge University Press, 2015).
7. Peter L. Berger, *The Sacred Canopy: Elements of a Sociological Theory of Religion* (Garden City, NY: Doubleday, 1967), 3–28; Gérard Genette, *Narrative Discourse: An Essay in Method*, trans. Jane E. Lewin (Ithaca, NY: Cornell University Press, 1980); Jerome Bruner, *Acts of Meaning* (Cambridge, MA: Harvard University Press, 1990); Thomas DeGloma, *Seeing the Light: The Social Logic of Personal Discovery* (Chicago: University of Chicago Press, 2014); Erin F. Johnston, "'I Was Always This Way...': Rhetorics of Continuity in Narratives of Conversion," *Sociological Forum* 28, 3 (2013), 549–73. Importantly, the role models in these conceptions of narrative usually are not static figures who are depicted as "good" or "bad" characters but are dynamic figures who dramatize the differences between "good" and "bad" by moving across the symbolic boundaries separating the two.
8. The concept of dialogic comparisons is from Bakhtin, *The Dialogical Imagination*; see also Michael Gardiner, "Alterity and Ethics: A Dialogical Perspective," *Theory, Culture, and Society* 13, 2 (1996), 121–143, who relates dialogism to Buber's discussion of "I-It" and "I-Thou" distinctions and Levinas's emphasis on relational meaning as well as Bakhtin; and on the cognitive construction of categories as "schemas," see Roy D'Andrade, *The Development of Cognitive Anthropology* (New York: Cambridge University Press, 1995); Paul DiMaggio, "Culture and Cognition," *Annual Review of Sociology* 23 (1997), 264–87; and Andrei Boutyline and Laura K. Soter, "Cultural Schemas: What They Are, How to Find Them, and What to Do Once You've Caught One," *American Sociological Review* 86, 4 (August 2021), 728–58.
9. In *Communities of Discourse: Ideology and Social Structure in the Reformation, the Enlightenment, and European Socialism* (Cambridge, MA: Harvard University Press, 1989), 13, I discussed discursive fields as symbolic spaces or structures involving an opposition of binary concepts that provides the fundamental categories in which thinking can take place and defines the range of problems that can be addressed.
10. Paul Ricoeur, "The Metaphorical Process as Cognition, Imagination, and Feeling," *Critical Inquiry* 5, 1 (1978), 143–59.
11. See especially the discussions of transgressions across categories and the treatment of metaphors in Mary Douglas, *Purity and Danger: An Analysis of the Concepts of Pollution and Taboo* (New York: Routledge, 1966); George Lakoff and Mark Johnson, *Metaphors We Live By* (Chicago: University of Chicago Press, 1980); and George Lakoff, *Women, Fire, and Dangerous Things* (Chicago: University of Chicago Press, 1987).
12. The symbolic contrasts between that which is unknown and that which is known, such as between heaven and earth, are ones I have discussed at greater length in *The God Problem: Expressing Faith and Being Reasonable* (Berkeley and Los Angeles: University of California Press, 2012).
13. George Whitefield, *The Works of the Reverend George Whitefield* (Edinburgh: Edward and Charles Dilly, 1771), 20, 421; Rosenwein, *Generations of Feeling*, 272, notes that "happiness" as a term relating to heaven and the soul appears to have increasingly been used in place of "felicity" during the seventeenth century.
14. John Locke, *An Essay Concerning Human Understanding* (Oxford, UK: Clarendon Press, 1894 [1689]), 337.

15. Carville V. Earle, "Environment, Disease, and Mortality in Early Virginia," in *The Chesapeake in the Seventeenth Century: Essays on Anglo-American Society*, eds. Thad W. Tate and David L. Ammerman (Chapel Hill: University of North Carolina Press, 1979), 96–122; Edwin J. Perkins, *The Economy of Colonial America*, 2nd ed. (New York: Columbia University Press, 1988).
16. Thomas Haweis, *The Communicant's Spiritual Companion* (London: E. Dilly, 1764), 139.
17. Thomas Haweis, *The Path to Happiness Illustrated and Explained, Being a Concise View of the Genuine Tendency of Christian Principles* (Boston: E. Lincoln, 1802 [1796]), 3.
18. "Some Account of the Conversion and Happy Death of Margaret Carr," *Arminian Magazine* 20 (May 1797), 237–41.
19. "Meditations on the Happiness of Heaven, No. V," *Western Christian Monitor*, May 1, 1816.
20. Jonathan Edwards, *A Faithful Narrative of the Surprising Work of God in the Conversion of Many Hundred Souls in Northampton* (Boston: S. Kneeland, 1738 [1736]), 20.
21. Ebenezer Pemberton, *Sermons on Several Subjects* (Boston: Daniel Henchman, 1738), 18.
22. John Wesley, *Sermons on Several Occasions* (New York: Ezekiel Cooper, 1806), 171.
23. Thomas Brooks, *Heaven on Earth; or, A Serious Discourse Touching a Well-Grounded Assurance of Men's Everlasting Happiness and Blessedness* (London: John Hancock, 1657), 88. Brooks (1608–1680), unlike Thomas Hooker and John Cotton whose views he shared, did not come to America, but his writing circulated widely in the colonies as well as in England.
24. Jonathan Mitchel, *A Discourse of the Glory to Which God Hath Called Believers by Jesus Christ* (Boston: B. Green, 1721), 235.
25. James Janeway, *Heaven Upon Earth; or, the Best Friend in the Worst of Times* (London: Milbourn, 1669), 72–5. Janeway (1636–1674), who preached in London during and after the Black Plague of 1665 and the Great Fire of 1666, and who died of tuberculosis, was considered to have been nearly as influential through his writing as John Bunyan; *Heaven Upon Earth* was distributed widely in North America in editions published in 1710 and 1730, and in an 1847 edition that included an essay about the Janeways and the times in which they lived; it was published again in several twenty-first-century editions, including in 2006 and 2018.
26. Philanthropos, *A Letter to the Unconverted* (New York: James Parker, 1768).
27. William J. Scheick, *Authority and Female Authorship in Colonial America* (Lexington: University Press of Kentucky, 1998), 73.
28. David Brainerd, *An Extract of the Life of the Late Rev. David Brainerd*, ed. John Wesley (London: W. Cock, 1815), 67.
29. James Blair, *Our Saviour's Divine Sermon on the Mount* (London: J. Brotherton, 1740), 140.
30. Max Weber, *The Protestant Ethic and the Spirit of Capitalism*, trans. Talcott Parsons (New York: Charles Scribner's Sons, 1958 [1920]); among the many criticisms of Weber's thesis, several that are particularly relevant to considerations about religion and pleasure are David Little, "Max Weber Revisited: The 'Protestant Ethic' and the Puritan Experience of Order," *Harvard Theological Review* 59, 4 (October 1966), 415–28; Paul Seaver, "The Puritan Work Ethic Revisited," *Journal of British Studies* 19, 2 (Spring 1980), 35–53; Peter Wagner, "Puritan Attitudes towards Physical Recreation in 17th Century New England," *Journal of Sport History* 3, 2 (Summer 1976), 139–51; and C. John Summerville, "The Anti-Puritan Work Ethic," *Journal of British Studies* 20, 2 (Spring 1981), 70–81. A careful reading of the Protestant Ethic and the Spirit of Capitalism suggests that Weber was less interested in early modern Protestantism's disavowal of worldly pleasure as has often been assumed, as he was in the rationally disciplined approach to life that was advanced in the Calvinist traditions; on this point, see especially Philip S. Gorski, *The Disciplinary Revolution: Calvinism and the Rise of the State in Early Modern Europe* (Chicago: University of Chicago Press, 2003).
31. John Shower, *Heaven and Hell, or the Unchangeable State of Happiness or Misery for All Mankind in Another World* (London: Heptinstall, 1700), 183–4.
32. Richard Baxter, *The Saints' Everlasting Rest* (London: Thomas Tegg, 1842 [1650]), 62, 82–6, 187; N. H. Keeble, *Richard Baxter: Puritan Man of Letters* (New York: Oxford University Press, 1982).
33. Jonathan Edwards, *A Treatise on Religious Affections* (New York: Shepard Kollock, 1746), 277–78; among the discussions of Edwards's treatment of religious affections that provide historical context, see especially Ava Chamberlain, "The Grand Sower of the Seed: Jonathan Edwards's Critique of George Whitefield," *New England Quarterly* 70, 3 (September 1997), 368–85; and Wayne Proudfoot, "From Theology to a Science of Religions: Jonathan Edwards and William James on Religious Affections," *Harvard Theological Review* 82, 2 (April 1989), 149–68.

34. This literature is reviewed in Bruce C. Daniels, "Did the Puritans Have Fun? Leisure, Recreation and the Concept of Pleasure in Early New England," *Journal of American Studies* 25, 1 (April 1991), 7–22.
35. "On Religious Joy," *Weekly Amusement* (April 5, 1766), 217.
36. Thomas Watson, *A Body of Practical Divinity Consisting of above One Hundred and Seventy Six Sermons on the Lesser Catechism Composed by the Reverend Assembly of Divines at Westminster* (London: Ingram, Dichman, and Hamilton, 1741), 445.
37. "On the Increase of the Saints in Heaven in Knowledge, Holiness, and Joy," *Methodist Magazine* 22 (May 1799), 247–51; and William Beveridge, *Of the Happiness of the Saints in Heaven* (London: Thomas Speed, 1695), 4–5; the text was a reprint of a sermon preached before the queen at Whitehall on October 12, 1690; Beveridge's influence on Wesley is described in Frank H. Baker, *John Wesley and the Church of England* (London: Epworth Press, 1970), 16.
38. John Rowe, *Heavenly-Mindedness, and Earthly-Mindedness in Two Parts* (London: Francis Tyton, 1672), 104.
39. See also the extended treatment of desire and sensation, which includes a discussion of the facial nerves and muscles involved in laughing and expressing joy, in Cotton Mather, *The Christian Philosopher: A Collection of the Best Discoveries in Nature, with Religious Improvements* (London: Eman. Matthews, 1721).
40. "The Happiness of Heaven," *The Christian's, Scholar's, and Farmer's Magazine* 1, 1 (April/May 1789), 41.
41. Robert C. Fox, "The Character of Mammon in Paradise Lost," *Review of English Studies* 13, 49 (1962), 30–9.
42. Philip Vickers Fithian, *Journal and Letters, 1767–1774* (Carlisle, MA: Applewood Books, 1900), 17.
43. Funeral sermon for Richard Baxter in 1691 by Rev. William Bates, "Some Further Account of the Reverend Richard Baxter," *Piscataqua Evangelical Magazine* 1, 3 (May 1, 1805), 81–3; see also Rev. Willian Tong, *An Account of the Life and Death of Mrs. Elizabeth Bury* (London: Matthews, 1720); deathbed narratives were often evoked from the dying person or the person's loved ones to prove that the person was indeed redeemed; see, e.g., Sarah Rivett, "Tokenography: Narration and the Science of Dying in Puritan Deathbed Testimonies," *Early American Literature* 42, 3 (2007), 471–94; John J. Navin, "'Decrepit in Their Early Youth': English Children in Holland and Plymouth Plantation," in *Children in Colonial America*, ed. James Marten (New York: New York University Press, 2007), 206–26; David E. Stannard, *The Puritan Way of Death: A Study in Religion, Culture, and Social Change* (New York: Oxford University Press, 1977).
44. "Memoir of Mr. Samuel Buell," *Christian's, Scholar's, and Farmer's Magazine* 2, 2 (Jun/Jul 1790), 150–2.
45. "The Believer's Conquest Over Death," *Massachusetts Baptist Missionary Magazine* 2, 4 (December 1808), 119.
46. Solomon Williams, *A Sermon Preached to the First Society in Lebanon on Occasion of the Much Lamented and Untimely Death of Mr. David Trumble* (Boston: J. Draper, 1740).
47. "The Life and Death of Two Young Ladies, Contrasted," *Experienced Christian's Magazine* 1 (January 1797), 175–86, 293–365.
48. Cotton Mather, *Magnalia Christi Americana* (Hartford, CT: Silas Andrus, 1820), 560.
49. Jonathan Edwards, *A Careful and Strict Enquiry into the Modern Prevailing Notions of That Freedom of Will Which Is Supposed to Be Essential to Moral Agency, Virtue and Vice, Reward and Punishment, Praise and Blame* (London: J. Johnson, 1775), 372. Edwards's understanding of divine joy is discussed in Perry Miller, "Jonathan Edwards to Emerson," *New England Quarterly* 13, 4 (December 1940), 589–617. For a wide-ranging treatment of understandings about natural disasters and divine punishment, see also Jan Wim Buisman, *Lightning in the Age of Benjamin Franklin: Facts and Fictions in Science, Religion, and Art* (Leiden: Leiden University Press, 2023), especially pp. 71–110.
50. John R. Knott, "John Foxe and the Joy of Suffering," *Sixteenth Century Journal* 27, 3 (Autumn 1996), 721–34.
51. Hezekiah Butterworth, *The Story of the Hymns; Or, Hymns that Have a History* (New York: American Tract Society, 1875), 118–9.
52. Mark G. Spencer, "Hume's Reception in Eighteenth-Century Philadelphia," *Rivista di Storia della Filosofia* 62, 3 (2007), 287–308. On gloom and melancholy, David Hume, *Dialogues Concerning Natural Religion* (London, 1779), Part XII, 259.

53. Letter from Adam Smith dated November 9, 1776, included in Benjamin Rush, "Contrast between the Death of a Deist and a Christian," *The United States Magazine, A Repository of History, Politics, and Literature* 1 (February 1779), 65–72, reprinted in *The Christian's Magazine* 1, 3 (January 3, 1806), 294–303, and reprinted in *Hume's Reception in Early America*, ed. Mark G. Spencer (New York: Bloomsbury Academic, 2017), 479–88.
54. George Horne, *Letters on Infidelity* (London: Clarendon Press, 1786), 24.
55. John Mitchell Mason, "Remarks on the Accounts of the Death of David Hume, Esq and Samuel Finley D.D.," *Christian's Magazine* 1, 4 (January 4, 1806), 419–28.
56. "Some Remarks on the Nature, Causes, Dangerous Errors, and Infectious Spread of the Present Religious Enthusiasm in America," *The United States Magazine* (October 1779), 411.
57. "Authentic Narrative: Of a Conversion from Deism," *New York Missionary Magazine* (April 1, 1803), 130.
58. David E. Stannard, *The Puritan Way of Death: A Study in Religion, Culture, and Social Change* (New York: Oxford University Press, 1977); see also the deathbed narrative of Sarah Prince in George M. Marsden, *Jonathan Edwards: A Life* (New Haven, CT: Yale University Press, 2003), 496–7.
59. "Biography: A Brief Account of the Conversion, Experience, and Death of Miss Patty Long," *Massachusetts Baptist Missionary Magazine* 1, 5 (September 1805), 157.
60. Bruce C. Daniels, "Sober Mirth and Pleasant Poisons: Puritan Ambivalence toward Leisure and Recreation in Colonial New England," *American Studies* 34, 1 (Spring 1993), 121–37.
61. Gilbert Tennent, *Twenty Three Sermons upon the Chief End of Man* (Philadelphia: William Bradford, 1743), 15, 19, 104, 134.
62. John Norton, *Memoir of John Cotton* (New York: Saxton & Miles, 1842), 92.
63. Clement Elis, *The Summe of Christianity* (London: Rogers, 1699); the relationship of godly living and happiness shifted over the years to one about moral living and happiness, which was supported in social psychology experiments showing that hypothetical persons who were described as living moral lives were perceived to be happier than persons leading dissolute lives; Jonathan Phillips et al., "True Happiness: The Role of Morality in the Folk Concept of Happiness," *Journal of Experimental Psychology* 146, 2 (2017), 165–81; these results were considered by the study's authors to contradict the view that happiness could be experienced just as well by someone who had just committed murder, e.g., as argued in Daniel Gilbert, *Stumbling on Happiness* (New York: Vintage Books, 2006), 36–7.
64. Matthew P. Brown, *The Pilgrim and the Bee: Reading Rituals and Book Culture in Early New England* (Philadelphia: University of Pennsylvania Press, 2007); Hambrick-Stowe, *The Practice of Piety*; Stephen Kahlberg, *Max Weber's Comparative-Historical Sociology* Today (Chicago: University of Chicago Press, 1994), 200, argues that "respectable demeanor" was one of the lasting legacies of early American asceticism.
65. John Wesley, *The Works of the Reverend John Wesley*, vol. 2 (New York: Emory and Waugh, 1831), 512; Benjamin Franklin, whose theology was different from Wesley's, nevertheless expressed a somewhat similar view: "As I should be happy to have so wise, good and powerful a Being my Friend, let me consider in what manner I shall make myself most acceptable to him. Next to the praise due to his wisdom, I believe he is pleased and delights in the happiness of those he has created; and since without virtue man can have no happiness in this world, I firmly believe he delights to see me virtuous, because he is pleased when he sees me happy." Benjamin Franklin, "Articles of Belief and Acts of Religion, 20 November 1728," www.founders.archives.gov.
66. Wesley, Works, 230.
67. Bernard Capp, "'Jesus Wept' but Did the Englishman? Masculinity and Emotion in Early Modern England," *Past & Present* 224 (August 2014), 75–108, quote on page 87.
68. "Authentic Narrative of a Conversion from Deism," *New York Missionary Magazine* (April 1, 1803), 130.
69. Elizabeth Bury (1644–1720), as quoted in William Tong, *An Account of the Life and Death of Mrs. Elizabeth Bury* (London: J. Penn, 1720), 103–4.
70. "Memoirs of the Life of the Rev. William Burkitt," *The Experienced Christian's Magazine* 1 (December 1796), 233.
71. Cotton Mather, *Diary of Cotton Mather, 1681–1724* (Boston: Massachusetts Historical Society, 1911), 515.
72. Francis Asbury, *Journal of Rev. Francis Asbury* (New York: Eaton and Maine, 1800), 258.
73. Valeri, "Conversion, Free Will, and the Affections in Eighteenth-Century New England," 41.

74. Gilbert Tennent, *The Necessity of Religious Violence in Order to Obtain Durable Happiness* (New York: William Bradford, 1735), 19–20, 27, 36, 43.
75. William Throop, *A Sermon Occasioned by the Unspeakable Loss in the Death and Delivered at the Funeral of Brinley Sylvester, Esq.* (Boston: William Throop, 1753); Ambrose Clancy, "1700s-Era Document Sheds New Light on Island History," *Shelter Island Reporter*, October 10, 2021; Epher Whitaker, *History of Southold, L.I.: Its First Century* (Southold, NY: Orange Chronicle, 1881), 260.
76. Charles Chauncy, *Seasonable Thoughts on Religion in New England: A Treatise in Five* Parts (Bedford, MA: Applewood Books, 1743), 126; Charles Chauncy, "Enthusiasm Described and Caution'd Against. A Sermon Preach'd at the Old Brick Meeting-House in Boston, the Lord's Day after the Commencement, 1742," Evans Early American Imprint Collection, quod.lib.umich.edu. Chauncy (1705–1787) was educated at Harvard, ordained in 1727 as a Congregationalist minister, and was a leading critic of George Whitefield and the "enthusiasm" of the Great Awakening.
77. Zabdiel Adams, "The Nature, Pleasure and Advantages of Church Musick. A Sermon Preached at a Lecture in the First Parish of Lancaster, on Thursday April 4, 1771," Evans Early American Imprint Collection, quod.lib.umich.edu. Zabdiel Adams (1739–1801) was educated at Harvard, ordained in 1764 and served as a minister in Lunenburg, Massachusetts.
78. David W. Music, "The Early Reception of Isaac Watts's Psalms of David Imitated," *The Hymn* 69, 4 (Autumn 2018), 14–20; Christopher N. Phillips, "Cotton Mather Brings Isaac Watts's Hymns to America; or, How to Perform a Hymn without Singing It," *New England Quarterly* 85, 2 (June 2012), 203–21. Although it has been argued that the popularity of Watts's hymns possibly reflected a more optimistic cultural ethos, a close analysis of Watts's own theology concluded that he believed that true joy could be realized only in heaven, and thus by dying, even though he urged Christians to be joyful anyway; Louise Joy, "Morbid Pathos in Isaac Watts' Philosophy of Affectionate Religion," *Literature and Theology* 27, 3 (September 2013), 297–312.
79. Isaac Watts, *Hymns and Spiritual Songs in Three Books* (London: Thomas and John Fleet, 1772), 6. Isaac Watts (1674–1748) composed more than 600 hymns, including the perennial favorite "Joy to the World" in 1719. Rochelle A. Stackhouse, "Isaac Watts: Composer of Psalms and Hymns," in *Hymns and Hymnody: Historical and Theological Introductions, Vol. II: From Catholic Europe to Protestant Europe*, eds. Mark A. Lamport, Benjamin K. Forrest, and Vernon M. Whaley (London: Lutterworth Press, 2019), 197–209.
80. E.g., one of the more popular guidebooks was Haweis, *The Path to Happiness Illustrated and Explained.*
81. The associations among piety, virtue, and "public happiness" have been extensively examined in works such as Jeffrey Rosen, *The Pursuit of Happiness: How Classical Writers on Virtue Inspired the Lives of the Founders and Defined America* (New York: Simon and Schuster, 2024); Andrew Burstein and Nancy Isenberg, *Madison and Jefferson* (New York: Random House, 2010); Eric R. Schlereth, *An Age of Infidels: The Politics of Religious Controversy in the Early United States* (Philadelphia: University of Pennsylvania Press, 2013); and Jeffrey H. Morrison, *John Witherspoon and the Founding of the American Republic: Catholicism in American Culture* (Notre Dame: University of Notre Dame Press, 2005).
82. Reverend George Horne, "The Blessing of a Cheerful Heart," *Arminian Magazine* 19 (July 1796), 352–8.
83. Percival Stockdale, *Thirteen Sermons to Seamen Preached on Board of His Majesty's Ship, Leander, in the Bay of Gibraltar* (London: J. Deighton, 1791), 233.
84. Thomas Nettleton, *A Treatise on Virtue and Happiness* (Glasgow: R. Urie, 1759), 163.
85. James S. Lambert, "'Raised unto a Cheareful and Lively Beleeving': The 1587–90 Diary of the Puritan Richard Rogers and Writing into Joy," *Studies in Philology* 113, 2 (Spring 2016), 254–81.
86. Alec Ryrie, *Being Protestant in Reformation Britain* (New York: Oxford University Press, 2013), 311; similar arguments about the importance of diary writing are included in Tom Webster, "Writing to Redundancy: Approaches to Spiritual Journals and Early Modern Spirituality," *Historical Journal* 39 (1996), 33–56; and Andrew Cambers, *Godly Reading: Print, Manuscript and Puritanism in England, 1580–1720* (Cambridge, UK: Cambridge University Press, 2011). Paul S. Seaver, *Wallington's World: A Puritan Artisan in Seventeenth Century London* (Stanford: Stanford University Press, 1985) is a fascinating account of Puritans' emotional struggles and expectations of heavenly joy drawn from Nehemiah Wallington's extensive journaling.

87. Elizabeth Griffith, "On Temper, as It respects the Happiness of the Married State," *Massachusetts Magazine* 6, 6 (June 1794), 346.
88. "Mirth, Cheerfulness," *Massachusetts Sentinel*, August 14, 1784.
89. Hugh Blair, *Sermons* (New York: Harper, 1826 [1777]), 129, 624.

Chapter 2

1. On situations and emotional practice, John F. Rauthmann et al., "The Situational Eight DIAMONDS: A Taxonomy of Major Dimensions of Situation Characteristics," *Journal of Personality and Social Psychology* 107, 4 (2014), 677–718; see also John F. Rauthmann, Ryne A. Sherman, and David C. Funder, "Principles of Situation Research: Towards a Better Understanding of Psychological Situations," *European Journal of Personality* 29 (2015), 363–81; and David Diehl and Daniel McFarland, "Toward a Historical Sociology of Social Situations," *American Journal of Sociology* 115, 6 (May 2010), 1713–52, who focus on cognitive framing in situations; on spaces, Thomas F. Gieryn, "A Space for Place in Sociology," *Annual Review of Sociology* 26 (2000), 463–96; Ng, "The Problem of *Place*," 185–204; on situated power, Mary C. Murphy, Claude M. Steele, and James J. Gross, "Signaling Threat: How Situational Cues Affect Women in Math, Science, and Engineering Settings," *Psychological Science* 18, 10 (2015), 879–85; on affordances, Tia DeNora, *Music in Everyday Life* (Cambridge: Cambridge University Press, 2000). My work on situations and feelings in found in *What Happens When We Practice Religion: Textures of Devotion in Everyday Life* (Princeton, NJ: Princeton University Press, 2020), 42–76; and on religion's institutional power in the management of time and space, *Religion's Power: What Makes It Work* (New York: Oxford University Press, 2023), 106–18.
2. Randall Collins, "Interaction Ritual Chains and Collective Effervescence," in *Collective Emotions: Perspectives from Psychology, Philosophy and Sociology*, eds. Christian von Scheve and Mikko Salmela (New York: Oxford University Press, 2014), 299–311, quote on page 300; see also Randall Collins, *Interaction Ritual Chains* (Princeton, NJ: Princeton University Press, 2004), 48–50.
3. Daniel W. Stowell, "Murder at a Methodist Camp Meeting: The Origins of Abraham Lincoln's Most Famous Trial," *Journal of the Illinois State Historical Society* 101, 3/4 (Fall-Winter 2008), 219–34; Robert Bray, "Abraham Lincoln and the Two Peters," *Journal of the Abraham Lincoln Association* 22, 2 (Summer 2001), 27–48; Mark Twain's reference to a camp meeting appears in *The Adventures of Huckleberry Finn* and in the March 4, 1866, note titled "The New Wildcat Religion," online at twainquotes.com; whether Nat Turner's insurrection was inspired by a camp meeting or enabled by White Southerners being away at a camp meeting has been discussed in John W. Cromwell, "The Aftermath of Nat Turner's Insurrection," *Journal of Negro History* 5, 2 (April 1920), 208–34; Makungu M. Akinyela, "Battling the Serpent: Nat Turner, Africanized Christianity, and a Black Ethos," *Journal of Black Studies* 33, 3 (January 2003), 255–80; and Charles F. Irons, *The Origins of Proslavery Christianity: White and Black Evangelicals in Colonial and Antebellum Virginia* (Chapel Hill: University of North Carolina Press, 2008), 133–68.
4. Among the many informative studies of camp meetings, the ones I have found most helpful include Charles A. Johnson, *Frontier Camp Meeting: Religion's Harvest Time* (Dallas: Southern Methodist University Press, 1955); Kenneth O. Brown, *Holy Ground: A Study of the American Camp Meeting* (New York: Garland, 1992); Ellen Eslinger, *Citizens of Zion: The Social Origins of Camp Meeting Revivalism* (Knoxville: University of Tennessee Press, 1999); Randall Balmer, *Mine Eyes Have Seen the Glory: A Journey into the Evangelical Subculture in America* (New York: Oxford University Press, 2014 [1989]), 226–45; Walter Brownlow Posey, *Frontier Mission: A History of Religion West of the Southern Appalachians to 1861* (Knoxville: University Press of Kentucky, 1966), 22–40; Jonathan Cooney, "The Shout Heard 'Round the World: Similarities and Differences between American and English Camp Meetings," *Methodist History* 50, 1 (October 2011), 40–53; Russell E. Richey, "From Quarterly to Camp Meeting: A Reconsideration of Early American Methodism," *Methodist History* 23, 1 (July, 1985): 199–207; Roger Robins, "Vernacular American Landscape: Methodists, Camp Meetings, and Social Respectability," *Religion and American Culture* 4, 2 (Summer 1994), 165–91; Samuel Avery-Quinn, *Cities of Zion: The Holiness Movement and Methodist Camp Meeting Towns in America* (Lanham, MD: Lexington Books, 2019); and Taves, *Fits, Trances, and Visions*, 104–34. The literature on camp meetings is rich in descriptive information and in relating camp meetings to theological questions about revivalism; my aim here is to say more about the roles of social interaction, the management of camp meetings, and happiness.

5. Some writers argue that joy is fundamentally different from happiness, not merely in how the words are commonly used but also in their neurobiological manifestations—a point that may be true in terms of the intensity of arousal and the cognitive frameworks used to interpret the feelings; however, camp meeting leaders and participants spoke about both joy and happiness (and gladness) and often used the terms interchangeably. On the overlap of joy and happiness, see also this statistical study in which there was a .85 correlation in respondents' use of the terms, Fleir J.M. Laros and Jan-Benedict E. M. Steenkamp, "Emotions in Consumer Behavior: A Hierarchical Approach," *Journal of Business Research* 58, 10 (October 2005), 1437–45.
6. Rosenwein, *Emotional Communities in the Early Middle Ages*.
7. John H. Wigger, *Taking Heaven by Storm: Methodism and the Rise of Popular Christianity in America* (New York: Oxford University Press, 1998), 97, argues that camp meetings were "readily adaptable to existing Methodist style and practice," building especially on Methodists' quarterly meetings (and sometimes held in place of or in conjunction with quarterly meetings) that brought clergy and local pastors together, included preaching services, and provided time for fraternizing; the camp meetings, in which much larger numbers of people, mostly nonclergy, participated, then, followed the same pattern of organizing services.
8. The will of John Childs (1770–1829), dated March 7, 1829, included a 40-acre tract to be sold to pay his debts and listed the names of his eight children; "Slave Manumissions in Alexandria Land Records, 1790–1863," freedmenscemetery.org, shows John Childs having enslaved at least five adults and nine children; several of the adults were old enough that they may have attended the 1807 camp meeting on Childs' farm. Childs' wife, Margaret Adams, was the daughter of Methodist minister Reverend Wesley Adams; the Childs' son, John Wesley Childs (1800–1850) was also a minister and became a prominent leader of the Methodist Episcopal Church South when the denomination split in 1844 over slavery; John Ellis Edwards, *Life of Rev. John Wesley Childs* (Richmond, VA: John Early, 1862).
9. A Spectator, "Communication," *Alexandria Daily Advertiser*, August 22, 1807; the writer did not indicate that Childs was a minister and that Childs may have preached but did say that several ministers preached, which was customary at camp meetings; Edwards, *Life of Rev. John Wesley Childs*, indicates that the younger Childs was converted at a camp meeting and was engaged in preaching at camp meetings by about 1822.
10. Ibid. David Richard Kasserman, *Fall River Outrage: Life, Murder, and Justice in Early Industrial New England* (Philadelphia: University of Pennsylvania Press, 1986), 41, notes that religious authorities considered camp meetings' remote settings advantageous because "spiritual conversion was more easily attained in an environment in which individuals were removed from all contact with their usual lives."
11. An 1809 sketch by Benjamin Henry Latrobe reproduced in Wigger, *Taking Heaven by Storm*, 95, shows a camp meeting laid out in a semicircle near a wooded stream with approximately a hundred tents arranged in two half circles, about fifteen rows of benches, a center aisle, and a preaching platform.
12. Anna Vemer Andrzejewski, "The Gazes of Hierarchy at Religious Camp Meetings, 1850–1925," *Perspectives in Vernacular Architecture* 8 (2000), 138–57.
13. "Camp Meeting," *New York Evangelist*, September 13, 1834; curiosity as the reason people attended camp meetings resembles arguments in the social science literature about attendance at twenty-first century revival meetings; see, e.g., Mikko Heimola, "Threats of Hellfire and Jumping for Heavenly Joy: Manifest Emotionalism as a Solution to the Problem of Machiavellian Hypocrites in Religious Revivals," *Method & Theory in the Study of Religion* 26, 4/5 (2014), 508–32; as Heimola suggests, though, people who attended only from curiosity were likely to be regarded as hypocrites, which suggests that they may have had a disincentive to attend at all, unless there were other incentives, one of which was undoubtedly to feel that they were among the redeemed, even if they did not experience exuberant emotion, and another of which was apparently the pleasure of mingling with friends and neighbors.
14. Frederick Douglass, *My Bondage and My Freedom* (New York: Miller, Orton & Mulligan, 1855), 193–94.
15. Cynthia Lynn Lyerly, *Methodism and the Southern Mind, 1770–1810* (New York: Oxford University Press, 1998), 62, reports an account of an instance in which an enslaver in Kentucky "took a 'wagonful' of slaves to a camp meeting and they 'rofessedly converted.' Once home, however, 'finding their lives by no means a practical comment upon the Scriptures which he daily

read for their instruction, he watched the opportunity for sending them all to another camp meeting to be converted over again.'"

16. Jarena Lee, *Religious Experience and Journal of Mrs. Jarena Lee, Giving an Account of her Call to Preach the Gospel* (Philadelphia: Jarena Lee, 1849), 27; Sojourner Truth, *Narrative of Sojourner Truth: A Northern Slave* (New York: Sojourner Truth, 1853), 115–19.
17. "News Article," *Vermont Chronicle*, October 18, 1833.
18. Emily P. Burke, *Reminiscences of Georgia* (Oberlin, OH: J. M. Fitch, 1852), 241.
19. Letter from Rev. George Addison Baxter to Rev. Dr. Archibald Alexander, reprinted in William W. Woodward, "Surprising Accounts of the Revival of Religion in the United States of America," *American Review and Literary Journal* 2, 2 (April 1802), 156–58, also published in William Wallis Woodward, *Increase of Piety, or the Revival of Religion in the United States of America* (Philadelphia: Woodward, 1802), 56–66, and in religious periodicals of the day such as the *Connecticut Evangelical Magazine*. George Addison Baxter (1771–1841) was a Presbyterian minister; Archibald Alexander (1772–1851), also a Presbyterian, was president of Hampden-Sydney College at the time of the letter from Baxter and from 1812 to 1851 was president of Princeton Theological Seminary. The letter was written at the time when Presbyterian leaders were divided about the "enthusiasm" evident in revival meetings and thus reflected Baxter's effort to show that the meeting was both orderly and beneficial to those participating. The historiography that has depended almost exclusively on Baxter's letter has rarely questioned the claim that 20,000 people participated. Participation was undoubtedly furthered by the popularity of the main preacher involved and may have been facilitated by the Cane Ridge Meeting House's location only a few miles from the road connecting Lexington and Cincinnati. However, other aspects of the location and of Baxter's account suggest that the number was probably inflated: the letter does not state that 20,000 were actually present, instead that "It is generally supposed that at many places, there were not less than eight, ten, or twelve thousand people. At one place called Cane Ridge meeting house, many are of opinion there were not less than twenty thousand"; the letter also states that "an hundred and forty wagons [came] loaded with people," which implies either that each wagon on average was impossibly loaded with 143 people or that vast numbers came on foot. A subsequent letter from Baxter to Alexander (April 25, 1833) did not mention the 20,000 claim but addressed questions about the bodily movements that appeared to have been a "mysterious disease" among some of the participants at revival meetings (blog.richmond.edu).
20. "Camp Meeting," Connecticut Courier, August 24, 1825; reprinted from *The Friendly Visitor*, August 12, 1825; included in *The Friendly Visitor: Being a Collection of Select and Original Pieces, Instructive and Entertaining* (New York: J. C. Totten, 1825), 263.
21. Albert Raboteau, *Slave Religion: The Invisible Institution in the Antebellum South* (New York: Oxford University Press, 2004), 223–24.
22. Harriet Beecher Stowe, *Dred: A Tale of the Great Dismal Swamp*, ed. Judie Newman (Edinburgh: Edinburgh University Press, 1992 [1856]), 314–49.
23. *Report of the Trial of the Rev. Ephraim K. Avery, Methodist Minister, for the Murder of Sarah Maria Cornell* (New York: W. Stodart, 1833); the case is described in detail in Kasserman, *Fall River Outrage*, who notes the role of Sarah's friendships.
24. Opportunities for socializing at camp meetings were likely to have been especially appealing to rural women who otherwise had few occasions for socializing; see, e.g., Lyerly, *Methodism and the Southern Mind*, 116.
25. "Revival in Dunkirk, N.Y." *Boston Recorder*, October 9, 1833.
26. Riley B. Case, *Faith and Fury: Eli Farmer on the Frontier, 1794–1881* (Indianapolis, IN: Indiana Historical Society, 2018), 71.
27. Rev. H. Vincent, *A History of the Wesleyan Grove, Martha's Vineyard, Camp Meeting* (Boston: Geo. C. Rand & Avery, 1858), 60.
28. "Camp Meeting," *Connecticut Courant*, September 4, 1826.
29. David Hempton, *Methodism: Empire of the Spirit* (New Haven: Yale University Press, 2005), 97, as reported by Catharine Williams, *Fall River: An Authentic Narrative*, ed. Patricia Caldwell (New York: Oxford University Press, 1993).
30. "The Revival Meeting or The Rioters Routed," *Boston Investigator*, April 8, 1840, was a fictional account of a Methodist meeting at which a young gentleman was threatened with expulsion by the police for apparently smiling too much rather than taking the event seriously; he explained to the sexton in charge, "I am an observer of human nature and I am either delighted or astonished when I witness any exhibition of nature which transcends my previous conceptions."
31. William Ellery Channing, "On Music," reprinted in *Weekly Messenger*, August 15, 1838.

32. The phrase "getting happy" was used by Black and White participants alike, possibly more often by the former, and was employed by critics as a way of suggesting that those who experienced it were moved by passion rather than by understanding and were possibly hypocritical or shallow in their convictions.
33. "Revival of Religion," *Merrimack Gazette*, October 1, 1803.
34. "The Camp Meeting," *Washington Federalist* [Georgetown, DC], April 30, 1804.
35. "The Camp Meeting," *Savannah Evening Ledger*, October 15, 1811.
36. Lorenzo Dow, *The Life, Travels, Labors, and Writings of Lorenzo Dow* (New York: C. M. Saxton, 1859).
37. A first-person account of the Cane Ridge revival by another Presbyterian minister also mentioned people falling down but said nothing about crying out or ecstasy; Rev. John Evans Finley, "Dear Uncle," *Philadelphia Gazette*, February 24, 1802.
38. "Raleigh, NC," *Cumberland Register* [Carlisle, PA], October 29, 1805.
39. "The History of the 'Jirks,'" *New York Telescope*, 2, 38 (February 18, 1826), 150–51.
40. Zilpha Elaw, *Memoirs of the Life, Religious Experience, Ministerial Travels and Labors of Mrs. Zilpha Elaw, an American Female of Color* (London: Zilpha Elaw, 1846), 22–23.
41. "Presbyterian Camp Meetings," *Philadelphian*, January 29, 1830.
42. Taves, *Fits, Trances, and Visions*, 100–2.
43. Dickson D. Bruce Jr., *And They All Sang Hallelujah: Plain-Folk Camp-Meeting Religion, 1800–1845* (Knoxville: University of Tennessee Press, 1974), 5.
44. Rev. B. W. Gorham, *Camp Meeting Manual, a Practical Book for the Camp Ground* (Boston: H.V. Degen, 1854), 52–4.
45. "Camp Meeting at Haverhill, N.H.," *Zion's Herald*, July 4, 1827.
46. See the concerns about insanity, fanaticism, suicide, and financial abuse in "Discontinuance of the Protracted Meeting," *New York Herald*, May 3, 1841; and "West Cambridge Affairs," *Trumpet and Universalist Magazine*, September 10, 1842.
47. "Troubles in New Bedford," *Trumpet and Universalist Magazine*, September 24, 1842.
48. "Protracted Meeting in Illinois," *Christian Watchman*, February 24, 1843.
49. "Camp Meeting Scenes—Who Are Responsible?" *Christian Intelligencer*, October 16, 1845.
50. Some evidence suggests that religious authorities were especially concerned when the spirit moved a person to speak who was poor, a woman, or Black; see, e.g., Philip N. Mulder, *A Controversial Spirit: Evangelical Awakenings in the South* (New York: Oxford University Press, 2002). An ethnographic study that describes these challenges to authority in another context is Meredith B. McGuire, *Pentecostal Catholics: Power, Charisma, and Order in a Religious Movement* (Philadelphia: Temple University Press, 1982).
51. "Camp Meeting at Shiloh," *New Hampshire Observer* [Concord, NH], October 19, 1833.
52. "Father Boehm's Memories of a Hundred Years," *The Methodist*, January 23, 1875; see also Erika K. R. Stalcup, "The Wesleys: Charles and John," in *Hymns and Hymnody: Historical and Theological Introductions*, eds. Mark A. Lamport, Benjamin K. Forrest, and Vernon M. Whaley (London: Lutterworth Press, 2019), 210–25.
53. Chris Armstrong, "'Wrestling Jacob': The Central Struggle and Emotional Scripts of Camp-Meeting Holiness Hymnody," in *Singing the Lord's Song in a Strange Land: Hymnody in the History of North American Protestantism*, eds. Edith L. Blumhofer and Mark A. Noll (Tuscaloosa: University of Alabama Press, 2004), 171–95.
54. "Revival Efforts," *Christian Herald*, December 8, 1842.
55. Charles G. Finney, *Lectures on Revivals of Religion* (New York: Leavitt, Lord & Co., 1835), 370.
56. "Family Piety," *Christian Intelligencer*, December 28, 1839.
57. "Religious Enjoyment," *Boston Recorder*, July 15, 1836.
58. Balmer, *Mine Eyes Have Seen the Glory*, 226, noted that one incomplete list compiled in 1987 included 114 camp meetings. The Asbury Camp Meeting in Hamilton, Massachusetts, and the Ocean Grove Camp Meeting in Ocean Grove, New Jersey, were among several of the early associations that were in operation in the twenty-first century. The history of the Ocean Grove Camp Meeting is described in Troy Messenger, *Holy Leisure: Recreation and Religion in God's Square Mile* (Minneapolis: University of Minnesota Press, 1999).
59. Vincent, *A History of the Wesleyan Grove*, 202–4.
60. Rev. A. C. Rose, "Camp Meetings," *Northeastern Christian Advocate*, August 27, 1858.
61. "Camp Meeting and Revivals," *Zion's Herald*, December 20, 1826.
62. "Holston Annual Conference," *Zion's Herald*, February 2, 1825.

63. Henty M. Field, "A New Measure or Two," *The Evangelist*, October 24, 1861; a New York Presbyterian minister, Rev. Field, asserted that the enthusiasm at revival meetings was waning and that Wednesday evening prayer meetings were so poorly attended that a leader could fire a pistol through the room in almost any direction without hitting anyone; "church sociables" held once a month, he believed, could be a remedy. Church socials, as they were more commonly named, grew in popularity over the next half century, usually meeting on a weekday evening from about 7 p.m. to 10 p.m. and including refreshments or a light supper, entertainment, and time for informal conversation. Catharine Beecher, Henry Ward Beecher, Mark Twain, Edith Wharton, Willa Cather, William Dean Howells, L. Frank Baum, and Edna Ferber all wrote about them. Brief mention of church sociables also appears in such academic works as Christian O. Paiz, *The Strikers of Coachella: Rank-and-File History of the UFW Movement* (Chapel Hill: University of North Carolina Press, 2023); John Strangeland and Aline MacMahon, *Hollywood, the Blacklist, and the Birth of Method Acting* (Knoxville: University Press of Kentucky, 2022); Daniel E. Sutherland, *Expansion of Everyday Life, 1860–1876* (Little Rock: University of Arkansas Press, 1889); and Lynne Marks, *Revivals and Roller Rinks: Religion, Leisure, and Identity in Late-Nineteenth-Century Small-Town* Ontario (Toronto: University of Toronto Press, 1996).
64. Julie Wilhelm, "'All the Fervor of a Camp Meeting': Race and Revivalism in Uncle Tom's Cabin," *Papers on Language and Literature* 56, 2 (Spring 2020), 107–39.
65. Raboteau, *Slave Religion*, 59–68, 129–33, quote on page 225; Melville J. Herskovits, *The Myth of the Negro Past* (Boston: Beacon Press, 1958). Erika Bourguignon, "Ritual Dissociation and Possession Belief in Caribbean Negro Religion," in *Afro-American Anthropology: Contemporary Perspectives on Theory and Research*, eds. Norman E. Whitten and John F. Szwed (New York: Free Press, 1970), 88; on enslavement and happiness, see especially the debate in the Virginia House of Delegates in the wake of Nat Turner's rebellion, Erik S. Root, *Sons of the Fathers: The Virginia Slavery Debates of 1831–32* (New York: Lexington Books, 2010), which acknowledged in passing that happiness and slavery were incompatible.

Chapter 3

1. John Brand, *Observations on Popular Antiquities, Chiefly Illustrating the Origin of Our Vulgar Customs, Ceremonies, and Superstitions* (London: J. Johnson, 1777); quote on page 129 of the 1841 edition, edited by Henry Ellis (London: Charles Knight, 1841).
2. Weber, *The Protestant Ethic and the Spirit of Capitalism*, 113.
3. The phrase "regulated improvisation" is from Pierre Bourdieu, *Outline of a Theory of Practice* (New York: Cambridge University Press, 1977), 21, which refers to situational adaptations within the constraints of social norms and asymmetries of power; on improvisation, see George E. Lewis and Benjamin Piekut, eds., *The Oxford Handbook of Critical Improvisation Studies, 2 vols.* (New York: Oxford University Press, 2016); on ceremonial events, see Molly Farneth, *The Politics of Ritual* (Princeton, NJ: Princeton University Press, 2023); on festival studies, see Judith Mair, ed., *The Routledge Handbook of Festivals* (New York: Routledge, 2018).
4. Studies of the "commercialization" of emotions, such as Hochschild, *The Managed Heart*, e.g., emphasize the influence of a single, centralized authority, such as the airline company for whom flight attendants work; yet authority in those instances is also dispersed, as studies such as Wingfield, "The (Un) Managed Heart," 197–212, and Julia Cooke, *Come Fly the World* (New York: Mariner Books, 2022), have shown. Similarly, in religious contexts, authority may be formally exercised by the patriarchal hierarchy, but studies of gendered relationships have consistently emphasized ways in which patriarchal authority is transgressed; e.g., see Candace West and Don H. Zimmerman, "Doing Gender," *Gender and Society* 1, 2 (June 1987), 125–51; Kelly H. Chong, "Negotiating Patriarchy: South Korean Evangelical Women and the Politics of Gender," *Gender and Society* 20, 6 (2006), 697–724; and R. Marie Griffith, *God's Daughters: Evangelical Women and the Power of Submission* (Berkeley and Los Angeles: University of California Press, 1997).
5. The historiography of ladies' fairs is sparse, but see Colleen McDannell, "Going to the Ladies' Fair: Irish Catholics in New York City, 1870–1900," in *The New York Irish*, eds. Ronald H. Bayor and Timothy J. Meagher (Baltimore: Johns Hopkins University Press, 1997), 234–51.
6. John Adams to Abigail Adams, July 3, 1776, quoted in J. Patrick Mullins, "Yankee Continentalism: The Provincial Roots of John Adams's Vision for American Union, 1775–1776," in *Revolutionary Prophecies: The Founders and America's Future*, eds. Robert M. S. McDonald

and Peter S. Onuf (Charlottesville: University of Virginia Press, 2021), 51; "The Village Fair," *The European Magazine and London Review* 49 (May 1806), 375, author identified only as JML.

7. Carolyn J. Lawes, *Women and Reform in a New England Community, 1815–1860* (Lexington: University Press of Kentucky, 2000), 47.
8. "Ladies' Sewing Societies and Charity Fairs," *Philadelphia Recorder*, January 16, 1830.
9. Silas B. Howe, "An Address," *Zion's Herald* [Boston, MA], August 3, 1825.
10. "Communication," *Alexandria Gazette*, June 28, 1826.
11. "Ladies' Fair," *Daily National Journal* [Washington, DC], April 20, 1827.
12. "Editor," *Republican Star and General Advertiser* [Easton, MD], October 9, 1827.
13. "Fair to Be Held Today," *Daily National Intelligencer* [Washington, DC], December 28, 1827.
14. "Ladies' Fair at Washington," *Hampshire Gazette* [Northampton, MA], January 16, 1828.
15. "The Ladies Fair," *Philadelphia Inquirer*, October 31, 1829, reprinted from the *Baltimore Republican.*
16. "Poetry," *The Fredonian* [New Brunswick, NJ], March 11, 1829, reprinted from the *Virginia Free Press.*
17. "Ladies' Fairs," *Boston Recorder*, May 23, 1832.
18. "Ladies' Sewing Societies and Charity Fairs," *Philadelphia Recorder*, January 16, 1830.
19. "Miscellany: Ladies' Fairs," *Boston Recorder*, May 2, 1832.
20. Henry P. Phelps, *Story of the Albany Orphan Asylum* (Albany, NY: Albany Engraving Company, 1893), 25.
21. William H. Seward, *Autobiography* (New York: Appleton, 1877), 430.
22. Kelly Hays, "Boston Furnituremakers and the New Social Media, 1830–1860," in *Boston Furniture, 1700–1900*, eds. Jobe Brock, Gerald W. R. Ward, and Lynn McCarthy (Charlottesville: University of Virginia Press, 2016), 335–49.
23. "Ladies' Fair," *Salem Gazette* [Salem, MA], April 26, 1933.
24. "Monument Fair," *Bellows Falls Gazette* [Bellows Falls, VT], September 19, 1840.
25. Timothy Shay Arthur, "The Ladies' Fair," *Philadelphia Saturday Courier* (1842) reprinted in *The Rural Repository*, April 9, 1842.
26. "Ladies' Fairs," *Weekly Messenger*, November 29, 1843.
27. "New York Ladies' Fancy Fairs," *New York Herald*, December 23, 1858; "Strawberry Festival," *Daily Missouri Republican*, May 16, 1859.
28. "Baby Show," *New York Herald*, February 27, 1854.
29. "The Baby Show," *New York Times*, June 6, 1855.
30. "California Gossip," *New York Times*, January 10, 1860.
31. "Church Gambling," *Boston Investigator*, April 23, 1845.
32. "Anti-Slavery Fair," *The Liberator*, December 20, 1834.
33. "A British Nobleman in America," *Baltimore Sun*, January 6, 1851.
34. Maria Weston Chapman, "The Twelfth Massachusetts Anti-Slavery Fair," *The Liberator*, August 29, 1845.
35. "Anti-Slavery Fairs," *National Anti-Slavery Standard*, December 1, 1855.
36. "Letter from Fairfax County," *Alexandria Gazette*, December 1, 1859.
37. "Doesticks Attends a Charitable Fair," *Plattsburgh Republican*, March 10, 1855.
38. "Adventures with Fair Ladies," *Columbus Gazette*, January 13, 1860.
39. "Ladies' Fair at Aiken," *Charleston Tri-Weekly Courier*, November 5, 1863.
40. "The Soldiers' Festival," *New York Daily Tribune*, April 5, 1864; John H. Gourlie, *Final Report of the Treasurer and Finance Committee of the Metropolitan Fair* (New York: John F. Trow, 1864); Kerry L. Bryan, "Civil War Sanitary Fairs," *Encyclopedia of Greater Philadelphia* (2012), online at philadelphiaencyclopedia.org.
41. Mary Elizabeth Wilson Sherwood, *An Epistle to Posterity: Being Rambling Recollections of Many Years of My Life* (New York: Harper & Brothers, 1897), 88–89 and "Memories of 1861–64: The Sanitary Commission," *New York Times*, May 28, 1898; Gourlie, *Final Report.*
42. E. W. Winthrop, "Ladies' Fair," *The American Freedman*, 1866, 155.
43. "The Freedmen's Fair," *Chicago Tribune*, December 23, 1864; "The Freedmen's Fair," *Missouri Democrat* [St. Louis, MO], July 2, 1868.
44. An unsigned letter to the editor reprinted in Caroline Cowles Richards, *Village Life in America, 1852–1872* (New York: Henry Holt, 1913), 203.
45. "Fair of the Cuban Ladies' Relief Association," *New York Herald*, April 20, 1869; "First New York Cavalry Cuban Liberators," *Daily Morning Chronicle* [Washington, DC], July 26, 1869.
46. "German Ladies' Fair," *Missouri Republican* [St. Louis, MO], October 1, 1870.

47. "The Fair Delusion," *Missouri Republican* [St. Louis, MO], November 6, 1870.
48. The principal architect was James Renwick Jr., the rising star still in his thirties who had supervised the construction of the Croton Reservoir for the Croton Aqueduct that carried water into the city, designed the Grace Episcopal Church, won the competition for the Smithsonian Institution Building in Washington, DC, and would over the next two decades design many other Gothic Revival structures including buildings at Vasser and Columbia.
49. William J. McClure, "On Church Fairs," *Journal of the Fair*, October 28, 1878.
50. "The Cathedral Fair," *New York Herald*, October 27, 1878.
51. "The Cathedral Fair," *Irish American Weekly*, November 2, 1878.
52. "Grand Catholic Fair at New York," *Cincinnati Commercial Tribune*, October 20, 1878.
53. *Journal of the Fair*, October 28, 1878.
54. "Scenes at the Cathedral Fair," *New York Tribune*, November 2, 1878.
55. "The Cathedral Fair," *New York Herald*, November 10, 1878.
56. Mary A. Sadlier, "Our Fair," *Journal of the Fair*, October 24, 1878.
57. "Scenes at the Cathedral Fair," *New York Tribune*, November 2, 1878.
58. "Church Fairs," *New York Times*, April 26, 1879; "Church Fairs," *New York Times*, December 18, 1868.
59. "Servant Girls," *New York Times*, December 21, 1872; "A Spiteful Woman's Irish Girls," *Irish American Weekly*, January 5, 1878; "A Servant Girl Takes Poison," *New York Times*, October 20, 1875.
60. "The New Cathedral Solemn Blessing of the Edifice," *Irish American Weekly*, June 7, 1879; "The New Cathedral Dedication," *New York Tribune*, May 26, 1879.
61. "Twenty Youngsters Earn $55 for Clayton Street Baptist Church," *Montgomery Advertiser*, November 1, 1914.
62. "Church Rummage Sale Causes Chicago Riot," *Grand Forks Daily Herald* [Grand Forks, ND], May 16, 1915.
63. The late nineteenth- and early twentieth-century reinvention of folk festivals as modern, pedagogic events was in considerable measure the work of Mary Master Needham, Percival Chubb, Amalie Hofer, Bertha Hofer, Mary K. Simkhovitch, Dorothy Gladys Spicer, and a few others. See especially Mary Master Needham, *Folk Festivals: Their Growth and How to Give Them* (New York: B.W. Hersch, 1912); Percival Chubb, *Festivals and Plays in Schools and Elsewhere* (New York: Harper & Brothers, 1912); Amalie Hofer, "The Significance of Recent National Festivals in Chicago," *Proceedings of the Second Annual Playground Congress* (New York: Playground Association of America, 1909), 74–85; and Katharine Lord, Alice Minnie Herts Heniger, and Howard Bradstreet, eds., *A Guide and Index to Plays, Festivals, and Masques: For Use in Schools, Clubs, and Neighborhood Centers* (New York: Harper & Brothers, 1913).

Chapter 4

1. Theodore Roosevelt, *Realizable Ideals* (San Francisco: Whitaker & Ray-Wiggin, 1912), 55.
2. Jean-Jacques Rousseau, *Emile*, trans. Allan Bloom (New York: Basic Books, 1979), 293, 314, where Rousseau associates durable happiness with "practicing our duties" and having a "good conscience"; see Rafeeq Hasan, "Autonomy and Happiness in Rousseau's Justification of the State," *Review of Politics* 78, 3 (Summer 2016), 391–417; Stephen Salkever, "Rousseau and the Concept of Happiness," *Polity* 11 (1978–79), 27–45; Rousseau associated durable happiness with clarity of conscience.
3. The idea of situated emotional practices contributing to durable happiness has been examined in several interesting empirical studies; see especially Rebecca M. Warner and Kerryellen G. Vroman, "Happiness Inducing Behaviors in Everyday Life: An Empirical Assessment of 'The How of Happiness,'" *Journal of Happiness Studies* 12 (2011), 1063–82; R. A. Emmons and M. E. McCullough, "Counting Blessings versus Burdens: Experimental Studies of Gratitude and Subjective Well-Being in Daily Life," *Journal of Personality and Social Psychology* 84 (2003), 377–89; and M. Joseph Sirgy, "Positive Balance: A Hierarchical Perspective of Positive Mental Health," *Quality of Life Research* 28 (2019), 1921–30.
4. Sydney E. Ahlstrom, *A Religious History of the American People* (New Haven: Yale University Press, 1972), 785–804; Heath W. Carter, "Social Gospels Thrived Outside the Church," *Church History* 84, 1 (March 2015), 199–202.
5. "Slum Expert on St. Louis Work," *St. Louis Post Dispatch*, March 29, 1900.

6. Wendy J. Deichmann, "The Social Gospel as a Grassroots Movement," *Church History* 84, 1 (March 2015), 203–6; Cornelius L. Bynum, "'An Equal Chance in the Race for Life': Reverdy C. Ransom, "Socialism, and the Social Gospel Movement, 1890–1920," *Journal of African American History* 93, 1 (2008), 1–20.
7. Barry Hankins, *God's Rascal: J. Frank Norris and the Beginnings of Southern Fundamentalism* (Lexington: University Press of Kentucky, 1996); David R. Stokes, *The Shooting Salvationist: J. Frank Norris and the Murder Trial That Captivated America* (New York: Steerforth Press, 2011).
8. W.E.B. Du Bois, *The Philadelphia Negro: A Social Study* (Philadelphia: University of Pennsylvania Press, 1899), 207; the social outreach of several other African American churches was described in R. R. Wright Jr., "Social Work and Influence of the Negro Church," *Annals of the American Academy of Political and Social Science* 30 (November 1907), 81–93.
9. Edward Judson, "The Church in Its Social Aspect," *Annals of the American Academy of Political and Social Science* 30 (November 1907), 2.
10. Charles Stelzle, "Presbyterian Department of Church and Labor," *Annals of the American Academy of Political and Social Science* 30 (November 1907), 28–32; William J. Kerby, "Social Work of the Catholic Church in America," *Annals of the American Academy of Political and Social Science* 30 (November 1907), 45–54.
11. "School Which Turns Out Domestics Settles Problem," *Grand Rapids Evening Press*, December 14, 1901; located in Luray, Virginia, the school's graduates were prepared to meet the growing demand for domestic service in Pittsburgh; "Tennessee Town History: From Freedom to the Future," tenntownnia.weebly.com; founded in 1893 in conjunction with Sheldon's Central Congregational Church, the kindergarten helped launch the career of Elisha Scott who would serve as one of the attorneys in *Brown v. Board of Education*.
12. Richard Hofstadter, *The Age of Reform: From Bryan to FDR* (New York: Knopf, 1955), 152, emphasized that the progressive reform movements varied in their leaders' views of religion but enjoyed widespread pastoral support.
13. Gary Scott Smith, *The Search for Social Salvation: Social Christianity and America, 1880–1925* (Lanham, MD: Lexington Books, 2000); Northern Baptist, Methodist, and Presbyterian pastors were prominent leaders in the Social Gospel movement; for a listing of denominations that generally favored or opposed Social Gospel ideas, see Melissa Wilde, *Birth Control Battles: How Race and Class Divided American Religion* (Berkeley and Los Angeles: University of California Press, 2019), 50–55; or Melissa Wilde, "Fewer and Better Children: Race, Class, Religion, and Birth Control Reform in America," *American Journal of Sociology* 119, 6 (May 2014), 1710–60.
14. Data collected in 1893 and 1894 showed density of 143.2 persons per acre in Manhattan but density of 964.4 in the city's eleventh ward; Jason Barr and Teddy Ort, "Population Density across the City: The Case of 1900 Manhattan," Rutgers University, Newark, Working Paper #WP2014-005 (March 2014); the canvass of the city conducted by the Federation of Churches and Christian Workers also documented a doubling in the number of persons per dwelling; "Results of a Religious Canvass in New York," *The Independent*, October 16, 1896.
15. Magali Sarfatti Larson, *The Rise of Professionalism: A Sociological Analysis* (Berkeley and Los Angeles: University of California Press, 1977), discusses the cultural significance of growth in the professions; the growth of specific professions is suggested by the increase between 1880 and 1910 in the number of physicians from approximately 85,000 to 151, 000 and among teachers from 227,000 to 599,000; *Bureau of the Census, Thirteenth Census of the United States, Vol. IV: Population 1910* (Washington, DC: Government Printing Office, 1914).
16. White House, *Proceedings of the Conference on the Care of Dependent Children* (Washington, DC: Government Printing Office, 1909); orphanages, many of which were under church sponsorship, were currently caring for some 93,000 children; on hospitals, see Paul Starr, *The Social Transformation of American Medicine: The Rise of a Sovereign Profession and the Making of a Vast Industry* (New York: Basic Books, 1982).
17. George Unwin, Philip Unwin, and David H. Tucker, "History of Publishing," *Encyclopedia Britannica*, 2023, www.britannica.com/topic/publishing.
18. Walter Rauschenbusch, *Christianizing the Social Order* (New York: Macmillan, 1912), 220.
19. Du Bois, *Philadelphia Negro*, 396.
20. Beth L. Bailey, *From Front Porch to Back Seat: Courtship in Twentieth Century America* (Baltimore: Johns Hopkins University Press, 1988); by the 1910s, concerns were being expressed about "joy riding" and the moral implications of the automobile; concerns about the churches' failure to attract working class people were common in the Social Gospel literature.
21. Jane Addams, *A New Conscience and an Ancient Evil* (New York: Macmillan, 1912), 210.

22. Gary Dorrien, "Social Salvation: The Social Gospel as Theology and Economics," in *The Social Gospel Today*, ed. Christopher H. Evans (Louisville, KY: Westminster John Knox, 2001), 101; Christopher H. Evans, "The Social Gospel as 'the Total Message of the Christian Salvation,'" *Church History* 84, 1 (March 2015), 196–8.
23. Samuel Zane Batten, *The New Citizenship: Christian Character in Its Biblical Ideals, Sources, and Relations* (Philadelphia: Union Press, 1898), 23.
24. Ibid, 184.
25. A. W. Stevens, "Social Aspect of Labor," *Springfield Republican*, April 1, 1906.
26. "Contemporary Thought," *Dallas Morning News*, May 24, 1910.
27. Rauschenbusch, *Christianizing the Social Order*, 226, 250, 470.
28. Stevens, "Social Aspect of Labor."
29. Batten, *The New Citizenship*, 210–11.
30. John A. Ryan, *A Living Wage: Its Ethical and Economic Aspects* (New York: Macmillan, 1906).
31. Elbert Hubbard, "Remember the Weekday to Keep It Holy," *Denver Post*, October 31, 1903.
32. Batten, *The New Citizenship*, 218.
33. "Cheerful Giving," *Baltimore Sun*, March 19, 1898.
34. Joseph Wilson Cochran, "The Church and the Working Man," *Annals of the American Academy of Political and Social Science* 30 (November 1907), 13–27.
35. Rauschenbusch, *Christianity and the Social Crisis*, 246.
36. Rev. W. M. Puffer, "Church to Stand for Social Service," *Grand Rapids Press*, January 16, 1914.
37. Rev. E. P. Stevens, "Young People's Work," *Northern Christian Advocate* [Syracuse, NY], December 14, 1892.
38. "Joyful Service," *The Guide* [Oklahoma City, OK], July 4, 1901.
39. Dr. C. B. Mitchell, "Not Sinful to Be Happy," *Plain Dealer*, October 26, 1903.
40. "Freedom of Christian Service," *Northern Christian Advocate*, January 13, 1897.
41. "The Value of Cheerfulness," *Crockery and Glass Journal*, August 20, 1903; "Locomotive Terminals," *American Engineer and Railroad Journal*, August 1, 1904.
42. "Thanksgiving," *Idaho Statesman*, November 30, 1905.
43. Theodore Roosevelt, "Only Way to Serve the Lord and the State Is with the Whole Heart," *Courier-Journal*, October 26, 1903.
44. "Contemporary Thought," *Dallas Morning News*, September 10, 1912; "What Doest Thou Here," *Kansas City Times*, November 9, 1913.
45. Elbert Hubbard, "Little Sermons," *Baltimore American*, April 2, 1905; Elbert Hubbard, "Habit the Master," *Fort Worth Star-Telegram*, August 16, 1913; many of Hubbard's short essays were reprinted in Alice Hubbard, ed., *An American Bible* (East Aurora, NY: Roycrofters, 1918).
46. "In Teachers' Hands," *Boston Daily Globe*, May 14, 1907.
47. Lily H. Montagu, "The Happiness of Work," *Women Workers*, October 28, 1902.
48. Ryan, *A Living Wage*, 52–65; Rauschenbusch, *Christianizing the Social Order*, 199, expressed a similar idea in arguing for reforms that upheld the right to work: "As long as the happiness of the workers rests on the personal character of employers, it is insecure. What is granted as a favor when the directors feel cheerful may be canceled when they feel hard up. We must set our faces toward a thoroughgoing change in the relation between the two great economic classes."
49. Batten, *The New Citizenship*, 200.
50. Stevens, "Young People's Work," 1892.
51. "Country Bars Are Devil's Own Recruiting Station, Declares Pastor of White Temple," *Oregonian*, September 20, 1909; Brougher (1870–1967) moved from Portland to Los Angeles in 1910 where he pastored the large Temple Baptist Church, was elected president of the Southern California Baptist Convention in 1914, officiated at the marriage of actors Douglas Fairbanks and Mary Pickford in 1920, and delivered the funeral oration for Will Rogers in 1935.
52. Lyman Abbott, *The Life that Really Is* (New York: Wilbur B. Ketcham, 1899), 294.
53. "Torrey Preaches to Women," *Chicago Daily Tribune*, October 21, 1907.
54. Rauschenbusch, *Christianity and the Social Crisis*, 278.
55. Addams, *Twenty Years at Hull House* (New York: Macmillan, 1912), 184.
56. Rauschenbusch, *Christianizing the Social Order*, 320.
57. Susan Curtis, *A Consuming Faith: The Social Gospel and Modern American Culture* (Baltimore: Johns Hopkins University Press, 1991), 228–78; in the 1950s essays produced by the National Council of Churches' Division of Christian Education were still encouraging churches to be more joyful, lamenting the fact that cemeteries were too often placed near churches, and relating anecdotes about young people not wanting to go to church because the services were

dreary; see, e.g., Roy L. Smith, "Christianity Not Opposed to Deep Joy," *Columbia Record*, November 22, 1958; and Roy L. Smith, "Good Religion Brings Person Real Pleasure," *Columbia Record*, December 14, 1957.

58. Diane Winston, *Red-Hot and Righteous: The Urban Religion of the Salvation Army* (Cambridge, MA: Harvard University Press, 1999).
59. For an account of the Brooklyn Sunday school parade in the 1870s, see "Brooklyn's Fine Children: Today's Sunday School Parade in the Sister City," *New York Herald*, May 23, 1877; on the Wilkes-Barre parade, see "Six Thousand in the Sunday School Parade," *Wilkes-Barre Times-Leader*, March 26, 1913; the numbers of children in the parades ranged from 7,000 in Beaumont to 50,000 in Gulfport.
60. Religious periodicals and newspapers frequently carried stories of this kind; see, e.g., "Winston-Salem Notes," *Reformer* [Richmond, VA], January 27, 1900.
61. Rauschenbusch, *Christianity and the Social Crisis*, 311; Washington Gladden, *Social Salvation* (New York: Houghton, Mifflin and Company, 1902), 231.
62. Rauschenbusch, *Christianity and the Social Crisis*, 68, 70, 308, 365; Rauschenbusch, *Christianizing the Social Order*, 360.
63. Paul Carter, *The Decline and Revival of the Social Gospel* (Ithaca, NY: Cornell University Press, 1954); Donald Meyer, *The Protestant Search for Political Realism* (Berkeley and Los Angeles: University of California Press, 1960); Ahlstrom, *Religious History*, 921–26; Gary Dorrien, *Social Ethics in the Making: Interpreting an American Tradition* (New York: Wiley-Blackwell, 2011).
64. Julie Golia, *Newspaper Confessions: A History of Advice Columns in a Pre-Internet Age* (New York: Oxford University Press, 2021); Other columnists whose writing appeared for shorter periods included Barbara Boyd's "Heart and Home Talks" in the 1910s, Edith Johnson's "Happiness Chats" and Dr. Leonard Keene Hirshberg's "Secrets of Health and Happiness" in the 1920s, Winifred Sweet Black who wrote as Annie Laurie in the 1930s, George Antheil whose "Boy Advises Girl" columns appeared from 1937 to 1945, Abbe Wallace Service whose "Advice on the Problems of Life" appeared in Black newspapers in the 1940s, Hubbard Hoover and Isabelle Macrae Hoover who wrote "Pursuit of Happiness" columns in the 1950s, and Norman Vincent Peale whose extended career included confident living columns in the 1950s and 1960s.
65. Bessie R. Murphy, "Conquer Your Worries or Happiness Departs," *Atlanta Constitution*, November 27, 1921.
66. Doris Blake, "Happiness and Thrill Chasing Often Confused," *Chicago Daily Tribune*, July 15, 1932.
67. Kate Gannett Wells, "Little Happinesses," *Boston Cooking School Magazine of Culinary Science and Domestic Economics* 16 (June 1911), 8–9.
68. Edith Johnson, "Where Happiness Is and Is Not Found," *Boston Daily Globe*, April 22, 1922.
69. Dorothy Dix, "To Achieve Happiness, Stop Borrowing Trouble," *Baltimore Sun*, March 9, 1932.
70. Dorothy Dix, "Recipe for Happiness," *Baltimore Sun*, April 7, 1925.

Chapter 5

1. J. L. Gillin, "The Sociology of Recreation," *American Journal of Sociology* 19, 6 (May 1914), 825–34.
2. G. Stanley Hall, *Jesus, the Christ, in the Light of Psychology* (Garden City, NY: Doubleday, 1917), 419.
3. See especially the influential contributions of Georg Simmel and Everett C. Hughes, "The Sociology of Sociability," *American Journal of Sociology* 55, 3 (November 1949), 254–61; Johan Huizinga, *Home Ludens: A Study of the Play-Element in Culture* (Boston: Beacon, 1950 [1938]); and Roger Caillois, *Man, Play, and Games*, trans. Meyer Barash (New York: Free Press, 1961).
4. On religion and athletic teams, several detailed histories are available, especially Randall Balmer, *Passion Plays: How Religion Shaped Sports in North America* (Chapel Hill: University of North Carolina Press, 2022); Annie Blazer, *Playing for God: Evangelical Women and the Unintended Consequences of Sports Ministry* (New York: New York University Press, 2015); and William J. Baker, *Playing with God: Religion and Modern Sport* (Cambridge, MA: Harvard University Press, 2007).
5. Matteo Bortolini, *A Joyfully Serious Man: The Life of Robert Bellah* (Princeton, NJ: Princeton University Press, 2021).

6. Robert N. Bellah, "Transcendence in Contemporary Piety," in Robert N. Bellah, *Beyond Belief: Essays on Religion in a Post-Traditional World* (New York: Harper & Row, 1970), 196–208.
7. In this regard, Bellah serves as a scholar whose work reflected a wide range of influences among contemporary writers, especially in identifying transcendence as a crucial concept in the evolution of modern religion, and whose long career of scholarship was itself influential.
8. Peter L. Berger and Thomas Luckmann, *The Social Construction of Reality* (Garden City, NY: Doubleday, 1966).
9. Herbert W. Richardson, "Three Myths of Transcendence," in *Transcendence*, eds. Herbert W. Richardson and Donald R. Cutler (Boston Beacon Press, 1969), 98–113.
10. Wilfred Cantwell Smith, *Faith and Belief* (Princeton, NJ: Princeton University Press, 1979), 133.
11. Robert N. Bellah, *Religion in Human Evolution* (Cambridge, MA: Harvard University Press, 2011), 276.
12. Ariel Glucklich, *The Joy of Religion: Exploring the Nature of Pleasure in Spiritual Life* (New York: Cambridge University Press, 2019), 74.
13. James Sellers, *Theological Ethics* (New York: Macmillan, 1966), 62–3.
14. Alfred Schutz, The *Problem of Social Reality: Collected Papers I*, ed. Maurice Natanson (The Hague: Martinus Nijhoff, 1962), 329–49; Alfred Schutz, *Literary Reality and Relationships: Collected Papers VI*, ed. Michael Barber (New York: Springer, 2013), 345–46; see also Taves, *Religious Experience Reconsidered*, 36.
15. These arguments posed questions about what the "self" was in these instances; E.g., was there one part of the self, perhaps a "true self," that remained constant or was the self fungible enough that it lost continuity and stability during moments of self-transcendence; these questions were the focus of a large literature; among the varying perspectives, see especially Charles Taylor, *Sources of the Self: The Making of the Modern Identity* (Cambridge: Harvard University Press, 1989); Antonio R. Damasio, *Descartes' Error: Emotion, Reason, and the Human Brain* (New York: Penguin, 1994); and Kenneth J. Gergen, *The Saturated Self: Dilemmas of Identity in Contemporary Life* (New York: Basic Books, 1991).
16. On Cox's contributions, see especially Harvey Cox, *The Feast of Fools: A Theological Essay on Festivity and Fantasy* (Cambridge, MA: Harvard University Press, 1969).
17. Johan Huizinga, as quoted in Willem Otterspeer, *Reading Huizinga* (Amsterdam: Amsterdam University Press, 2010), 120–21; and on Bellah's later references to Schutz and Huizinga, see especially *Religion in Human Evolution*, chapter 2. See also Thomas S. Henricks, *Play Reconsidered: Sociological Perspectives on Human Expression* (Urbana: University of Illinois Press, 2006), 1–26.
18. Bellah drew from Jerome Bruner as well as from Piaget in developing his ideas about parallels between childhood development and religious evolution; for a good discussion of how play was conceptualized by these and other writers, see Thomas S. Henricks, "Play as Self-Realization: Toward a General Theory of Play," *American Journal of Play* 6, 2 (Winter 2014), 190–213.
19. "Dr. Bushnell's Phi Beta Discourse," *Christian Register*, September 2, 1848; Horace Bushnell, *Work and Play* (London: Alexander Straham, 1864 [1848]).
20. *Christian Watchman*, August 31, 1848.
21. Horace Bushnell, *Christian Nurture* (New York: Charles Scribner, 1861 [1847]), 338–65; Theodore T. Munger, *Horace Bushnell: Preacher and Theologian* (Boston: Houghton, Mifflin, 1899), 329, includes a statement by Bushnell's daughter recalling "the daily, after-dinner romps, not lasting long, but most vigorous and hearty at the moment."
22. Bushnell, *Work and Play*, 6–7.
23. Ibid., 10, 33–34.
24. Ibid., 11.
25. John White Chadwick, "Work and Play," *Christian Register*, May 4, 1872.
26. Herbert Spencer, *Principles of Sociology* (New York: D. Appleton, 1906), 19.
27. Chadwick, "Work and Play."
28. Rev. J. A. Benton, "Work and Play," *Pacific*, January 16, 1868.
29. Rev. R. A. White, "Should Furnish Pleasure," *Wisconsin Weekly Advocate*, April 12, 1906.
30. Henry S. Curtis, "The Growth, Present Extent and Prospects of the Playground Movement in America," *Pedagogical Seminary* 16 (January 1, 1909), 344–50.
31. Chubb, *Festivals and Plays in Schools and Elsewhere*, 17; Dorothy Gladys Spicer, *Folk Festivals and the Foreign Community* (New York: The Womans Press, 1923), 18–20; Jane Addams, *The Long Road of Woman's Memory* (New York: Macmillan, 1916), 112.

32. Thorstein Veblen, *The Theory of the Leisure Class: An Economic Study of Institutions* (London: George, Allen & Unwin, 1899), 295–300; while these remarks focused on sports and religious devotion among men, Veblen's equally keen observations about women emphasized women's traditional "ancillary" roles and the changes among modern women that focused on work, self-expression, and emancipation; see especially pages 354–62.
33. William James, *The Varieties of Religious Experience: A Study in Human Nature* (London: Longmans, Green, and Co., 1903).
34. Huizinga, *Homo Ludens*; Eric Voegelin, "Review of Homo Ludens: Versuch einer Bestimmung des Spielements der Kultur," *Journal of Politics* 10, 1 (February 1948), 179–87.
35. Rev. A. B. Kendall, "What's Wrong and What's Right with the Movies?" *Herald of Gospel Liberty* 119, 36 (September 8, 1927), 36–37; "Librarian Declares Child's Mind 'Burned' by Movies," *Courier-Journal*, February 8, 1921; Rev. Charles E. Schaeffer, "What about the Movies? What's Wrong?" *Herald of Gospel Liberty* 119, 38 (September 22, 1927), 38.
36. Jürgen Moltmann, *Theology of Play*, trans. Reinhard Ulrich (New York: Harper & Row, 1972), 2, 12–13.
37. Roger Caillois, *Man and the Sacred*, trans. Meyer Barash (Urbana: University of Illinois Press, 2001 [1959], 159.
38. Ibid., 212.
39. Absorption as total immersion in some imagined reality as the crucial feature of play is emphasized in Peter Stromberg, *Caught in Play: How Entertainment Works on You* (Stanford, CA: Stanford University Press, 2009).
40. Caillois, *Man and the Sacred*, 19.
41. Mary Charles Bryce, "Play and Players in a Religious Context," *Liturgy* 2, 1 (1981), 14–21.
42. Robert K. Johnston, *The Christian at Play* (Grand Rapids, MI: Wm. B. Eerdmans, 1983).
43. Among the works that generated the most criticism were Harvey Cox, *The Secular City* (New York, Macmillan, 1965); Cox, *Feast of Fools*; and David L. Miller, *Gods and Games* (New York: Harper & Row, 1971).
44. On the history of fandom, see Daniel Cavicchi, "Fandom Before 'Fan,'" *Reception: Texts, Readers, Audiences, History* 6 (2014), 52–72; and Kristina Busse, *Framing Fan Fiction: Literary and Social Practices in Fan Fiction Communities* (Iowa City: University of Iowa Press, 2017); among numerous works on churches and popular music, see especially Leah Payne, *God Gave Rock and Roll to You: A History of Contemporary Christian Music* (New York: Oxford University Press, 2024).
45. Matthew Hodge, "Faith and Fandom: Pop Culture Villainy in Twenty-First-Century Spirituality," *International Journal of Religion and Spirituality in Society* 14, 3 (2023), 1–24; Michael A. Elliott, "Fandom as Religion: A Social Scientific Assessment," *Journal of Fandom Studies* 9, 2 (February 2021), 107–22; Mark Duffett, "I Scream Therefore I Fan? Music Audiences and Affective Citizenship," in *Fandom: Identities and Communities in a Mediated World*, 2nd ed., eds. Jonathan Gray, Cornel Sandvoss, and C. Lee Harrington (New York: New York University Press, 2017), 143–57; Candy Leonard, "Beatles Fandom: A De Facto Religion," in *Fandom and the Beatles: The Act You've Known for All These Years*, eds. Kenneth Womack and Kit O'Toole (New York: Oxford University Press, 2021), 19–54.
46. Hodge, "Faith and Fandom: Pop Culture Villainy in Twenty-First-Century Spirituality"; Philip Goff, "Religion and Popular Culture," in *The Columbia Guide to Religion in American History*, eds. Paul Harvey, Edward J. Blum, and Randall Stephens (New York: Columbia University Press, 2012), 295–308; David Chidester, "The Church of Baseball, the Fetish of Coca-Cola, and the Potlatch of Rock 'n' Roll: Theoretical Models for the Study of Religion in American Popular Culture," *Journal of the American Academy of Religion* 64, 4 (Winter 1996), 743–65; Cristina Rocha, *Cool Christianity: Hillsong and the Fashioning of Cosmopolitan Identities* (New York: Oxford University Press, 2024), 52–75; Josiah Kidwell, "The Sanctuary of the Spectacle: Megachurches and the Production of Christian Celebrities and Consumers," *Journal of Media and Religion* 20, 2 (2021), 53–64; Guy Marchessault, "Is Religion Compatible with Media Entertainment?" in *New Media and Communication Across Religions and Cultures*, eds. Isaac Nahon-Serfaty and Rukhsana Ahmed (New York: IGI Global, 2014), 66–80.
47. Alasdair MacIntyre, *After Virtue: A Study in Moral Theory*, 2nd ed. (Notre Dame, IN: University of Notre Dame Press, 1984).
48. Daniel Bell, "Religion in the Sixties," *Social Research* 38, 3 (Autumn 1971), 447–97, argued that theology in the 1950s had emphasized the depravity and imperfection of human nature

and that religious writings in the 1960s reflected "a new optimism about human nature and human powers" (p. 447). Bell argued that contemporary religious practice focused on self-transcendence and cathartic experience but lacked "the sustained force that a continuing system of transcendental meaning can provide" (p. 487).

49. Norman O. Brown, *Love's Body* (Berkeley and Los Angeles: University of California Press, 1996 [1966]), 245.
50. Wade Clark Roof, *Spiritual Marketplace* (Princeton, NJ: Princeton University Press, 2000), 19–20.
51. R. Marie Griffith, *Moral Combat: How Sex Divided American Christians and Fractured American Politics* (New York: Basic Books, 2017).
52. Alex Comfort, *The Joy of Sex: A Gourmet Guide to Love Making* (New York: Crown, 1972).
53. Georges Bataille, *Eroticism* (London: Marion Boyars, 2006 [1957]); on Bataille's contributions to sociology through his discussion of eroticism, see Chris Shilling and Philip A. Mellor, "Sociology and the Problem of Eroticism," *Sociology* 44, 2 (June 2010), 435–52; and on the transgressive aspects of eroticism in Bataille's work, see Maryline Lukacher, *Maternal Fictions: Stendhal, Sand, Rachilde, and Bataille* (Durham, NC: Duke University Press, 1994).
54. Anthony J. Steinbock, *Knowing by Heart: Loving as Participation and Critique* (Evanston, IL: Northwestern University Press, 2021), 64–76.
55. Audre Lorde, *The Uses of the Erotic: The Erotic as Power* (Berkeley, CA: Crossing Press, 1978), 53.
56. Ken Wilber, "Foreword," in *Transcendent Sex: When Lovemaking Opens the Veil*, ed. Jenny Wade (New York: Paraview Pocket Books, 2004).
57. Walt Whitman, "Is It Right to Dance?" *The Collected Writings of Walt Whitman*, eds. Herbert Bergman, Douglas A. Noverr, and Edward J. Recchia (New York: Peter Lang, 1998), 334.
58. Arguments and official statements against dancing by Baptist, Catholic, Congregational, Disciples, Episcopal, Methodist, and Presbyterian groups are included in William Edward Biederwolf, *The Christian and Amusements* (Chicago: Glad Tidings Publishing, 1911).
59. Sylvanus Stall, *Self and Sex Series: What a Young Man Ought to Know* (Philadelphia: Vir Publishing, 1897), 243.
60. Judith L. Hanna, "Dance under the Censorship Watch," *Journal of Arts Management Law and Society* 29, 1 (2002), 1–13; Sabrina D. MisirHiralall, "Dance as Portrayed in the Media," *Journal of Aesthetic Education* 47, 3 (Fall 2013), 72–95. One of the more interesting illustrations of faith communities' changing views toward dancing was Judson Memorial Church in the Greenwich Village neighborhood of New York City, which was founded by Baptist pastor Edward Judson and named for Judson's father, the missionary Adoniram Judson, and by 1962 was the home of the Judson Dance Theatre that held concerts and dance performances; Sally Banes, "The Birth of the Judson Dance Theatre: 'A Concert of Dance' at Judson Church, July 6, 1962," *Dance Chronicle* 5, 2 (1982), 167–212.
61. Leslie Gotfrit, "Women Dancing Back: Disruption and the Politics of Pleasure," *Journal of Education* 170, 3 (1988), 122–41; Angela McRobbbie, "Dance and Social Fantasy," in *Gender and Generation*, eds. Angela McRobbie and Mica Nava, 130–61 (New York: Macmillan, 1984).
62. On themes of transcendence that deny the body, and how dance contrasts with those themes, see Sondra Fraleigh, *Dancing Identity: Metaphysics in Motion* (Pittsburgh: University of Pittsburgh Press, 2004).
63. Ronald Cagne, Thomas A. Kane, and Robert VerEecke, *Introducing Dance in Christian Worship* (Washington, DC: Pastoral Press, 1984); David L. Johns, "Sometimes You Just Gotta Dance: Physical Expressiveness in Worship," *CrossCurrents* 52, 2 (Summer 2002), 200–11; Pamela Dickey Young, *Re-Creating the Church: Communities of Eros* (Harrisburg, PA: Trinity Press International, 2000); Kathleen Turner, *And We Shall Learn through the Dance: Liturgical Dance as Religious Education* (Eugene, OR: Pickwick Publications, 2021).
64. Time spent in nature was relatively unproblematic for faith communities to accept as a playful source of self-transcendence. See Bron Taylor, *Dark Green Religion: Nature Spirituality and the Planetary Future* (Berkeley and Los Angeles: University of California Press, 2010), 42–70, on the history of spiritual conceptions of nature.
65. Emily A. Thorson and Michael Serazio, "Sports Fandom and Political Attitudes," *Public Opinion Quarterly* 82, 2 (Summer 2018), 391–403; Carole M. Cusack, "Sports," in *The Oxford Handbook of the Study of Religion*, eds. Michael Stausberg and Steven Engler (New York: Oxford University Press, 2016), 472–81; Kevin Dixon, "Sport, Spectatorship, and Fandom," in *The Oxford*

Handbook of Sport and Society, ed. Lawrence A. Wenner (New York: Oxford University Press, 2022), 967–87.

66. Cottingham, *Practical Feelings*, 69–97.
67. Although marketing explicitly in terms of happiness had been resisted on grounds that it cheapened happiness ("selling happiness at Satan's price," as an 1870s poem stated), there was a long history of exceptions, starting in the 1910s and early 1920s with the Happiness Candy Company selling "happiness in every box," coal companies selling "happiness by the ton," amusement park developers promising "real profits in selling happiness," and motor car dealers assuring buyers that the car would "promote your happiness." Post–World War II developments in universities and the military that contributed to happiness as a business are discussed in Daniel Horowitz, *Happier? The History of a Cultural Movement That Aspired to Transform America* (New York: Oxford University Press, 2018).
68. E.g., Randy Alcorn, *Happiness* (Carol Stream, IL: Tyndale House, 2015); Max Lucado, *Jesus* (Nashville, TN: Nelson Books, 2020); Joel Osteen, *Think Better, Live Better: A Victorious Life Begins in Your Mind* (Nashville, TN: Faith Words, 2016); Brian Edgar, *The God Who Plays: A Playful Approach to Theology and Spirituality* (Eugene, OR: Cascade Books, 2017); James Martin, *Between Heaven and Mirth: Why Joy, Humor, and Laughter Are at the Heart of the Spiritual Life* (New York: HarperOne, 2012); Devin LaVore, *God Is So Much Fun* (Scotts Valley, CA: CreateSpace Publishing, 2018); Dante Stack, *Fun with Jesus A Manic Odyssey through the Extra Books about Christ* (Broken Arrow, OK: Stockade, 2019); Roberta Grimes, *The Fun of Loving Jesus* (Normal, IL: Afterlife Research and Education Institute, 2022); and Rex McGregor, *Laugh with Jesus: The Funniest Comedian of All Time* (Scotts Valley, CA: CreateSpace Publishing, 2012). Online media included a monthly devotional magazine called *Joy!* and classes offered by "Enjoying Jesus Ministries." YouTube videos and podcasts included series such as "Having Fun with God" and "Having Fun with Jesus in Your Heart." Fun with Jesus was also featured in episodes of the popular film series "The Chosen" and in the lyrics of upbeat Christian music such as "Crazy" and "With Us." Merchandise included such items as the "Holy Happiness Party Poncho," "Double Your Fun with Jesus" t-shirts, and "Dancing with Jesus" bobbling figurines.
69. Felicity Dale, "Forward," in *Having Fun with God*, ed. Suzette Lambert (Scotts Valley, CA: CreateSpace Publishing, 2016).
70. A theology of Jesus as a "laugh maker" was developed in Brian Edgar, *Laughter and the Grace of God: Restoring Laughter to Its Central Role in Christian Faith and Theology* (Cambridge, UK: Lutterworth Press, 2019); previous rebrandings of Jesus were described in Richard Wightman Fox, *Jesus in America: Personal Savior, Cultural Hero, National Obsession* (San Francisco: Harper San Francisco, 2004).
71. Beth Snyder Bulik, "Churches Get Religion on Marketing," *Advertising Age*, 80, 17 (May 11, 2009), 4, 33; Editors, "The Joy-Driven Life: Death to Deadly Earnest Discipleship!" *Christianity Today*, December 1, 2009.
72. Office of Public Information, "New United Methodist Ad Campaign Addresses Loneliness," United Methodist Church, October 30, 2019, umc.org; Office of Public Information, "United Methodist Spring Advertising Campaign Encourages Togetherness," *ResourceUMC*, March 24, 2022, resourceumc.org.
73. "Let the Good Times Roll: 5 Practical Ways to Embrace Joy in Your Church," *Christianity Today*, July 11, 2023.

Chapter 6

1. Gary Wolf, "The Data-Driven Life," *New York Times Magazine*, April 28, 2010; Natasha D. Schüll, "The Data-Based Self: Self-Quantification and the Data-Driven (Good) Life," *Social Research* 86, 4 (Winter 2019), 909–30; Minna Ruckenstein and Mika Pantzar, "Beyond the Quantified Self: Thematic Exploration of a Datistic Paradigm," *New Media and Society* 19, 3 (March 2017), 401–18.
2. James A. Russell, "A Circumplex Model of Affect," *Journal of Personality and Social Psychology* 39, 6 (1980), 1161–78; Gary Wolf, "A Penny for Your Deepest Thoughts," *Salon*, January 11, 2008; Gary Wolf, "Measuring Mood and Emotion," *Quantified Self*, August 11, 2021, quantifiedself.com.
3. Jon Cousins, *Nudge Your Way to Happiness: The 30 Day Workbook for a Happier You* (Stanford, CA: Zodora Books, 2021); these examples were reported on the Quantified Self website, quantifiedself.com/blog.

4. Jason Pridmore and Yijing Wang, "Prompting Spiritual Practices through Christian Faith Applications: Self-Paternalism and the Surveillance of the Soul," *Surveillance and Society* 16, 4 (2018), 502–16.
5. Spirituality Habit Tracker, mellamind.com; Michelle Faverio et al., "Online Religious Services Appeal to Many Americans, but Going in Person Remains More Popular," Pew Research Center, June 2, 2023, pewresearch.org.
6. Tamar Sharon and Dorien Zandbergen, "From Data Fetishism to Quantifying Selves: Self-tracking Practices and the Other Values of Data," *New Media and Society* 19, 11 (November 2017), 1695–709.
7. Vaike Fors et al., *Imagining Personal Data: Experiences of Self-Tracking* (New York: Routledge, 2020), 85–98.
8. Chen and Huang, "Christians and Buddhists Are Comparably Happy on Twitter," 1–8.
9. Ritter, Preston, and Hernandez, "Happy Tweets," 243–9.
10. Gina Neff and Dawn Nafus, *Self-tracking* (Cambridge, MA: MIT Press, 2016); Ranganathan Chandrasekaran, Vipanchi Katthula, and Evangelos Moustakas, "Patterns of Use and Key Predictors for the Use of Wearable Health Care Devices by US Adults: Insights from a National Survey," *Journal of Medical Internet Research* 10 (October 2020), e22443.
11. John Wesley, *Explanatory Notes Upon the New Testament* (New York: Soule and T. Mason, 1818), 653.
12. Henry Ward Beecher, "Slow Development of Christian Character," *New York Herald*, December 14, 1874.
13. M. Scott Peck, *The Road Less Traveled: A New Psychology of Love, Traditional Values and Spiritual Growth* (New York: Simon & Schuster, 1979); James Dobson, *Dare to Discipline* (Chicago: Gospel Light, 1972); Richard J. Foster, *Celebration of Discipline: The Path to Spiritual Growth* (New York: Harper & Row, 1978).
14. Lawrence Kohlberg, *Essays on Moral Development* (New York: Harper & Row, 1981); James W. Fowler, *Stages of Faith: The Psychology of Human Development and the Quest for Meaning* (New York: Harper Collins, 1981); Kenneth Boyack, Robert Duggan, and Paul Huesing, "Catholic Faith Inventory: A Tool for Fostering Spiritual Growth," *New Catholic World* 229 (May/June 1986), 123–28; P. L. Benson, M. J. Donahue, and J. A. Erickson, "The Faith Maturity Scale: Conceptualization, Measurement, and Empirical Validation," *Research in the Social Scientific Study of Religion* 5 (1993), 1–26; P. C. Hill et al., "Conceptualizing Religion and Spirituality: Points of Commonality, Points of Departure," *Journal for the Theory of Social Behaviour* 30, 1 (2000), 51–77; Chang-Ho C. Ji, "Faith Maturity and Doctrinal Orthodoxy: A Validity Study of the Faith Maturity Scale," *Psychological Reports* 95, 3 (December 2004), 993–98.
15. Thomas Merton, *Spiritual Direction and Meditation* (Collegeville, MN: Liturgical Press, 1960); Gerald O'Collins, *The Spirituality of the Second Vatican Council* (Mahwah, NJ: Paulist Press, 2014).
16. Owen Chadwick, *John Cassian* (Cambridge, UK: Cambridge University Press, 1968); Kate O'Brien, *Teresa of Avila* (New York: Sheed & Ward, 1951); Justin McCann, ed., *The Rule of Saint Benedict* (Westminster, MD: Newman Press, 1952).
17. Ariel Glucklich, *Everyday Mysticism: A Contemplative Community at Work in the Desert* (New York: Oxford University Press, 2017).
18. Illouz, *Saving the Modern Soul*; Steven M. Tipton, *Getting Saved from the Sixties*: Moral *Meaning in Conversion and Cultural Chan*ge (Berkeley and Los Angeles: University of California Press, 1982).
19. Spiritual discipline was not meant to imply a theology of salvation achieved by "works" but something closer to the biblical idea of sanctification. This clarification was emphasized in the work of such writers as Dallas Willard, *The Spirit of the Disciplines: Understanding How God Changes Lives* (New York: HarperCollins, 1988); Donald S. Whitney, *Spiritual Disciplines within the Church: Participating Fully in the Body of Christ* (Chicago: Moody, 1996); and Philip Nation, *Habits for Our Holiness: How the Spiritual Disciplines Grow Us Up, Draw Us Together, and Send Us Out* (Chicago: Moody, 2016).
20. Irving I. Zaretsky and Mark P. Leone, *Religious Movements in Contemporary America* (Princeton, NJ: Princeton University Press, 1975); Charles Y. Glock and Robert N. Bellah, eds., *The New Religious Consciousness* (Berkeley and Los Angeles: University of California Press, 1976); Peter B. Clarke, ed., *Encyclopedia of New Religious Movements* (New York: Routledge, 2006).

21. George Gallup Jr. and D. Michael Lindsay, *Surveying the Religious Landscape: Trends in U.S. Beliefs* (New York: Morehouse, 1999); Wuthnow, *All in Sync: How Music and Art Are Revitalizing American Religion* (Berkeley and Los Angeles: University of California Press, 2003), 20, 37.
22. Leonnardo Blair, "More Americans Say They Want to 'Grow Spiritually,'" *Christian Post*, January 24, 2023, christianpost.com; Taylor Orth, "Most Americans Endorse At Least Some Aspects of the New-Age Spiritual Movement," YouGov, November 29, 2022, today.yougov.com; Wade Clark Roof, *A Generation of Seekers: The Spiritual Journeys of the Baby Boom Generation* (San Francisco: Harper San Francisco, 1993), 79.
23. Caryle Murphy, "Navigation for the Inward Journey," *Washington Post*, September 13, 2003.
24. Mark Chaves, *Congregations in 21st Century America: National Congregations Study* (Durham, NC: Duke University, 2021), 32–33.
25. On the role of therapy, well-being programs, and positive psychology centers in promoting happiness as self-development, see Horowitz, *Happier?*.
26. Christopher P. Scheitle, *Beyond the Congregation: The World of Christian Nonprofits* (New York: Oxford University Press, 2010) demonstrated the significant extent to which professionalized religious occupations were diversifying beyond congregations; Wendy Cadge, *Spiritual Care: The Everyday Work of Chaplains* (New York: Oxford University Press, 2022) provides a valuable overview of changes in organized religion associated with the development of professionalized chaplaincy careers serving outside of traditional congregation settings; David Hollinger, *Christianity's American Fate: How Religion Became More Conservative and Society More Secular* (Princeton, NJ: Princeton University Press, 2022) is one of the best treatments of the fallout from decline in mainline Protestantism; Ryan P. Burge, *The Nones: Where They Came From, Who They Are, and Where They Are Going* (Minneapolis: Fortress Press, 2023) is a rich source of information on numeric trends, as is Mark Chaves, *American Religion: Contemporary Trends* (Princeton, NJ: Princeton University Press, 2017).
27. Evelyn Underhill, *The Ways of the Spirit*, ed. G. A. Brame (New York: Crossroad, 1990), 62.
28. Natasha A. McLennan Tajiri, "Attentiveness to God: Contemplative Presence in Spiritual Direction" (PhD dissertation, Institute of Transpersonal Psychology, Palo Alto, CA, 2009).
29. Thomas DeGloma, "Awakenings: Autobiography, Memory, and the Social Logic of Personal Discovery," *Sociological Forum* 25, 3 (September 2010), 519–40.
30. Timothy Keller, *Making Sense of God: Finding God in the Modern World* (New York: Penguin, 2016), 79.
31. Tilden Edwards, "Developing Leaders for Contemplative Groups," *The Way* 75 (1992), 67–75.
32. Kathleen Cahalan, "How the Practice of Lectio Divina Heals and Transforms," in *Christian Practical Wisdom: What It Is, Why It Matters*, eds. Dorothy C. Ball et al. (Grand Rapids, MI: Eerdmans, 2016), 47.
33. Thomas Grant Lengyel, "Recovering the Disciplines: A Comparative Study on the Spiritual Disciplines as Expressed in the Lives, Teaching and Ministry of Jonathan Edwards, Charles Finney and Richard Foster" (D. Min Dissertation, Duke Divinity School, 2018), 11.
34. In their study of parenting, Christian Smith and Amy Adamczyk, *Handing Down the Faith: How Parents Pass Their Religion on to the Next Generation* (New York: Oxford University Press, 2021), found a strong emphasis among Muslims, Hindus, and Buddhists, as well as among Protestants and Catholics, on spiritual discipline.
35. Erin F. Johnston, "Failing to Learn, or Learning to Fail? Accounting for Persistence in the Acquisition of Spiritual Disciplines," *Qualitative Sociology* 40 (2017), 353–72.
36. Examples are given in Dorothy C. Bass, ed., *Practicing Our Faith: A Way of Life for a Searching People* (Minneapolis: Fortress Press, 1997); Gretchen Ronnevik, *Ragged: Spiritual Disciplines for the Spiritually Exhausted* (Irvine, CA: New Reformation Publications, 2021); and Mason King, *Spiritual Disciplines: How to Become a Healthy Christian* (Brentwood, TN: B&H Publishing, 2023).
37. Seung-Ho Baek and Sophia Seung-Yoon Lee, "Changes in Economic Activity, Skills and Inequality in the Service Economy," *Development and Society* 43, 1 (2014), 33–57.
38. Phoebe Moore and Andrew Robinson, "The Quantified Self: What Counts in the Neoliberal Workplace," *New Media and Society* 18, 11 (December 2016), 2774–92; for a persuasive argument about the contradictions inherent in the "neoliberal" marketized social order, see Nancy Fraser, "The End of Progressive Neoliberalism," *Dissent*, January 2, 2017.
39. Nancy J. Ault, "Theological Reflection and Spiritual Direction," *The Australasian Catholic Record* 90, 1 (January 2013), 81–91.

40. Joerg Stolz and Jean Claude Usunier, "Religions as Brands? Religion and Spirituality in Consumer Society," *Journal of Management, Spirituality and Religion* 16, 1 (2019), 6–31; Mara Einstein, "The Evolution of Religious Branding," *Social Compass* 58, 3 (2011), 331–38; Bulik, "Churches Get Religion on Marketing," 33–7.
41. Luca Mavelli, "Neoliberalism as Religion: Sacralization of the Market and Post-Truth Politics," *International Political Sociology* 14 (2020), 57–76.
42. Sarah Igo, *Average Americans: Surveys, Citizens, and the Making of a Mass Public* (Cambridge, MA: Harvard University Press, 2007), 289.
43. Paul Froese, *On Purpose: How We Create the Meaning of Life* (New York: Oxford University Press, 2015), 82.
44. Francisco J. Buera and Joseph P. Kaboski, "The Rise of the Service Economy," *The American Economic Review* 102, 6 (2012), 2540–69.
45. Mitchell Barnes, Lauren Bauer, and Wendy Edelberg, "Nine Facts about the Service Sector in the United States," *Economic Facts* (September 2022), brookings.edu; "Clergy and Community Service Occupations," DataUSA, 2023, https://datausa.io/profile/soc/clergy?compare=community-social-service-occupations. On occupational specialization trends, see Claude S. Fischer and Michael Hout, *Century of Difference: Diversity and Unity Among Americans, 1900–2000* (New York: Russell Sage Foundation, 2006), 107–10, which uses Theil's index of diversity to calculate diversity of occupational categories as classified by the US Census, showing an index value of 1.0 in 1900 rising to 1.5 by 1960, and 2.16 in 2000.
46. Nancy Tatom Ammerman, *Sacred Stories, Spiritual Tribes: Finding Religion in Everyday Life* (New York: Oxford University Press, 2013), 66; David Bronkema, "The Challenges and Promises of Spiritual Metrics: Understanding the Dynamics at Play and Guidelines for Best Practices," in *Towards an Understanding and Practice of Spiritual Metrics*, ed. David Bronkema, Mark Forshaw, and Ellen Strohm (Unpublished manuscript, Joint Learning Initiative on Faith and Local Communities, 2016), https://jliflc.com
47. Sally K. Gallagher, *Getting to Church: Narratives of Gender and Joining* (New York: Oxford University Press, 2017), 98–125.
48. James Wellman, Katie E. Corcoran, and Kate J. Stockly, *High on God: How Megachurches Won the Heart of America* (New York: Oxford University Press, 2019), 161.
49. Gerardo Marti, *Hollywood Faith: Holiness, Prosperity, and Ambition in a Los Angeles Church* (New Brunswick, NJ: Rutgers University Press, 2008), 177.
50. Jason Garner, "What Is Your Metric for Spiritual Growth?" *The Tattooed Buddha*, January 16, 2020.
51. Erin F. Johnston, "The Feeling of Enlightenment: Managing Emotions through Yoga and Prayer," *Symbolic Interaction* 44, 3 (August 2021), 576–602.
52. Elizabeth Barrett Browning, "Aurora Leigh," in *Oxford Book of English Mystical Verse*, eds. D.H.S. Nicholson and A.H.E. Lee (Oxford: Clarendon Press, 1917).
53. Quentin Smith, *The Felt Meanings of the World: A Metaphysics of Feeling* (West Lafayette, IN: Purdue University Press, 1986), 151.

Chapter 7

1. Portions of this chapter are drawn with permission from Robert Wuthnow, "Religion, Democracy, and the Task of Restoring Trust," *Daedalus, the Journal of the American Academy of Arts and Sciences* 151, 4 (Fall 2022), 1–15, which benefited from the helpful suggestions of Henry Brady, Kay Schlozman, and the *Daedalus* editorial staff.
2. Laurie Goodstein, "Willow Creek Church's Top Leadership Resigns over Allegations against Bill Hybels," *The New York Times*, August 8, 2018; and Laurie Goodstein, "How the Willow Creek Church Scandal Has Stunned the Evangelical World," *The New York Times*, August 9, 2018.
3. "Jim Bakker Resigns His TV Ministry," *Washington Post*, March 19, 1987.
4. John Dart, "Swaggart Steps Down after Public Confession," *Los Angeles Times*, February 22, 1988.
5. Laurie Goodstein, "Episcopal Church Ex-Treasurer Gets 5 Years for Embezzlement," *Washington Post*, July 11, 1996.
6. Matt Carroll, Sacha Pfeiffer, and Michael Rezendes, "Church Allowed Abuse by Priest for Years," *Boston Globe*, January 6, 2002.
7. Office of Attorney General, Commonwealth of Pennsylvania, *Report I of the 40th Statewide Investigating Grand Jury* (Harrisburg, PA, 2018).
8. Robert Downen, Lise Olsen, and John Tedesco, "Abuse of Faith," *Houston Chronicle*, February 10, 2019.

9. Sarah Pulliam Bailey, Susan Svriuga, and Michelle Boorstein, "Jerry Falwell Jr. Resigns as Head of Liberty University," *Washington Post*, August 25, 2020; the Falwell scandal became the focus of a documentary, *God Forbid: The Sex Scandal That Brought Down a Dynasty* (2022).
10. On the relationship of emotional harm and religious harm from such scandals, see Jordan Morehouse and Laura L. Lemon, "Beyond Reputational and Financial Damage: Examining Emotional and Religious Harm in a Post-Crisis Case Study of Hillsong Church," *Public Relations Review* 49, 1 (March 2023), 1–20.
11. Jeffrey Guhin, "In the Theological Sense, Jerry Falwell Jr.'s Scandal Is Profoundly Sad," *Slate*, August 26, 2020.
12. Jeffrey M. Jones, "Confidence in U.S. Institutions Down; Average at New Low," Gallup, July 5, 2022, news.gallup.com/poll.; similarly, the General Social Survey documented a decline in "a great deal" of confidence in organized religion from 45 percent in 1974 to 21 percent in 2018; GSS Data Explorer, NORC at the University of Chicago. To the extent that these trends were influenced by specific events, the two sharpest declines in the Gallup data were around the time of the Bakker and Swaggart scandals in 1987 and 1988 and the public exposure of the Catholic sex scandals in 2001 and 2002.
13. Celina Tabor, "About 30% of American Adults Are Now Religiously Unaffiliated," *USA Today*, December 15, 2021.
14. Shadi Hamid, "America without God," *The Atlantic*, April 2021, theatlantic.com; Richard Just, "How Religion Can Help Put Our Democracy Back Together," *Washington Post*, October 28, 2020.
15. See the literature review and empirical analysis in John Brehm and Meg Savel, "What Do Survey Measures of Trust Actually Measure?" in *Trust in Contemporary Society*, ed. Masamichi Sasaki (Leiden, Netherlands: Brill, 2019), 233–60, and the approaches discussed in Eric M. Uslaner, "The Study of Trust," in *The Oxford Handbook of Social and Political Trust*, ed. Eric M. Uslaner (New York: Oxford University Press, 2018), 2–14; on trust and happiness, see especially Benjamin Radcliff, *The Political Economy of Human Happiness* (New York: Cambridge University Press, 2013).
16. Everett Carll Ladd Jr., "The Polls: The Question of Confidence," *Public Opinion Quarterly* 40 (4) (Winter 1976–1977), 544–52.
17. Among books and articles providing background on clergy scandals, see Anson Shupe, *Spoils of the Kingdom: Clergy Misconduct and Religious Community* (Urbana: University of Illinois Press, 2007); Mark T. Mulder and Gerardo Marti, *The Glass Church: Robert H. Schuller, the Crystal Cathedral, and the Strain of Megachurch Ministry* (New Brunswick, NJ: Rutgers University Press, 2020); and Susan Harding, *The Book of Jerry Falwell: Fundamentalist Language and Politics* (Princeton, NJ: Princeton University Press, 2000), 247–69.
18. E.g., see Bhojraj Bhatta, "Success without Happiness Is Bill Hybels," August 10, 2018, vojraj.blogspot.com.
19. Bart Gingerich, "Jerry Falwell Jr.'s Sad Story," *MinistryWatch*, February 2, 2022, ministrywatch.com.
20. Joshua Gamson, "Normal Sins: Sex Scandal Narratives as Institutional Morality Tales," *Social Problems* 48, 2 (2001), 185–205, quote on page 198.
21. Another example of evangelical publications responding to church scandals is the sixteen-episode podcast, The Rise and Fall of Mars Hill, produced by Mike Cosper under the auspices of *Christianity Today*.
22. R. Albert Mohler Jr., "Why I Am a Baptist," *First Things*, August 2020.
23. Pew Research Center, "In U.S., Decline of Christianity Continues at Rapid Pace, October 17, 2019, www.pewresearch.org.
24. These factors affecting young adults are discussed in Robert Wuthnow, *After the Baby Boomers: How Twenty- and Thirty-Somethings Are Shaping the Future of American Religion* (Princeton, NJ: Princeton University Press, 2007); these factors also underscore that declining trust and participation in religion should not be attributed principally to church scandals, even though church scandals have been a contributing factor; e.g., see the helpful discussion of the relationship of Catholic scandals with attitudes toward the church's handling of the scandals and rates of defection in Burge, *The Nones*, 58–61.
25. Michael Hout and Claude S. Fischer, "Why More Americans Have No Religious Preference: Politics and Generations," *American Sociological Review* 67, 2 (2002), 165–90; and David E. Campbell, "The Perils of Politicized Religion," *Dædalus* 149, 3 (Summer 2020), 87–104.

26. E. J. Dionne Jr., "Trump Is Weaponizing Evangelicals' Mistrust. And He's Succeeding," *The Washington Post*, August 21, 2019.
27. Ralph Keyes, *The Post-Truth Era: Dishonesty and Deception in Contemporary Life* (New York: St. Martin's Press, 2004).
28. Christian Smith, *American Evangelicalism: Embattled and Thriving* (Chicago: University of Chicago Press, 1998).
29. Andrew L. Whitehead and Samuel L. Perry, *Taking America Back for God: Christian Nationalism in the United States* (New York: Oxford University Press, 2020).
30. Diana Butler Bass, "Nothing Is as It Was: American Religion Is Changing and We Need a New Story," *The Cottage*, October 13, 2020.
31. Robert Jones, *Dueling Realities: Amid Multiple Crises, Trump and Biden Supporters See Divergent Priorities and Futures for the Country: Findings from the American Values Survey* (Washington, DC: PRRI, 2020).
32. Aleem Maqbool, "Coronavirus: Pastor Who Decried 'Hysteria' Dies after Attending Mardi Gras," *BBC News*, April 6, 2020.
33. Emily McFarlan Miller, "Willow Creek Names NAE Head, 3 Others to Oversee Hybels Investigation," *Religion News Service*, September 18, 2018.
34. "Catholic Church Sex Abuse Scandal Lawsuit Investigation," *Top Class Actions*, October 25, 2022, topclassactions.com.
35. Gamson, "Normal Sins"; Willow Creek Community Church Independent Advisory Group, Report of the Independent Advisory Group (South Barrington, IL: Willow Creek Community Church, 2019); Emily McFarlan Miller, "Willow Creek Conforms New Sexual Harassment Claims," MinistryWatch, January 29, 2020; and Daniel Burke, "Catholics Are Losing Faith in Clergy and Church after Sexual Abuse Scandal," CNN, January 11, 2019.
36. Dave Tell, "Jimmy Swaggart's Secular Confession," *Rhetoric Society Quarterly* 39, 2 (2009), 124–46; Susan Wise Bauer, *The Art of the Public Grovel: Sexual Sin and Public Confession in America* (Princeton, NJ: Princeton University Press, 2008), 143–51.
37. Kate Shellnutt, "Willow Creek Investigation: Allegations against Bill Hybels Are Credible," *Christianity Today*, February 28, 2019.
38. Douglas, *Purity and Danger*.
39. James Madison, The Federalist, No. 10: "The Same Subject Continued: The Union as a Safeguard Against Domestic Faction and Insurrection," *New York Packet*, November 23, 1787.
40. Kent Greenawalt, *From the Bottom Up: Selected Essays* (New York: Oxford University Press, 2016), 39. On democracy and healthy skepticism toward political claims, see Mark Warren, "Trust and Democracy," in *The Oxford Handbook of Social and Political Trust*, ed. Uslaner, 77–97.
41. An approach that emphasizes contention as a feature of pluralism is Chantal Mouffe, "Religion, Liberal Democracy, and Citizenship," in *Political Theologies: Public Religions in a Post-Secular World*, eds. Hent De Vries and Lawrence E. Sullivan (New York: Fordham University Press, 2006), 318–26; see also Chantal Mouffe, *Agonistics: Thinking the World Politically* (London: Verso, 2013); and Chantal Mouffe, "Deliberative Democracy or Agonistic Pluralism?" *Social Research* 66, 3 (Fall 1999), 745–58.
42. Robert Wuthnow, *Why Religion Is Good for American Democracy* (Princeton, NJ: Princeton University Press, 2021) is where I have developed these arguments about religious groups' diverse engagement in public policy.
43. Kenneth L. Woodward, "Religion and Presidential Politics: From George Washington to Donald Trump," *Commonweal*, September 1, 2020.
44. Jessica Hamar Martínez, *Americans Express Increasingly Warm Feelings toward Religious Groups* (Washington, DC: Pew Research Center, 2017), www.pewresearch.org.

Index

For the benefit of digital users, indexed terms that span two pages (e.g., 52–53) may, on occasion, appear on only one of those pages.